No Other Choice

An Autobiography

GEORGE BLAKE

SIMON & SCHUSTER

NEW YORK · LONDON · TORONTO · SYDNEY · TOKYO · SINGAPORE

SIMON & SCHUSTER
Simon & Schuster Building
Rockefeller Center
1230 Avenue of the Americas
New York, New York 10020

Manufactured in the United States of America

1   3   5   7   9   10   8   6   4   2

Library of Congress Cataloging in Publication Data
Blake, George, 1922–
No other choice: an autobiography/George Blake.
p.   cm.
"Originally published in Great Britain by Jonathan Cape, Ltd."
—T.p. verso.
1. Blake, George, 1922–   . 2. Spies—Soviet Union—
Biography.   3. Spies—Great Britain—Biography.   4. Espionage,
Soviet—Great Britain.   I. Title.
UB271.R928575   1990
327.1′2′092—dc20
[B]   91-14711
CIP
ISBN: 0-671-74155-1

Introduction
by
Phillip Knightley

In the history of British espionage no spy arouses such passion, such a conflict of emotions, as George Blake. Convicted of working for the KGB while serving as an officer in Her Majesty's Secret Intelligence Service, Blake was sentenced in London in 1961 to forty-two years' imprisonment for his treachery, the longest term ever imposed under English law.

His damage to Western intelligence was so great – he confessed to having passed to the KGB a copy of every important official document which had come into his hands – that his trial was held in camera and the British government did its best to persuade the media to conceal the fact that Blake had ever been in intelligence work.

The scanty news that 'leaked' after his trial suggested that he had been a traitor of the first magnitude. It was said that he had 'undone most of the work of British intelligence since the end of the war', that he had given the KGB the name of every British agent behind the Iron Curtain, and, most damaging of all in the public view, he had been responsible for the deaths of 42 of them – hence his sentence, 'a year for each life betrayed'. One history of British intelligence tells of these events under the revealing chapter heading, 'The Blake Catastrophe'.

Once he was behind bars, Blake, to the relief of the authorities, dropped out of the news. Then, when he had served barely five-and-a-half years of his forty-two, Blake made a spectacular escape from

Wormwood Scrubs prison, West London, confounded the police, and vanished. He surfaced in the Soviet Union, a year later. There he settled quietly into Moscow life with a new Russian wife. (His British one, by whom he had three sons, had met someone else and had started divorce proceedings just before Blake's escape.) He avoided Western journalists and shunned any publicity.

Periodically the press would return to Blake's story because there were so many unanswered questions. When, for example, had Moscow recruited him? One version had Blake loyal to Britain until he was brainwashed as a prisoner in a Communist prisoner-of-war camp during the Korean war. Another was that he had been a Communist since a teenager and had been cunningly inserted into British intelligence as a KGB penetration agent, an act made possible by the failure of our security services to check his background thoroughly. Some said Blake had done it all for money and that his hands were stained with the blood of agents who had trusted him; others that he was an ideological spy, besotted by Marxism, who believed his work for the KGB was in the best interests of world peace. But despite the many books and articles, the real Blake remained an enigma.

My own interest in Blake, always strong, revived in 1988 when, after an intermittent correspondence over a twenty-year period, I went to Moscow for six days of interviews with Kim Philby, the other SIS officer who had also worked for the KGB. Philby had fled to Moscow from Beirut in 1963. (He had been in Lebanon at the same time as George Blake but the two had never met. In fact, neither knew of the other's work for the KGB until they were exposed.)

In the course of my conversations with Philby, Blake's name often came up. The two exiles had been friends. They had visited each other's apartments, married Russian women who were themselves friends – Blake's wife, Ida, had introduced Philby to his future wife, Rufa. There had been parties at Blake's dacha and Philby had taken an avuncular interest in Blake's son by Ida, Misha. Then the two men had fallen out and drifted apart. But when Philby died in May, 1988, Blake had attended the KGB ceremonies to mark the occasion.

I wrote to Blake soon afterwards, passing the letter through Novosti, the Soviet press agency. This was necessary because, unlike Philby who had a box at the main Post Office in Moscow, Blake kept his address a secret. No one knew where he lived or what he did. Whereas Philby had given an interview to the *Sunday Times* in 1967 and photographs of him in Moscow had appeared in the Western press, Blake had remained in the shadows. So in my letter I suggested that we meet and that I should write about him as I had written about Philby – as objectively as possible.

I had an indirect reply via Novosti saying that Blake would consider my request when he had finished writing his own book, an account of his life. As this was obviously going to take some time, I put the matter out of my mind. Then, in June this year, Blake got in touch and said he would be able to spare me a couple of days before he went on his family summer holiday the following week.

It had been winter when I saw Philby, the countryside covered in snow, the Moscow streets thick with slush. The Berlin Wall was still up and the end of the Cold War was not even in sight. Now our plane flew over a Russia green with the warmth of summer, and instead of a KGB car to take me to Philby's flat, there was a Russian taxi-driver quoting the fare to the city in dollars. As we hurried down the highway past the monument that marks the limit of the German advance on Moscow, I wondered about the approaching meeting with Blake. Clearly this was going to be very different from Philby. I knew so much about Philby from his letters, from his own book, from conversations with members of his family who lived in London, and from interviews with his former colleagues in Britain and the United States, that the eventual meeting was no real surprise. He was as I expected – convivial, humorous, charming, an expansive host, and open in his defence of what he had done. How would Blake be?

We met at my hotel the morning after I arrived. A slight, neat man, looking younger than his sixty-eight years, dressed in a striped blue shirt, no tie, grey trousers, red socks and suede slip-on shoes, he looked very Russian, so the guard on the hotel door at first refused to allow him to enter the lobby, much to Blake's annoyance. Why is it that men of great dash and daring, men who tackle fate with two hands, appear so ordinary when you meet them?

Blake was wary of me. He did not want to start the interviews immediately. 'We need to get to know each other a bit first,' he said. I suggested a drink in the hotel's hard currency bar that evening, or a meal in one of the new Moscow restaurants that take only Western credit cards. He was appalled. 'I don't approve of those sort of places,' he said. He suggested instead a short drive to the Moscow University look-out and a walk in the nearby park.

I found him at first a retiring man, not easy to draw out, careful in the extreme. (He had, for example, parked his car a long way from the hotel because, he said, he could not be certain that there would be parking close-by, and to drive around the block again might make him late.) He wanted to know exactly what we would be doing over the next two days, how I planned to approach our talks, had I read his book, how would what I write differ from it, where and when would my material appear.

That first morning we steered clear of his spying career, talking instead in general terms of what was happening in the Soviet Union, of Kim Philby and of Donald Maclean, the British diplomat who defected to the USSR in 1951. He was pleased when I said that, as a result of what he had written about Maclean in his book, the West would have to reassess Maclean's life.

Then we spoke about his ninety-five-year-old mother who lives in Holland. She is obviously an important influence in his life and his face became animated when he talked of her. It causes him some pain that they can never again meet – she is too old to make the long trip to Moscow and he cannot go to Holland. 'The British might kidnap me,' he said, 'and the Dutch police would turn a blind eye.' I said that I thought this unlikely. 'You don't understand,' he said. 'The risk is much greater for me than it was for Philby or Maclean. They were never convicted of anything. But if the British authorities got hold of me, all they would have to do would be to put me back in my cell at Wormwood Scrubs.' He did not say it, but I got the feeling that this was the last thing Blake was going to allow to happen.

We met the next morning and drove to his apartment, bigger and better than most in Moscow, but very modest by Western standards. (It had once been a KGB 'safe house'.) There we talked for hours. Slowly he unbent and there emerged a man I was completely unprepared for. Unless Blake was playing some deep KGB game – and in the light of current world events what would be the point? – then we have to cast aside all our preconceptions about George Blake and think again.

As we went through his life together I realised that it was not just that of one of the most successful spies in history. It was not just an account of deceit, treachery and betrayal. It was the story of a man who risked his life from the time he was a teenager for what he believed in. He did not always win – he lost his liberty four times to four different régimes and has spent nearly nine years locked up. But, looking back on this, he does not complain. In fact he says that his times in prison have been among the most interesting and rewarding in his life. 'You cannot imagine the fascinating people I met in Wormwood Scrubs,' he says.

I know that this will infuriate the many people who revile George

Blake, but I decided that I was dealing with a very sincere man who is in the process of coming to terms with the fact that the side he chose forty years ago has lost the ideological battle. He is not bitter or unhappy about this; he accepts it. But it does not mean that his love affair with Russia is over – far from it. He says he has linked his fate with his adopted country 'and I will stay, come what may, for better or for worse, till death do us part.'

Blake is given to dramatic statements like this. But it is impossible to predict what path they will take. He is a man of complex and sometimes bewildering views. Among the people who helped him escape from Wormwood Scrubs were two members of the Campaign for Nuclear Disarmament. Yet Blake himself is a firm believer in the bomb and the nuclear deterrent. And just when I thought I had him catalogued as a typical Dutch Calvinist, he announced that he no longer considered himself a Christian. We then spent hours trying to fathom exactly what he is, and failed.

When I ventured that he must have hated Britain to have betrayed it so, he said that, on the contrary, he loves Britain and the British people and has the highest regard for them. He then embarked on a long and detailed criticism of the British class system and expressed bitterness that he had been treated differently from the other British KGB spies.

I was just absorbing this when he announced that he admires some of his ex-colleagues in SIS, and was reluctant to name them in his book, partly because of his SIS training in secrecy, and partly because the KGB is concerned lest he upset the new good relations between Britain and the Soviet Union. I expected him to be evasive about the agents he betrayed, or, like Philby, say it was war and people die in wars. But Blake freely admitted passing to the KGB the names of Communist bloc agents recruited by SIS. In fact, he said, he did not betray 42 agents but 'more likely four hundred'. But he feels fully justified in doing this because 'they were working against Communism'. And then, most astounding of all, he insisted that the KGB killed none of them and that some of them are not only alive and well today but working in the new democratic régimes in liberated Eastern Europe.

We returned to this subject when, on the second day, we drove down to his dacha in the countryside east of Moscow. Blake planned our outing carefully. We stopped on the outskirts of the city at a Georgian co-operative store that he knew and bought some suckling pig. (The butcher was mysteriously absent so Blake persuaded a helpful shop assistant to allow him into the butcher's section at the back of the store where he cut the meat himself.) We stopped again at a country market and bought some strawberries and plums.

After lunch we came back to the agents he had betrayed. Either he had blood on his hands, I said, or he did not. Why should we believe that the KGB had not executed as traitors the agents Blake had betrayed? 'Because I asked the KGB not to do so,' Blake said. 'I said that I would give them the names only on the guarantee that they would not be killed. They gave me that guarantee and I believe them.' Would he accept that other people might find this naive, or would not believe his story at all? 'Of course,' he said. 'But nevertheless it is true.' And to support his claim he pointed out – quite correctly – that it was not part of the Crown case against him at his trial that he had been responsible for the deaths of any agents, and, he said, nor had anyone ever been able to prove since that he had.

Our conversations were not all so serious. Blake has a keen sense of humour, particularly about the ironies of the intelligence world, and some of the stories he tells in his book could not have been invented by either John le Carré or Len Deighton at their best. Neither would have challenged their readers to believe what happened to Blake after he confessed to his SIS interrogators that he was indeed a KGB spy – they took him off for a weekend in the country! In a lovely house (surrounded by Special Branch officers) they chatted and took long walks (followed by police cars) and when it was time for tea on Sunday, George Blake, a good cook, made the pancakes.

Then there is his escape from Wormwood Scrubs. Blake says that far from being carried out with military precision – which led to rumours that it must have been organised by the KGB – it was marked by cock-ups and confusion and that the whole project was saved from disaster only by the loyalty and goodwill of his fellow prisoners.

Blake has not shirked the personal aspects of his life. He writes of the shock the revelation of his treachery caused his wife – she was eight months pregnant when he was arrested. He describes meeting this son in Moscow for the first time eighteen years later. But I leave the readers to decide whether they find something strange in Blake's writing when he is dealing with his relations with people close to him. Is it, as I believe, that Blake is ashamed at the personal betrayals that his greater treachery involved? Or is it possible, as someone who knows him says, 'There is a great chasm in George Blake's heart?'

Early on in our talks I asked George Blake why he had written this book. He said that he had at first been reluctant to do so. He had become used to a quiet, modest existence in Moscow with his family, his cocker spaniel Danny, his books, his record collection, and his not-too-demanding job at the Institute for World Economic and International Affairs. This is understandable. There must come a time when even the most daring adventurer grows tired of the risks and longs for a little of normal life. But in the early 1970s, the KGB urged him to write his story – no doubt for use as propaganda. Blake made a half-hearted attempt and produced a poor manuscript. The KGB put a very high price on it and when no Western publisher would meet it, the project lapsed. After *glasnost*, there were renewed offers for Blake's 'real story' and, after a lot of thought, Blake said, he wrote his autobiography again, this time with enthusiasm and without inhibition. In fact, he said, he delivered his second manuscript to his Western publisher *before* he showed a copy to his friends in the KGB.

But even in the new manuscript, the first drafts had a peculiar, detached tone. Blake recognised this. It was due, he told me, to a feeling that 'it all seemed as if it had happened to another person' and that he often had difficulty in relating the George Blake of today to, say, the teenage courier in the Dutch underground.

I sensed that it was not always a pleasant experience for George Blake to relive his life through his typewriter. But he has done it. I believe it is a frank and fair account – but without access to the archives of SIS and the KGB it is impossible to be sure – and that whether you hate him for the traitor to Britain that he is, whether you admire him as a man who had a revelation and whose principles forced him to act the way he did, or even if you believe, as Blake himself does, that fate ordained his path and he could as little change it as Canute could the tide, you will find this story compelling reading.

There is, as well, the book's political importance. As the Soviet Union is shaken by events as momentous as the Bolshevik Revolution itself, one man's account of why he attached himself to Communism, even when it meant betraying his country, his colleagues, his family and his friends, gives us valuable insight into a dangerous period of our history, one that, thankfully, now seems to be over.

Moscow
July, 1990

Foreword

It has, on various occasions, been suggested to me that I should write the story of my life. I once made a half-hearted attempt but it led nowhere. In the first place, it did not very much appeal to me to have to write about myself and reveal to all and sundry my actions and innermost thoughts. Also, as my life unfolded day by day before my eyes, it did not seem to me all that extraordinary and worth writing about. To do so might seem presumptuous. What is more, I have always been of the opinion that secret intelligence operations should remain secret and that those who are called upon to take part in them should remain silent, except perhaps within the small circle of those who are in the know, who are 'indoctrinated' as the term has it. Finally, I must say that I look upon espionage as an 'unfortunate necessity', or to put it more strongly 'a necessary evil', imposed on states by their rivalry and confrontation, by the existence of violent conflicts between nations and wars or the threat of wars and, as such, is a matter rather for regret than something to boast about or exult in.

Since my escape from prison and arrival in the Soviet Union, I have, therefore, tried to avoid meeting foreign journalists, eschewed publicity and in general been content to 'lie low'. In spite of this my name and the events with which it is connected have continued to crop up in the press or been referred to in books and, more often than not, they have been represented in a false light.

Meanwhile, great changes have taken place in the Soviet Union, Eastern Europe and the world as a whole. The Cold War has to all intents and purposes come to an end. *Glasnost*, which I welcome, with the irresistible urge to open up to the public gaze all aspects of life which were previously hidden, has become a fact of daily life in the Soviet Union. The pendulum has swung the other way. Many matters, which before nobody dare even whisper among intimate friends, are now shouted from the rooftops. In consequence, the suggestions, both from the Soviet and the British side, that I should write my story have become more insistent.

I objected that I was not a professional writer and that I doubted whether I could write a good and interesting book. Against this it was argued that the story would be worth writing simply as a record of the times; that as a man who had at the same time, been an officer of the British Secret Intelligence Service (SIS) and an agent of the Soviet Intelligence Service at the height of the Cold War, I had a unique story to tell which should be an interesting contribution to the history of that war. When it so happened that at about the same time my friends in England who had helped me to escape from prison were forced to come out in the open about their role in the escape, wrote a book about it and, in consequence, might stand trial with all the publicity this would bring with it, I yielded. I realised that whether I remained silent or wrote a book, whether I sought publicity or not, my name would still be mentioned in the mass media and I might as well give my side of the story, which so far had gone by default.

Many accusations have been made against me, many imputations cast upon me and many speculations and theories have surrounded my case. When a man who has acted strongly against a cause ends up by going over to the side of those whom he has combated, thereby undoing much of what his former friends and colleagues had achieved, it was inevitable that this should be so, all the more so as all this happened in a field of human activity which is carefully shielded from the eyes of the public and surrounded by great secrecy. I have always accepted this as part of the penalty which I naturally and justly incurred by going over to the Soviet side. I must say at once that many of these theories and speculations I was unaware of until very recently and some I may not know about even to this day. For the last twenty-five years I have had only irregular access to the British press and been unable to acquire the many books on espionage which have appeared in Britain in that time and in which my case has been discussed. I am therefore not in a position, nor have I tried, to answer or refute any of them specifically, except for two or three cases which have been especially brought to my notice. I realised that if I refuted some and left others unanswered simply because I did not know about them, I would create the impression that I could not do so and that therefore they must be true. I decided therefore that the best course was to content myself with giving a true account of my life and set out what happened so that it might be seen what did not happen; to relate the development of my thinking, describe the state from which I started and in which events and circumstances my opinions had their origin, how they grew and changed and how, in the end, this led me to embrace the cause of Communism; finally, how the ideal of building a Communist society, which to this day I consider the highest form of society mankind can achieve, affected my position and actions in that great conflict between East and West which, it now looks, has come happily to an end.

I have tried to tell the story without any embellishments or prevarications, avoiding, I hope, that cheap sensationalism with which matters connected with espionage are frequently made to look more exciting than they in reality are. The story itself will refute, I trust, those accusations, imputations and theories which are false and confirm those which are true.

It may well be asked but how can we believe him? He has over a long period successfully deceived us; how then can we believe him now? I have nobody to blame but myself for having put myself in a position where such a question can justly be asked. I must accept that together with other reproaches. I can only reply that I have tried to tell the truth as I see it, free from constraint of any kind, except only in so far as it affects the privacy of my family and friends. I am content to let readers draw their own conclusions and form their own judgment on whether what I say is true or not.

I should point out that by the very nature of my profession and activities I have never kept a diary or taken notes so that in this narrative I have had to rely entirely on my memory. It may, therefore, in certain respects be incomplete, especially in regard to operations which took place thirty to forty years ago. I have had no access to any documents which could have refreshed my memory or brought back certain facts. I have also forgotten the names of many people, one way or another involved, or remember them only incompletely. Rather than give wrong names, I have preferred to limit myself to general descriptions.

This book is not meant to be a justification or an apology. It is simply an explanation to which I think the British public, at least, is entitled. I have tried, as far as I am able, to explain myself, my opinions and actions, and state the facts whether they go against me or not.

G.B.
Moscow
31st March, 1990

Chapter One

Number 2 Carlton Gardens shares the secluded dignity of that quiet cul-de-sac between the Mall and Pall Mall with the private residence at Number 1 of the Secretary of State for Foreign Affairs. This fine old stuccoed town house with its heavy double green doors with brass knocker, its chandeliered marble entrance hall and monumental staircase with wrought-iron gilded banisters was to play an important part in my life. In the course of time it was to become the scene of two events, one which brought me much happiness and one much sorrow. It was there that I met and courted my future wife. It was there also that many years later the interrogations took place which led to my trial.

I entered this house for the first time on the occasion of the Queen's coronation on the 2nd of June 1953. In the narrow front garden overlooking the Mall stands had been erected for selected members of the Secret Intelligence Service to watch the coronation procession on its way to the Abbey. As a special mark of favour I was invited to join the champagne party which was held afterwards in the downstairs reception rooms.

In April of that year I had come back to England from Korea, where I had been working for the SIS and was subsequently taken prisoner. On my return I was called to Personnel to discuss a new appointment and seen by the Head of the Department, George

Pinney, whom I knew well. During the last year of the war, when he was working in the Political Department and I was a young beginner in the Dutch section, we had had frequent dealings. He greeted me cordially and informed me after the usual exchange of compliments – for he was a man of excellent manners – that it had been decided that I should remain on leave until the 1st of September. After that I was to join a comparatively new section called 'Y' located in 2 Carlton Gardens, which was concerned with highly secret operations of a technical nature against the Russians. The section was responsible for processing the material obtained from telephone tapping operations directed against Soviet targets in Austria and of microphone operations directed against missions of the Soviet Union and other socialist countries in the United Kingdom and other countries in Western Europe. The Head of section 'Y' needed a second-in-command who had a good knowledge of Russian and the choice had fallen on me. It was an interesting job, he continued and one, which if I did well, might favourably influence my career in the service. Section 'Y' was a new venture and receiving much attention from the senior members of the service. I would have every opportunity to bring myself to their notice.

My office was situated in a long, narrow room which must have been one of the bedrooms of the house since it had a large built-in wardrobe and, on one side, a bathroom now used as a storeroom for stationery. A room opening off it on the other side, presumably once a dressing-room, was now occupied by the secretaries of the Head of section 'Y', Colonel Tom Gimson, and myself.

Colonel Gimson had his office in the room next to theirs. It was large and sunny with french doors opening on a balcony overlooking the Mall and a rather fine ceiling. He was known to his staff as Tom and had not been long in the service. A career Guards officer, his last appointment before retiring from the Army had been that of commanding officer of the Irish Guards. He looked the part, every inch of his tall, straight figure. He always dressed with great care and in his discreet dark pinstripe he was a handsome man with a shy, somewhat wistful charm. He suffered from a knee complaint which caused him much pain and for which he vainly sought a cure. This, combined with his military bearing, conveyed to his movements a certain stiffness. He had joined SIS as had a number of other senior officers of the armed forces at a point when their career or their health precluded them from any further promotion. They had been found jobs commensurate with their position in which their experience could

6

be used and which enabled them to supplement their service pensions until the time came for them to retire altogether. They were therefore no longer bent on making a career and on the whole not jockeying for positions.

Ever since the days of Rahab, the whore of Jericho, and no doubt long before, the most valuable information and assistance has always been obtained from so called 'inside' agents i.e. persons in the enemy camp, who for various reasons best known to themselves are willing to work for the opposite side. Such people have always formed what one may call the 'conventional' forces of intelligence. In this field the superiority has, for a long time, lain markedly on the Soviet side. The reasons for this were, in my opinion, twofold. In the first place, the Soviet Union, as the recognised bulwark of the Communist cause, has been able to draw the allegiance of a large number of people who are attracted by its aims and ideals. Though nothing on earth would ever move them to betray their own country in favour of the national interests of another, they are, for ideological reasons, willing to work for the Soviet Union. The West has had no such advantage.

In the second place, the Soviet Union has been an embattled camp from its very foundation. It has therefore had to evolve for its protection a security system which is unknown in Western countries, and would, in fact, not be tolerated there. This system has generally succeeded in preventing Western intelligence agencies from gaining access to those people in the Soviet Union who might have been willing to work for them.

Faced with this problem early in the Cold War, ingenious heads in Western intelligence organisations began to ponder ways and means of getting round it. If valuable intelligence could no longer, or only as an exception, be obtained by the old 'conventional' methods, new 'unconventional' ones would have to be devised. In the British Secret Service one of these ingenious heads belonged to Peter Lunn. The son of Sir Arnold Lunn, the founder and head of the well-known travel agency of that name, who did so much to make skiing a popular British sport, Peter joined SIS during the war, like many others seconded from the armed services.

He was a small, slightly built man with prematurely grey and fast-receding hair. He spoke in a soft voice with a marked lisp. These features might create the impression on those who did not know him well that he was a timid and ineffective sort of person. Nothing was further from the truth. On the contrary, he was a zealot by nature, as he proved by everything he tackled. He was an ardent Roman Catholic and predictably a militant anti-communist. These characteristics, combined with strong will-power and considerable natural abilities, made him an extremely effective, hard working and successful intelligence officer. He also managed to be an enthusiastic skier and the father of a family, which, if I am not mistaken, ran into double figures.

Endowed with these qualities, he rose rapidly in the ranks of the Service. By 1947 he was in command of the Hamburg station, one of the many stations set up immediately after the war in Germany. Three years later he was appointed Head of the Vienna station, an important assignment in view of its common borders with Hungary, Czechoslovakia and Yugoslavia and the presence of Soviet occupation forces in Austria. Here, in a particularly stark form, he came face to face with the difficulties inherent in trying to penetrate the Soviet Union, the countries of the socialist bloc and more especially, the headquarters of the Soviet armed forces, located in such close proximity.

Of course, it was quite easy at that time to recruit large numbers of agents among the Austrians and displaced persons, and so create an impression of bustling activity. This is what had been done so far. It had provided large numbers of reports on troop movements, the location of HQ and military installations, mostly obtained by visual observation, of little value and difficult to check. Here and there black market contacts with Soviet military personnel had been established but these had seldom, if ever, led to the acquisition of hard intelligence. The problem had only been nibbled at. The core, finding out what went on inside the HQ of the Soviet Forces in Austria and the Vienna Commandatura, the repositories of the kind of information the Foreign Office and the War Office were vitally interested in, remained untouched. This state of affairs did not satisfy Peter Lunn.

One day, not long after he had taken over as Head of station, he happened to be leafing through a pile of reports from a source in the Austrian Post, Telegraphs and Telephone Administration. From these he noticed that a number of telephone cables, requisitioned by the Soviet Army and linking their HQ with several units, airfields and establishments in their zone of occupation, ran through the British and French sectors of Vienna. Suddenly the idea struck him that if those cables could be tapped and the conversations recorded, most valuable information might be extracted from them.

Of course, telephone tapping by the police and security services was nothing new, but such operations had mostly been directed at individual suspects and mainly for security purposes. The tapping for intelligence purposes of whole cables used by foreign armed forces was an entirely new and far-reaching development in espionage work.

Further study of the cable plans and investigation of the routes along which they ran showed that one of the most suitable places from which to carry out a tapping operation was a British Military Police post, right in front of which, at a distance of about six metres, ran a telephone cable which linked the Soviet HQ in Vienna with the military aerodrome at Swechat. A detailed plan was worked out.

Experts were called in and consulted. Mr Taylor, an extremely capable telephone engineer attached to the PTT Experimental Station at Dollis Hill, after studying the cable plan and other technical details obtained from our sources in the Austrian PTT, confirmed that the operation was feasible. Mr Balmain, a private mining consultant of considerable experience, agreed to build the tunnel and the chamber in which the tap was to be located. Firing everyone concerned in Head Office with his enthusiasm, Peter Lunn got the operation approved in record time. The necessary money was made available, the essential co-operation of the military authorities in Vienna was secured, and before long work was started. It involved digging a short tunnel from the basement of the police post, the placing of the tap and the setting up of a listening post with the necessary equipment and recording apparatus on the premises.

The operation was a greater success even than had been hoped for, and encouraged by this taps had been placed on two more Soviet cables. By the end of 1952 the material obtained from these two taps joined the material from the first tap which had been given the codename 'Conflict', in a steady flow of valuable intelligence, much appreciated by SIS customer departments.

One of these new operations, known by the codename 'Sugar', was run from premises occupied by a British firm dealing in imitation jewellery. It traded under the name 'Gablons', not very profitably but this did not matter much as it was financed by SIS and provided excellent cover for the listening post. The Viennese young women who visited the shop could hardly have imagined that right underneath their feet recorders were taking down the telephone conversations of senior officers in the Soviet military HQ.

The other operation, with the codename 'Lord', was run from a smart, modern villa in one of Vienna's fashionable suburbs surrounded by a green lawn kept in beautiful condition by an English major and his attractive young wife. They were a well-known and much appreciated couple in the mixed, international society of the Vienna of those days and the parties they gave frequently lasted until the early hours of the morning. I knew this major quite well from my days in the Dutch section of SIS, of which I was a member during the last year of the war. His name was John Wyke and he was, like me, partly of Dutch origin. At that time he had been involved in dangerous intelligence operations conducted from the liberated southern part of the Netherlands across the rivers into the northern part which was still occupied by the Germans.

The material obtained from these three operations reached such proportions that an overworked staff had to catch up with a three months' backlog and a monthly had become a fortnightly summary with several interim reports on special questions in between.

Very soon after the start of operation 'Conflict', it became clear that the two fluent Russian speakers who had been sent to Vienna to transcribe the tapped Soviet telephone conversations could not possibly cope with all the material that was flowing in. Additional staff had to be found. This was not easy. As anyone knows who has studied a foreign language one has to reach a really high standard to be able to follow telephone conversations. If it is borne in mind that the speakers in this case were not radio or TV announcers but military personnel using slang and technical terms and indulging in a great deal of bad language, it becomes clear that only one whose native tongue is Russian can effectively cope with such work. But such people were not easy to find, especially as they had to be absolutely reliable from a security point of view. Another difficulty was that there was a limit to the number of additional staff which the Vienna station could accommodate without drawing attention to its rapid expansion. It was therefore decided quite early on to transfer the processing side of the operation to London.

There was at that time in Head Office a small section, known by the symbol 'N' which, among such tasks as opening diplomatic mailbags undetected, when an opportunity to do so occurred, also studied conversations of foreign diplomats whose telephones were being tapped by MI5 for any matters of intelligence interest they might contain. The first impulse was therefore to make 'N' responsible for processing the 'Conflict' material. But 'N' was located in Head Office and incapable of physical expansion quite apart from the fact that its small staff of elderly and dignified linguists used to a leisurely pace of work were unlikely to be able to cope with a constant, heavy flow of traffic. So it was decided to set up an entirely new section with its own accommodation capable of expansion. This became all the more urgent as Peter Lunn, encouraged by the success of 'Conflict', was already putting forward plans for two more operations against specified Soviet cables in Vienna. It was in these circumstances that section 'Y' was born.

The broad base of the section was formed by the transcribers who listened to the tapes, which were flown in three times a week from Vienna by a special RAF plane. They took down the material which was then passed on to what constituted the second tier, a group of twelve Army and Air Force officers (some retired, some seconded), who had a good knowledge of Russian. Their job was to study the conversations, extract what intelligence they contained and combine it with information obtained from previous conversations into a regular intelligence bulletin on the Soviet armed forces in Austria. The third tier was formed by Colonel Gimson and his second-in-command assisted by four secretaries. They were responsible for the general running of the section and liaison with Head Office and customer departments. An important third member of this team was Mr Newall, the administrative officer, who had the difficult task of finding fluent and reliable Russian speakers.

Many of these he found among the descendants of the so-called St Petersburg English. For many generations a number of English merchants had lived in Russia, especially in St Petersburg, where they traded in timber and furs and set up factories. Though often married to Russian wives, they had remained English and usually sent their children back to England to be educated. These, as a rule, were bilingual in Russian and English. After the revolution the last generation of these merchants and industrialists left Russia and settled in England.

Other 'Y' transcribers were daughters of Russian émigrés, often women of noble origin, who had married Englishmen. Now, with their children mostly grown up, they were glad to have found quite unexpectedly interesting employment in which they could use their native tongue.

A third category of transcribers was formed by ex-Polish army officers. These were mostly rather stiff, well dressed, exceedingly polite and sometimes dashing gentlemen, who spoke Russian fluently with a strong Central European accent and called each other by their military rank. They were former members of the Polish intelligence service, which during the war operated from London under SIS control, and had remained in England. These different groups of transcribers gave 'Y' a distinct flavour of its own, quite unlike that of other SIS sections. The Russians in common with the English produce a large number of eccentrics and a combination of the two nationalities is likely to bring out this characteristic in a particularly accentuated form. Anyone who had dealings with the staff of 'Y' soon became aware of this. There was plenty of Slav temperament and moodiness about and it required a great deal of tact and careful handling to keep the peace and the machine running smoothly. Tom Gimson, with his excellent manners, patience and sad charm was the right man to accomplish this. I assisted him in this task as best I could.

It should not be forgotten that the work of a transcriber of telephone conversations is very exacting. Sometimes the lines are not very clear or the speech is slurred and individual words or whole parts of a sentence are difficult to make out. The passage has then to be played over and over again or somebody else has to listen and give his opinion before it begins to make sense. This requires a lot of patience and can be a heavy strain on the nerves. It is not surprising that this led sometimes to hysterics, especially among the women transcribers, if somebody in the room inadvertently made a noise just at the moment when the person trying to make out what a word was thought she had got it right and had to start all over again, or when there was a sharp difference of opinion on what the indistinguishable word was. It often took a lot of diplomacy to soothe ruffled feeling. From this point of view Tom was an ideal head of 'Y'. When he spoke as equal to equal with a Polish ex-colonel, all the latter's accumulated bitterness, born of dashed hopes and ambitions and the loneliness of émigré existence, melted away. He felt himself, for a moment at least, an important man again, even though he spent his day with earphones on in a small basement room, behind a recording machine.

Nobody, not in the know, passing 2 Carlton Gardens would have guessed the skulduggery, including my own, that went on and the passions that flared up behind the stately façade of this aristocratic London town house.

Much of my work consisted in liaising with the War Office and the Air Ministry. Often they were interested in specific items which they asked us to look out for in the transcribed material. If the required information was available I would write it up in a special report. In addition I was responsible for the processing of material obtained from microphone operations. This I found a rather frustrating job as, at any rate in my experience, these operations seldom produced hard intelligence. At best they were useful as an auxiliary in that they might provide information on the character, habits and contacts of the person against whom they were directed and thus might facilitate his recruitment.

There were at that time among the senior officers in SIS, especially among those who were directly in control of 'Y' many who believed that the future of spying lay in the technical field and that in time the human element would become less and less important. Although to some extent they have been proved right I do not fully share that view. A great deal of military intelligence which in the last war could only be obtained by large numbers of agents, is now acquired by technical means such as satellites. There remain, however, important elements such as the opponent's true intentions and plans, which can only be obtained through the man who sits in the inner councils. Besides every technical innovation in the intelligence field sooner or later, and usually sooner, leads to the invention of some piece of equipment which sets it at nought. But then I may be biased in my view.

Be that as it may, the fact is that when I came to 'Y' technical operations were very much 'in' and no self-respecting station commander could afford not to have a microphone operation going or to have one at least in the planning stage. As a result numerous reels with the 'take' from these operations arrived in Head Office and as most of the targets were Russian or Central European it was only natural that 'Y', with its large numbers of Russian and Polish transcribers and play-back equipment, should be given the task of processing this material.

Although, as I have said, several such operations were in progress in the sense that the microphones were actually installed on the target premises and working, the amount of audible conversations obtained was very small. There were several reasons for this. In the first place it was often difficult to get access to the flat or office itself and the microphone had to be installed through a so-called probe from adjoining premises. Since in practice this could only be done with the co-operation of the intelligence service of the country in which the target was situated this restricted microphone operations to those countries with intelligence services with which SIS had a close liaison. Furthermore the offices or living quarters in which a microphone was placed were often not chosen because of the importance of the official who occupied them but because of their accessibility. There were other difficulties. Lack of knowledge about the precise use of the rooms in a flat frequently reduced the operation to a game of chance.

It might be found that the microphone had been installed in a nursery or in a seldom-used guest room. Where conversations were recorded, background noises such as the radio, playing children or street noises through open windows made large parts of what was being said unintelligible. It is true to say that in all the material obtained from microphone operations that came my way during the time I worked in 'Y' we found not a single item of valuable intelligence. Of course, those were the days when that kind of operation was still in its infancy and it is quite possible that since then a lot has changed. As equipment and techniques improved and experience was gained, and with a certain amount of luck which is always an important element in intelligence operations, I do not exclude the possibility that there have been cases when important information was obtained that way.

My work necessitated contact with all the departments in 'Y' and soon I made friends both among the transcribers and the officers who analysed the material. These contacts and friendships arose because I liked the people concerned and they responded and not because I had an ulterior motive and specially sought them out. In my position I had access to all the relevant information in the normal course of my work and there was no need to milk people for more. In general I have never used my friendships and contacts in SIS for intelligence purposes and my relationships with people have always been based on mutual liking. Quite apart from the fact that inquisitiveness would have attracted attention and possible suspicion, the information I was able to obtain in the normal course of duties was sufficiently valuable and authentic not to have to ferret out additional facts from gossip and hearsay.

In the secretaries' room, adjoining mine, very much the principal person was Pam Peniakof, Tom Gimson's Personal Assistant. She was the widow of 'Colonel Popsky', the legendary White Russian who became famous during the war as the daring leader of a commando group operating in the Western desert. Her Russian name disguised a very English personality. She was tall, slim and very elegant. Her determined character and witty but sharp tongue made her a rather formidable figure. Tom Gimson, a man of gentle nature himself, was I think, a little afraid of her. But she was good fun and together with the three younger secretaries we formed a small working team which got on very well together.

The girls must have thought that the new man they were working for had some strange habits. Although I had returned from Korea in good health, the conditions in which we had been forced to live for nearly three years had left their mark on me. This took some time to wear off. For instance not having worn proper footwear, shoes were a heavy strain. As soon as I sat down at my desk and had reason to think that I would be undisturbed, off went my shoes and I felt a wonderful relief. The secretaries could not fail to notice this unusual habit which I don't think they had so far come across in other people they had worked for. When I explained the reason they were very sympathetic and one even brought me a pair of slippers. They showed equal understanding in the case of another habit which I had developed, and which personally worried me more. In Korea, where we lived in a small farmhouse without any work and for very long periods with nothing to read, the only pastime we had, apart from talking, consisted of walking up and down in a small courtyard. Our only lighting was a primitive oil lamp the oil supply for which frequently ran out. In the winter it was extremely cold and the days were short. In Korean houses the heating system consists of a fire which heats the stones of the mat-covered floor. It is a good heating system providing there is enough fuel. But it meant that in order to keep warm we had to lie on the floor and cover ourselves with old padded clothes. So boredom and the need to keep warm forced us to spend a great part of our time sleeping. In this way my organism had got used to a lot of sleep by day as well as by night and for quite a while after my return I found it almost impossible to keep my eyes open after lunch and experienced an almost irresistible urge to lie down and sleep. Fortunately it so happened that I was able to indulge in this without much difficulty. In the storeroom adjoining my office, the bath was still there but had been covered by boards. When I felt the urge to sleep too strongly, I would tell one of the girls who would then say to anyone who was looking for me that I was out. Having taken this precaution, I would lock myself in the bathroom and lie down on the boards with a pile of stationery under my head and soon be fast asleep. Half an hour later the girls would wake me and, much refreshed, I would carry on with my work. Only gradually did this sleepy sickness wear off. But thanks to the ideal arrangement of my office and the understanding attitude of the girls, knowledge about it remained restricted and it did not get me into difficulties.

Another effect of my Korean captivity was what amounted to almost an obsession with food. Three years of nothing else but a small bowl of rice and a little boiled cabbage three times a day, and sometimes not even that, had given me a keen appreciation of the pleasures of the palate. I took therefore to visiting various London restaurants two or three times a week, especially the smaller and more intimate ones which were springing up at that time in great profusion in the Chelsea and Kensington area. Naturally, I did not go there by myself but went with friends or invited a girlfriend. One of these was Gillian Allan, the youngest of the secretaries in the next room, a tall, attractive girl whose company I much enjoyed and whom I started to take out more and more often. I was at that time relatively well off and could afford to indulge in this fairly costly pastime. On my return, I had been paid my full accumulated salary for the three years I had been interned and, in addition, been given £500 in compensation for the loss of my personal effects. This made we wealthy to a degree I had never been before though, of course, in present terms my bank account was quite modest.

I had been working in 'Y' only a fortnight, when one day in the middle of September I received an urgent call from R5, the department in SIS responsible for counter-espionage and liaison with MI5. Melinda Maclean, the wife of the missing diplomat, Donald Maclean, had disappeared with her three young children from the address in Switzerland where she had been staying with her mother. It was suspected that she had fled to the Soviet Union to join her husband. There was a possibility that she might have travelled from Switzerland to the Soviet zone of Austria and been taken from there by military aircraft to Moscow. We were asked to look out for any unusual telephone conversations, especially on the Soviet air force lines, which might give an indication that this was so. We checked all the material of the relevant period carefully but found nothing that pointed to Melinda and her children having passed through Austria. Many years later in Moscow when we had become good friends I told her this story. She was highly amused that I should have been involved, even in a very indirect way, in the search for her. As it happened she had indeed passed through Austria and been taken from there by car to Prague from where she had been flown to Moscow.

In the very next month, October 1953, I met my Soviet contact for the first time in England. I left my office as usual shortly after six and walked in a leisurely way through Soho to Oxford Street. I had plenty of time. In an ABC I drank a cup of tea and ate a cake. It did not taste particularly nice, but then I had not much of an appetite. All the time I was watching to see if I was being followed, though there was no particular reason why I should be. I felt in my inside pocket if the folded paper I was going to hand over was still safely there. I then left the café and took the Underground at Charing Cross. As the train came in I waited till everyone had got on and then caught it at the last moment. At the next station I jumped off just as the doors were closing. I let two trains pass and got on the third, watching for any person who looked to me suspicious. I left at Belsize Park, again just before the doors closed. I now felt quite sure that I was not being followed and slightly more at ease walked to the exit, clutching a newspaper in my left hand as a sign that all was well. There were not many people about at that time and the further I went from the station the quieter it became. A man came slowly out of the fog walking towards me, also carrying a newspaper in his left hand. In his grey, soft felt hat and smart grey raincoat he seemed almost part of the fog. I recognised him as the man I had first met in April at Otpor, the frontier post on the border between China and the Soviet Union, when I was travelling on the Trans-Siberian railway on my way back from Korea to England.

He was a thick-set man of middle height, aged about fifty. He spoke English well but with a marked Slav accent. As we walked up the quiet street, I handed him a folded piece of paper which he put in his inside pocket. Without waiting for questions I began to explain to him that it was a list of top secret technical operations carried out by SIS against Soviet targets with a precise indication of their nature and location. They were divided into two parts: telephone tapping operations and microphone operations. Of these the telephone tapping operations were by far the most important as their location was Vienna. Like Germany, Austria had been divided after the war into four separate occupation zones: American, Soviet, British and French. Unlike Berlin, however, which had been divided into four sectors each administered separately by one of the four occupying powers, Vienna, though divided into four sectors, was administered jointly by the four powers and their military police jeeps which patrolled the city always carried an American, a Soviet, a British and a French soldier. This united front could not conceal, however, the sharp antagonism which at that time existed between the Western powers and the Soviet Union, an antagonism so intense that it was rightly called the Cold War. This war was fought according to all the rules of this new form of warfare: a great deal of mud-slinging and the utmost nastiness (always short of armed incidents) in the open, and a ceaseless, merciless struggle behind the scenes. This struggle was waged mainly by the various intelligence services which constituted the real armies with which this war was fought.

The microphone operations listed on the paper referred to

microphones installed in missions of the USSR and other socialist countries in the UK and other countries in Western Europe.

After I had explained the nature of the operations to him and answered some further questions, we made arrangements to meet again in a month's time in another London suburb and fixed reserve dates and meeting places in case one of us could not turn up at the appointed time. As we walked in deep conversation through the empty streets, turning at right angles so that our route took us back to the main road I felt my companion's attitude noticeably warming towards me. This was understandable. I had offered my services to the Soviets and they, as they had nothing to lose, had naturally accepted. But until they actually received information from me, they were in no position to evaluate whether my offer was genuine or whether I was a plant, acting on instructions from SIS. Being an experienced intelligence officer, as I later discovered my Russian friend was, he must have realised at once that the information I had just passed to him was too valuable and sensitive for any intelligence service to part with willingly and that it was very unlikely therefore that I was a plant. As far as he personally was concerned it seemed to me his suspicions left him there and then.

An hour later I was enjoying a late supper and a glass of wine in my mother's sitting-room. Not being married at that time, I was living with her in her flat in Baron's Court. My mother is a very good cook and this supper remained in my memory not only because I liked the food but mostly because the room seemed particularly cosy and secure after the damp foggy night outside and the dangers of the clandestine meeting I had just lived through.

I had warned my mother that I would be home late that evening as I was going to meet an old friend. She now asked me how I had found him after so many years. I told her in detail about a meeting I had had a few days earlier with a colleague from my days in Germany whom I had not seen since my return from Korea. It was a true account I gave her, the only departure from the truth being the time when it took place. Having had to live a life in which there has been much deception, I have nevertheless always tried to tell the truth as much as possible, or even better, to avoid saying anything at all. My boss in Korea, the late Vyvyan Holt, the British Minister in Seoul, once gave me a very good piece of advice. He drew my attention to the fact that most people are not particularly interested in your opinions or what you have to say, but very interested in voicing their own opinions and telling their own story. They are delighted if you listen to them attentively restricting yourself to making an occasional encouraging remark or asking for an elucidation. They will go away thinking you an interesting companion, who moreover fully shares their views, though, in fact, you have not stated your views at all but only listened with attention to theirs. Whenever possible I have tried to follow this advice and found in most cases that it worked.

That particular evening I realised full well that by having given this highly secret information to my Soviet contact, I had passed the point of no return. Strangely enough this gave me a feeling of relief very much like the experience of landing safely after my first parachute jump. An exhilarated feeling of achievement which comes whenever one has overcome fears and apprehensions.

The next time we met he brought me a small Minox camera on a short chain to measure the focal distance. He explained its working to me as we were walking along and it all seemed quite simple. At first I was somewhat taken aback as he showed me the camera. It looked rather bulky and large. I had expected something very small and sophisticated like a camera concealed in a button or a lighter. My Soviet contact explained to me that that sort of thing was all fancy stuff which looked impressive, but was, in fact, far from easy to operate and not very accurate. In his opinion a Minox was the best that was going for this sort of work and the easiest to handle. He persuaded me and I accepted the camera. After that almost every day whenever I went to my office I carried the Minox with me in the back pocket of my trousers in the same way as I carried my wallet in the inside pocket of my jacket. In this way I was always prepared as I never knew beforehand when I would find an interesting document on my desk and no other opportunity to photograph it than that day.

I am not by nature keen on photography, which has never been one of my hobbies. When I go on holiday I never take a camera with me and leave it to others to take photographs. Certainly my first efforts at photography were not a success and it took some practice and a certain amount of patient explaining on my Russian friend's part before the results were what they should be.

Throughout all that first year after my return to work, I continued to meet my Soviet contact, every month or three weeks. The meetings always took place after office hours at a pre-arranged place not far from an Underground station in one of the suburbs, usually in the northern part of London. Already at our second or third meeting I was able to pass to him a copy of the most recent 'Y' bulletin on the Soviet Armed Forces in Austria. It was a stencilled publication of some 30 to 40 pages which had high security grading and was distributed to selected SIS customers in the War Office, the Air Ministry, the Joint Intelligence Bureau (JIB) and the Foreign Office. A copy was also sent to Washington for the CIA. I now made sure that a copy also reached Moscow for the KGB. As the bulletins were numbered and strictly accounted for I could only do this by putting one together from pages which had been stencilled in excess of the required number as nearly always happened, and which, of course, were meant to be incinerated. I was able to do this by going to the stencilling room, to which I had access, when the two young secretaries who usually did the stencilling had gone for lunch or were otherwise engaged. I then hid the bulletin in my desk and took it out in the evening. This was of course a dangerous and rather unsatisfactory procedure. Although there was no great danger in taking documents out of the building as briefcases were not checked by the elderly watchman at the door, the material I had to pass to my Soviet contact was bulky and highly compromising both for him and for me if found on us. It was therefore much safer and simpler to photograph it.

Meanwhile, encouraged by the successes which marked the entry of SIS into the technical age, an even bolder enterprise was being contemplated. If it succeeded it would turn 'Y' into a vast organisation, almost a small intelligence service on its own and an unrivalled source of information on the Soviet armed forces.

In the middle of 1953, with the Vienna telephone taps producing a steady stream of valuable traffic, Peter Lunn, his reputation enormously enhanced and now one of the most powerful figures in the Service, was appointed Head of the Berlin station. If the post of SIS representative in Washington is considered the plum of the Service from a prestige point of view that of Head of the Berlin station was, at that time, far and away the most important from an operational aspect.

It is not surprising after his success in Vienna that Peter tackled the problem of getting intelligence on the Soviet armed forces stationed in East Germany in very much the same manner. With his usual energy, one of the first things he did was to set up a special technical section in the station at the head of which he put a British Post Office engineer on loan to SIS. This section was given the task of studying the intelligence obtained from sources in the East German telephone service with a view to working out plans for possible cable tapping operations.

It was not long before this section was able to put forward three concrete proposals. The most promising of these envisaged an operation against three Soviet cables, running close to the boundary of the American enclave at Alt Glienicke near Berlin which juts deeply into the Soviet zone. In order to carry out this operation it would be necessary to do two things: dig a tunnel advancing more than 600 yards into DDR territory, and obtain the co-operation of the Americans.

The number and size of the cables as well as the distance they were located from the sector boundary made this operation an infinitely more complex undertaking than anything that had been done in Vienna. Moreover, because of the permanent tension generated by the Berlin question, it was politically far more hazardous. When the preliminary discussions within SIS itself had been concluded and approval had been obtained in principle, the Foreign Office and the service ministries were consulted. The dividends expected from this operation were such that any hesitations on the part of the former were swept away by the enthusiasm of the latter. The general consensus was that the risks and expenses would be amply justified by the vast amount of hard intelligence that could be expected from this operation.

The two principal experts, Mr Taylor who was to make the tap, and Mr Balmain, who would have to supervise the construction of the tunnel, had already studied the project and given their verdict that it was practicable. The next step was to approach the CIA in Washington. As they had been regularly receiving the Vienna bulletins and at once saw the infinitely greater possibilities offered by the Berlin plan, which had been given the codename 'Stop-watch Gold', they needed no persuading and were at once enthusiastic. In February 1954 the CIA sent a strong team of their experts to London to begin detailed discussions and lay down the framework for future co-operation. The team of five officers was headed by Rowlett, who at that time was Head of the Soviet section in the CIA. Also present was Bill Harvey the Head of the CIA station in Berlin. This Texan had rather a Wild West approach to intelligence and, as if wishing to deliberately draw attention to this, always carried a six-shooter in an arm holster with him. Its unseemly bulge under his too-tight jacket looked somewhat incongruous in the quiet elegance of Tom Gimson's office in Carlton Gardens where the meetings were held.

The SIS side was led by George Young, then still Director of Requirements and soon to become Vice-Chief. Peter Lunn was there as the initiator of the project and Tom Gimson as the expert on the processing side. Other British authorities were called in as their aspect of the operation came up for discussion. I kept the minutes of the meeting.

The morning sessions were always prolonged over lunch to which each side entertained the other in one of the smarter West End restaurants. The afternoons were taken up with detailed discussions between the experts of both sides. The atmosphere was cordial and businesslike. The Americans were clearly anxious to get down to brass tacks and work out as quickly as possible a detailed plan for submission to Washington.

First the broad outlines of co-operation were laid down. The Americans would provide the money, the necessary cover facilities in Berlin and the manual labour required. The British would supply the technical equipment, the experts in the various fields and the monitoring staff. The processing and evaluation of the intelligence obtained would be carried out by joint CIA–SIS teams. The end product would be shared by the two services. As the processing centre would be located in London, it would be headed by an SIS officer with an American as his deputy.

In Berlin an American Army store would be built in the Alt Glienicke area to provide cover for the digging operation and to house the large monitoring station. The tunnel would run some twenty-four feet deep from the Army store along a cemetery to the Schoenefelder road under which ran the three Soviet cables. These contained direct trunk lines connecting the Soviet headquarters in Karlshorst with Moscow, as well as a large number of other military telephone lines. The taps themselves would be located in a shaft-like tapchamber only a few feet underground. The monitoring station, equipped with transformers, amplifiers, recording machines and the latest miscellaneous electronic equipment would be installed in vast chambers under the Army store. An elaborate alarm system would be installed which would give immediate warning if any unauthorised person penetrated the tunnel. Heavy sliding steel doors would secure the monitoring area from entry from the Eastern side. At the point where the tunnel crossed the zonal boundary it would be closed off by a barrier of sandbags. Finally a special air service would be laid on to fly the take daily to London for processing.

It might at this point be helpful to give a brief account of the general relationship between SIS and CIA at that time.

On the whole, co-operation between SIS and CIA was extremely close, though for reasons inherent in the character of these organisations there was always bound to be a certain amount of reserve on both sides. It is true that SIS, with its historic reputation and long experience, had been called in to act as midwife at the birth of CIA in the years immediately after the war when the USA had felt the need for a permanent intelligence service. In the person of Kim Philby, it had then had a guiding hand in the organisation of the new service and in the light of subsequent events it may possibly not have been the only guiding hand. But soon the young stripling had outgrown its mentor and, with far greater resources in money and manpower, had become the senior partner. Though its methods of operating were on the whole not to the liking of most SIS officers who, both by tradition and necessity, practised a more subtle approach and favoured more discreet ways of getting hold of intelligence, CIA, by sheer force of numbers and money, was able to produce far more information than SIS, with all its experience and know-how, could ever hope to lay hands on.

Contacts between SIS and CIA covered a wide field of activity. Some large-scale intelligence operations were jointly run. For instance, the British and Americans together financed and controlled for intelligence purposes the anti-Soviet émigré organisation, NTS. This operation, run under the code name 'Shrapnel', cost a lot of money, but produced poor results. Having come to the conclusion that NTS operations in the Soviet Union had come almost completely under Soviet control, SIS decided in 1955 to pull out and leave the tiresome job of dealing with Russian émigrés to its American partner.

This liaison between the British and American intelligence services was chiefly conducted through the SIS Washington station and CIA's station in London. The latter office had a large staff dealing with a number of Government departments (MI5, the Joint Intelligence Committee, the Joint Intelligence Bureau, the Foreign Office and others) but their main link was with SIS, which was broadly speaking responsible for their activities in the United Kingdom.

CIA often discussed plans and operations with SIS before informing the State Department of them. Care had to be taken therefore that no reference was made in Foreign Office telegrams to joint SIS–CIA operations or plans. Failure to observe this precaution had in the past resulted in the State Department becoming aware of CIA plans before they had been submitted to it for clearance, thus causing embarrassment to CIA and SIS relations.

There was an understanding that CIA would not recruit British citizens without SIS approval and SIS would not recruit American citizens without CIA approval. Equally CIA would not carry out intelligence operations in the United Kingdom without submitting details to SIS and obtaining its approval.

Not every one in SIS welcomed these close ties with the Americans. George Young, when he was Vice-Chief, said in one of his talks to senior SIS officers about Anglo-American relations in general, and SIS–CIA relations in particular: 'If we were in the position of England at the time of the first Elizabeth with the same unscrupulous adventurism of the first Elizabethans, the situation would not be difficult to play for our Government . . . But Britain would have to keep a free hand, as free as Elizabeth always left herself in her dealings with Spain, France, the Netherlands and the Muscovites. For better or for worse, we have thrown in our lot with the Americans. Interdependence has meant that we are embroiled more and more with CIA in any major project. It is the Prime Minister's policy "to carry the Americans with us", as the saying goes. The snag of course is that in a number of spheres of SIS–CIA co-operation the Americans might drag us back or even down with them and it is a delicate and difficult matter to handle.'

No doubt this was an expression of his personal views, but, I think, it is true to say that it reflected fairly accurately those tacitly held by the great majority of SIS officers.

I want to make it quite clear here that, apart from my involvement in the initial stages of operation 'Stop-watch Gold', the codename allotted by the SIS Registry Office to the Berlin tunnel operation, I have myself never at any stage in my career in SIS had any official contact with the CIA or been engaged in joint operations with that organisation.

When the Americans left they took with them to Washington detailed plans of every aspect of the operation. It so happened that two days later I had my regular meeting with my Soviet contact. I handed to him film of the minutes taken at the meetings together with the accompanying sketches and plans which I had been able to photograph in my office during lunchtime the previous day. I told him in broad outline about the Berlin project and pointed out to him the great secrecy with which the operation was surrounded and the necessity for taking particular care that any counter-measures the Soviet authorities might take should look natural and not create the suspicion that they were aware of what was afoot. My Soviet opposite number was much impressed with the audacity of the scheme and its magnitude and asked me to meet him again soon so that we could discuss it in more detail and I could keep him informed of any fresh developments.

When we met again a week later he told me that in view of the importance of the information and its secrecy he had taken the photographed documents to Moscow himself. There they were now being studied in order to work out appropriate protective measures. As far as he could see at this stage these would probably be limited to diverting the most important and secret traffic to other routes. He had, however, been especially instructed to assure me that no steps would be taken which could be interpreted as evidence that the Soviets knew or even suspected that their cables were no longer secure. The safeguarding of my position was considered of paramount importance. The operation would therefore be allowed to take its normal course. Indeed, it might be possible to make use of it to Soviet advantage.

How had it come about that I, who had been so proud on that morning in August 1944 when Colonel Cordeaux RM, Chief of the Northern Area (CNA), had told me in his office on the eighth floor of 54 Broadway Buildings that I was now a member of the legendary British Secret Service, so proud that I could hardly believe my luck, was now freely and willingly divulging information on the most sensitive and secret operations of that service to a representative of the Soviet Union? To explain this, I will have to start with the story of my life and above all relate how it shaped and changed, in the course of time, my religious and ideological convictions and brought me to the situation in which I now found myself.

Chapter Two

The first change in my life came when I was twelve. My father died. Up to then our family, consisting of my parents, my two younger sisters and myself had lived in comfortable circumstances in Rotterdam and later in Scheveningen, a fashionable seaside resort near The Hague. My father was the owner of a small factory manufacturing leather gloves, used by the riveters in the Rotterdam shipyards. The last years of his life were dogged by ill health and financial worries due to the heavy slump in shipbuilding following the Wall Street crash. These worries had hastened his end. We children had been little affected, however, by these gathering clouds as my mother, in spite of all the difficulties, had always managed to keep our home a haven of cosy security.

My father, Albert Behar, was Jewish and born in Constantinople, where his ancestors found refuge after their expulsion from Spain at the end of the fifteenth century. My grandfather was a wealthy carpet merchant who had many sons and daughters. The family's affluence lasted till my grandfather's death after which his elder sons managed to squander rapidly a considerable fortune. In my father's home on the Bosphorus Spanish was spoken and my grandmother in her letters to her many children, who, after the First World War, settled in various parts of Europe and the Middle East, would write in Spanish, but in Hebrew script.

Like most wealthy and educated oriental Jews my father's family looked to France as the fount of civilisation, culture and good taste. They were in love with all things French and while they might be indifferent or feel superior to the country in which they happened to live, they were ready to make any sacrifice for the country they idealised. But my grandfather, who died before the First World War, was evidently a prudent man who liked to hedge his bets. No doubt bearing in mind the German ascendancy in Turkey at that time, he sent some of his sons to study at German universities and some, because of his attachment to France, to French universities. My father, who was one of the younger sons, was sent to the Sorbonne. What exactly he studied there I never learnt. He had not been there very long when the First World War broke out. Passionately pro-French, he at once gave up his studies and volunteered for the Foreign Legion. Being a Turkish subject, I suppose this was the only way he could join the French Army. Much of this is surmise on my part as he never talked to us much about his background and early life. I know he served in the Foreign Legion because he told my mother and there was a photograph of him in a Legionnaire's uniform. How or why he subsequently transferred to the British Army, I do not know because he never told us. But I do know that at one time during the war he served with the British Army in Mesopotamia. Again I can only surmise that as a fluent Turkish speaker his knowledge of that language must have been required in that theatre of war in some intelligence function or other. He had a distinguished war record and when the war ended he had accumulated an impressive row of medals among them the MC and the French Croix de Guerre. He had also acquired British nationality. On several occasions he had been severely wounded and subsequently he never fully recovered his health. He was entitled to an invalid pension which he collected every month at the British Consulate in Rotterdam. His last posting before being demobilised had been with an army unit sent there to supervise the transit of British POWs passing through Holland on their way home from German prison camps. It was there that he met my mother, fell in love with her and decided to marry her.

My mother came from quite a different background. She belonged to a Dutch family which in the seventeenth century had moved from Westfalia to Rotterdam and, though originally engaged in trade, had later supplied many civil servants, doctors and ministers of the Church. Her father had been an architect in the service of the Rotterdam municipality and her maternal grandfather, who was of

27

Huguenot descent, an architect in government service. Ironically, he had been in charge of the building of a number of prisons in various parts of Holland and as a result his children were all born in different towns which are now known for their large prisons. My grandfather had died in the last year of the war, a victim of the epidemic of Spanish flu which was then sweeping Europe. My grandmother was left with five children: three daughters, the eldest of whom was my mother, and two boys, who were still in their teens. It was the eldest of my uncles, who, anxious to practise his English, struck up a casual acquaintanceship with my father and in due course invited him home for tea. This first visit was followed by many others and soon he was considered a friend of the family. My grandmother must have felt sorry for this lonely soldier in a foreign land while to the boys and girls he must have been a rather romantic figure. He was slightly built with a dark, handsome face which was marred, however, by two deep scars, one on each cheek, the result of flying shrapnel. This disfigurement was redeemed by his eyes which were large and dark and extremely beautiful. It was not surprising therefore that the three girls secretly fell in love with him. Of the three my mother was undoubtedly the most attractive. Aged twenty-three at the time she was tall and good looking with regular features framed in an abundance of fair hair. She had also great charm which throughout her life served her well as it disposed people of the most different kind well to her. She was exactly the type of woman oriental men fall for and, given the situation, it was almost inevitable that my father should fall in love with her. He started to ask her out and before long proposed to her. He still had some money left of his share in his father's inheritance and decided to use it to set up business in Rotterdam and settle there.

My grandmother had watched these developments with growing alarm. She naturally expected her daughters to marry Dutchmen of a solid background and was not at all keen on the idea of having as a son-in-law this dark foreigner about whom she knew very little and whose prospects seemed at the best uncertain. She would have been even more alarmed and her opposition to a marriage even stronger if she had known that my father was Jewish. Compared to some countries there is very little anti-semitism in Holland. This does not mean, however, that people of my grandmother's background were free of a certain amount of prejudice towards this ancient nation or above making the occasional snide remark when the talk was about Jews. Certainly she would not have welcomed a Jew with open arms as a member of the family. My father must have been aware of this and, realising that he was up against enough opposition as it was, decided not to make it worse by telling anyone, even my mother, that he was Jewish. Having set out on this course, he must have found it more and more difficult as time went on to broach the subject and so he kept silent. We only learned that he was Jewish after his death when I went to Egypt to live with his sister.

In view of my grandmother's opposition to the marriage and in order to avoid any awkward situations, the young couple went to London where they got married in the Chelsea register office in the presence of a few of my father's friends and without a religious ceremony. On their return to Rotterdam they settled in a large house in the oldest part of the town, a stone's throw away from the statue of Erasmus. I remember this statue well since as a small boy I watched it carefully on many occasions while playing in the little square in which it stood, having been told that he turned a page of the book he was holding every time the clock on the St Lawrence church nearby struck the hour. But however attentively I watched, I never caught him doing it. That part of the town, with its narrow alleys and small squares, has now disappeared having been entirely destroyed in the German bombardment of May 1940. The old house in which I was born and of which I remember very little was divided in two parts: on the ground floor was my father's office and the workshop, where the leather articles in which he traded were manufactured, while the upper floors were used as living quarters.

My grandmother was at first very angry at what amounted to an elopement and for a while even forbade her other children to visit my mother. But soon she relented and resigned herself to an accomplished fact especially when about a year later I, her first grandchild of whom from the very beginning she was very proud and fond, was born.

It so happened that I have fairly often had to change my name in the course of my life and the first change occurred very early on. My grandfathers on both sides were called Jacob, my Dutch grandfather in the Latin form, Jacobus. It was therefore decided that I should be called Jacob, in honour of one or both of them, as you like. Accordingly when, after the delivery, the family doctor asked my mother what I was to be called she said Jacob. When he returned in the evening to see how mother and child were doing he asked how little Jacob was getting on. To her great embarrassment my mother had to tell him that it was no longer Jacob, but George. What had happened was that on the way to register my birth my father had changed his mind. I was born on the 11th of November, 1922,

Armistice Day, and being a war veteran he decided at the last minute in a surge of patriotism to call me George in honour of the King of England. It was typical of my father that he did this on his own without first consulting my mother. The funny thing is that I never liked the name George and at home and by my relations I was never called by that name, but by the nickname Poek, which I was given very early on. Another strange thing is that later, when I started to read the Bible I felt a strong attraction to the personality of Jacob and to some extent identified myself with him. This was even before I knew that I was partly Jewish. Evidently the fact that my mother called me by that name in the first hours of my life must have left an impression. I have never liked the name George myself though this may be due in part to the fact that in Holland it is an unusual name and made me stand out from the beginning among my friends and school fellows as somebody slightly different. I much prefer incidentally to be called, as I have been for the last twenty-three years, by the Russian version, Gueorgi, which sounds more attractive to my ears.

From the very first my mother and her many relatives, in the first place my grandmother, my aunts and my uncles, played the most important part in my life. My father, though we loved him dearly and stood in awe of him, was a rather remote figure of whom we children saw comparatively little. This especially when, after a few years, we moved to a new flat on the outskirts of the town and he transferred his business to other premises in the centre. We then saw him only on Sundays or for a short time at breakfast. In those days it was the custom to put children to bed early and as he did not return home till well after eight we were asleep and never saw him in the evening, though he always came into our bedroom to cover us up and kiss us goodnight.

On Sundays he was often tired and preferred to stay at home with a good book rather than accompany my mother on the long walks on which she and her younger sister took us. His health was never very good and much of his energy was taken up by the struggle to keep his business going. He was up against many difficulties. He was a foreigner and did not speak Dutch. He also knew very little about the Dutch character and customs. This made him do things which in Dutch eyes seemed strange and instead of attracting customers put them off. These difficulties could have been to a large extent overcome if he had taken the trouble to learn the language and been willing to listen to my mother's advice, but this he stubbornly refused to do. The truth of the matter is that, in spite of his Jewish origins, he did not conform to the stereotype of the clever Jewish businessman. Nevertheless at times his affairs flourished and then he was in high spirits and spent money lavishly – much against my mother's sound common sense. At other times things went less well and then he was worried and depressed. It was my mother's great merit that among these fluctuations of fortune and moods she managed to keep the family boat on an even keel and sheltered us children as much as possible from their consequences.

My father spoke French as a native and English well, though how well I cannot judge since I myself did not learn to speak that language till after his death when I was thirteen and went to live with his relatives in Egypt. At home he spoke English with my mother, who, like most Dutch people spoke English much better than French, though she had learned both languages at school. We children spoke Dutch both at home with our mother and relations and, of course, at school and with our friends and as we saw comparatively little of our father did not learn to speak English. So there existed a rather unusual situation in our family where we children did not have a common language with our father. This lack of direct communication did not worry us very much as far as I can recall as, somehow, we managed to understand each other.

I can remember only one instance when it caused me great grief and mortification. The last three months of his life my father was in hospital in The Hague, where we were living then, dying of lung cancer, the result of a gas attack in the war. We knew he was going to die as the doctors had told my mother that his case was hopeless from the very beginning of his illness. Every day after school – I was at that time in my first year at the municipal Gymnasium – I went to visit him. He was lying in a cubicle with curtains around it which were usually open. One day, as I was sitting at his bedside, he asked me to close the curtain. Somehow I just could not make out what exactly it was he wanted, however much I tried. The more I tried the less I understood. He got angry with me and I felt desperate and was almost in tears. Fortunately, the man in the next cubicle who, being ill himself probably understood him better, told me what he wanted and all was well. But I shall never forget this experience, especially as he died shortly afterwards.

I suppose my father was always somewhat a stranger to me. As I've said, he was very foreign and had nothing Dutch about him. But any idea that I hated him and that this was my pyschological motive for what I later did and that, as Leo Abse has written, the British

Secret Service provided 'full facilities for George Blake to commit posthumous parricide', is absolute nonsense. My father's main influence in my early life was to give me a great respect for Britain and a dislike of Germany. That said, there is no doubt that I was closer to my mother. We are similar characters, we have a lot in common. After she was widowed at thirty-eight, I was the only man in the family. My mother has always been very loyal to me, a good friend as well as a good mother.

My mother's relations formed a close-knit family who, though not always agreeing, were very much taken up with each other and we saw a great deal of my grandmother, my aunts and uncles not to mention great aunts and uncles and cousins of various degrees of proximity. Being the eldest of her grandchildren, I was, from the very beginning, my grandmother's favourite. She was a tall, handsome woman with a high colour and beautiful white hair. Always dressed in long black gowns, as was the fashion for elderly women in those days, and walking with a black ebony stick because of a knee complaint, she had a rather imposing presence. She was a woman of strong character and always said exactly what she thought. Her children loved and respected her, but were a little bit afraid of her, as my grandfather must have been, who was, by all accounts, a mild and gentle mannered man. I simply adored her. My sisters and cousins were less enthusiastic and I think deep down resented the fact that I was her favourite. The family had no money of its own and she lived on a widow's pension from the Rotterdam municipality. Every month she had to go to the town hall to collect her pension. She would always take me with her and make a bit of an occasion of it. The town hall with its monumental staircase and long vaulted corridors with white and black marble tiles and heavy oak doors impressed me very much. It made me feel rather important, a kind of reflected glory that I too was in some way connected with this imposing building from which the town was governed. After she had received her money she would always take me to Heck's, one of the largest tearooms in Rotterdam in those days, where a small orchestra played light music and she treated me to cream cakes or icecream. My early life was not without male influence, in spite of my father's remoteness, as my two uncles devoted a lot of their free time to me. In summer they would take me sailing in their boat on the river Maas or for long bicycle rides along the straight roads and dykes along the canals which linked the many villages and small towns around Rotterdam. In winter, when there was ice, they took me with them when they went skating which I had learned to do quite well at the early age of five. My eldest uncle was then studying to become a hydrotechnical engineer. I remember visiting him with my grandmother while he was doing practical work draining polders. He was wearing high rubber boots and living in a wooden shed and what with all the sticky mud and water around it did not seem to me a profession I wanted to follow. When he finished his studies he was sent out by the Dutch government to the West Indies, got married and passed out of my life. My other uncle joined his brother-in-law's grain firm, also got married and later successfully set up his own grain business. He continued to play a role in my life till he died at the end of the Sixties. Both my uncles were very tall and it was my great hope as a boy that when I grew up I would be as tall as they were. For a long time I prayed every night that I might grow to be at least six feet tall. Although I myself never grew taller than about five foot seven, these prayers have evidently not been entirely without effect. One of my sons is six foot and the youngest, born in Russia, is six foot two.

My aunt Truus, short for Gertrude, my mother's youngest sister was another important person in my youth. She was the tallest of the three sisters with a rather sharp tongue and the same independent character as her mother. She had a great gift for story telling and the ability to make a quite ordinary everyday event into an interesting and amusing occurrence, imitating as she was telling it, the intonations, dialect or particularity of speech of all the persons involved. She never married and worked for a well-known Dutch banking firm. On her free Saturday afternoons she used to like taking me with her for long walks which often lasted three hours or more. I enjoyed accompanying her for during these walks she would tell me endless stories about distant relations or people in her office, whom, although I had never seen them, I got to know very well. These stories were mostly highly entertaining and at times I would shriek with laughter especially when she took people off. From these walks I have developed two lasting characteristics. One is that for me the highest form of humour remains somebody taking somebody else off. The other is that I developed the habit of listening rather than talking. So, partly out of laziness perhaps and partly out of a genuine interest in what other people have to say, I have always encouraged other people to do the talking, thus leaving myself free to listen or, occasionally, I must admit to simply switch off.

When I was five years old I went to the municipal primary school which was located at ten minutes' walking distance from where I lived.

From the very beginning I did well at school and one way or another was always among the four best pupils of the class. My favourite subject, however, was history – Dutch history, of course, at that point – and very early on I started reading historical novels about the Eighty Years War of the Dutch republic against Spain, the early journeys of discovery of the Dutch seafarers and the sea battles of de Ruyter and Tromp. In this I was much encouraged by my uncle Tom, who enjoyed reading these books himself, and then passed them on to me. Special heroes for me were the princes of Orange; William the Silent, a portrait of whom was hanging in my room, his sons and his great grandson the King – stadtholder William III. In consequence, I developed a great attachment to the House of Orange and when reading about the long drawn out struggle for power between the stadtholders and the powerful merchant oligarchy my sympathies were invariably on the side of the former.

Even earlier my imagination had been peopled by Biblical heroes: Abraham and Isaac, Jacob and Esau, Joseph and his brethren, Samson, David and Saul etc. The first book I was ever given as a present was an illustrated Children's Bible. With much pleasure I listened to and later read for myself the stories of the Old Testament. Their heroes made a deep impression on me, they seemed so much more exciting than those of the New Testament with whom I found it much more difficult to identify myself.

My mother's family belonged to the Remonstrant Church as the followers of the Dutch seventeenth-century theologian Arminius were called. He preached free will and universal salvation and put forward the view that because of Christ's atonement all men might be saved and not merely a pre-ordained elect, as the Dutch Reformed Church, more or less strictly adhering to Calvin's doctrine of predestination, held. The doctrinal controversies between the Arminians and the Calvinists led to civil strife in the Netherlands in the first two decades of the seventeenth century in which the rich merchant families of the large towns were generally on the side of the Arminians and the ordinary people, led by the stadtholder Maurits, son of William the Silent, on the side of the Calvinists. The struggle ended in a victory for the Calvinists when, in 1619, the Synod of Dort condemned Arminius as a heretic and expelled the Remonstrants from the Dutch Reformed Church. I write about this dispute in some detail as it coloured my religious and later my philosophical opinions. It might have been expected that since my family were Remonstrants my sympathies would have been with the followers of Arminius. In fact they were entirely on the side of the Calvinists and the Dutch Reformed Church. This was not of course because at the age of ten or so when I read about these quarrels, I knew what free will and predestination meant or understood what the controversy was about. It was simply this: the stadtholder was on the side of the Calvinists so, therefore, was I. It was only many years later, when I was able to understand the fundamental issues, that my initial sympathies led to a genuine belief in predestination and election by grace and later in determinism.

My early pleasure in books and interest in history should not be taken to mean that I did not enjoy playing with boys and girls of my own age. I had many friends both among my schoolfellows and boys and girls who lived in the neighbourhood. We played mostly in the street where the various games followed each other in a strict order established by some mysterious unwritten law governed by the seasons and just as immutable. Much of our free time we boys spent wandering on the river embankment and the many quays of the port. I enjoyed sitting on a bollard watching stately ocean liners being towed to their berths by busy small tugs. I spent many happy Wednesday afternoons, when there was no school, watching the traffic on the river and trying to determine the nationality of the ships that passed by their flags and what company they belonged to by the markings on their funnels. There is a well-known poem about Rotterdam which says that if you have spent your boyhood there you will feel at home anywhere in the world. Wherever you are you will encounter smells with which you were familiar in your youth when you played on the quayside – coffee from Brazil, spices from India, hides from Argentina, timber from Russia. Wherever you are you can say, here it smells as in Rotterdam. Perhaps that is why I have always felt quickly at home in whatever country I was predestined to live.

My relations with my sisters were very close and have remained so throughout our lives. We somehow felt that we were bound by a common destiny which nothing could sunder. There was only a difference of one year between us and so we played quite a lot together and with each other's friends. One of our favourite games was to play 'doctor'. I would transform the bathroom into a sort of operating theatre in which I was the doctor and my sisters were the patients. Or I would transform the attic into a church with benches made from boards and a makeshift pulpit. I, dressed in an old black gown of my grandmother would be the minister and my sisters would be the congregation. It is true, I enjoyed this game more than they did and I sometimes had to resort to bribery to get them to agree to join in.

Then in 1929 came the Wall Street crash. As the world crisis gathered strength it began to affect the fortunes of our family. As a result of the heavy slump in world trade many ships were laid up and, of course, no new ones were being built. This directly affected my father's business. Though he manufactured other leather articles as well, the bulk of his trade was the leather gloves, used by riveters in the dockyards. When they were laid off, no new orders for gloves were naturally forthcoming and he in turn had to sack a number of his work people. The firm of my aunt's husband, who was a grain dealer, was also badly affected and eventually went bankrupt. Like several other ruined and embittered middle-class people my aunt and uncle began to look towards national-socialism for salvation. At home the daily conversation centred round the ups and downs of business, the difficulties of paying creditors, how many people and who should be sacked and who kept on, whether there were signs that things were getting better or, on the contrary, worse. It was not only at home, but in the streets also that one noticed everywhere the signs of economic crisis. Shops in glaring red figures slashed prices in a desperate attempt to attract customers, many went bust and had to close down. Hundreds of thousands of people were soon without employment. They gathered every day around the labour exchanges where they had to have their cards stamped to prove that they were not clandestinely employed and therefore entitled to the modest unemployment benefit which was just enough to keep their families alive. Often there were meetings and demonstrations. The Salvation Army organised soup kitchens and collected clothes to help the needy. In my school there were several boys whose fathers were without work. I cannot say that at the age of ten or twelve this called forth a feeling of revolt in me against the injustice of a system which engendered all the misery I saw around me, but rather one of resignation as in the face of some enormous natural calamity which man was powerless to avert and had to accept as he had to accept illness and death. Indeed illness and death became inseparably linked in my memory with the world crisis.

As a result of constant financial worries, the struggle to keep his business going and the uncertainty of the future my father's already frail health began to deteriorate rapidly. When he came home from work he was often so exhausted that he could mount the stairs only with difficulty. On Boxing Day 1934 he took to his bed and did not get up again. My mother called the doctor who ordered him to be taken at once to hospital. The next day lung cancer was diagnosed and my mother was told that there was no hope of recovery.

This was the beginning of a difficult period. My mother had to take over the day to day running of my father's business in his absence and try to save what could be saved. Instead of looking after the home, she now had to go every day to work in Rotterdam. In addition, she wanted naturally to visit my father as often as possible. This was a great strain on her. To make sure that even if she could not go herself to the hospital somebody would come to see him, I took to going there every day after school often accompanied by my sisters. From the very beginning my mother had told us that there was no hope of him getting better. Even so I don't think it really sank in and part of me continued to believe that one day he would return home again. Although my father had not taken a very direct part in our upbringing, apart from of course providing for us, we loved him dearly and could not imagine life without him. As for my father himself, though he realised that he was very ill, I do not think he believed until perhaps the very last days that he was dying. He often talked about what he would do when he got out of hospital. One of his plans was to go and stay for a while with his mother, who was living in Nice at the time, to fully recover.

One morning in early April my father died. The evening before my mother had been called to the hospital as his condition had grown worse and she had spent the night there. I was cycling to school with my friend, as we did every morning, when she passed me in a taxi on her way home. She stopped the taxi and told me that my father had died. I told my friend who went on to school by himself and I returned home.

Although I had known that he was dying, it was still a heavy blow. He was buried from the hospital and as the coffin was closed I had not actually seen him in death. For a long time I continued to believe that he was really still alive somewhere and would unexpectedly turn up.

Meanwhile life went on. In the existing circumstances it had been quite impossible for my mother to keep my father's business going and soon after his death it went bankrupt. After all the outstanding debts had been paid, there were no assets left and we had nothing to live on. My mother's family helped as best they could, but they all lived on their salaries and did not have much money to spare. My mother began by letting two rooms in our house to two nurses from a nearby hospital. She was also a good cook so she started to cook evening meals for office girls in the neighbourhood. What with these sources of income, a small allowance from the national assistance and some stringent economies my mother managed to keep things going without too many drastic changes in our way of life.

Shortly before his death, when he must have realised that he was dying, my father had given my mother the address of one of his sisters, who was living in Cairo, and told her that she should turn to her for help.

This my mother did. My aunt was married to a banker, lived in a palatial house and had two sons in their early twenties. With them lived an unmarried younger sister of my father. The family was Jewish and very wealthy. They were very understanding and willing to help, but rather than send money regularly to my mother about whom, after all, they knew little or nothing, they suggested that I, as the only son, should come to Cairo to live with them and they would take charge of my education. This should help to ease my mother's financial situation and assure a good education for me.

At first my mother was rather taken aback by this offer and very reluctant to let me go. But after some thought and discussions with her family and friends she came to the conclusion that it would be in my interest to let me go. She felt that an upbringing in the wealthy and cosmopolitan surroundings of my aunt's home could only benefit me and provide a better preparation for life than the much more modest, rather narrow-minded and provincial way of life of a Dutch middle-class family at that time. My grandmother was much against my going, but as she was not in a position to offer much financial assistance, she also had, albeit reluctantly, to agree. As my mother would not have dreamt of sending me against my will, the final decision was left to me. When she asked me how I felt about it, I was torn. I was very much attached to my home, my Dutch relatives and, particularly, my grandmother and the thought of leaving them for the home of an unknown aunt and uncle, whose language I did not speak, frightened me. On the other hand, I was strongly attracted by the prospect of travelling to a far and exotic country and the entirely new life and adventures which awaited me there. It was this thirst for adventure and the unknown which proved the stronger and after a few days of thought, I told my mother that I would like to go.

Two months later, on a fine September evening, I stood on the deck of a Dutch cargo ship looking at the white dunes of Holland receding in the setting sun. The captain had promised my mother to keep an eye on me and to deliver me safely into the hands of my cousin, who would meet me in Alexandria. Among the crew was a young cabin boy, only two years older than myself, who turned out to be the brother of a boy I had been friendly with at school in Scheveningen. This gave me access to the crew's quarters, a world peopled in my eyes with 'real men' and quickly consoled me for the pangs of parting from my family. The crew was very kind to me and I think felt a bit sorry for me. The two weeks on board passed very quickly and much too soon for my liking our ship was slowly making its way past British warships and vessels from every nation to its berth in Alexandria harbour. There, on the quayside, my cousin Raoul was waiting for me to escort me to his parents' home in Cairo. As we drove off, the crew lined up on deck to wish me luck and wave farewell. My cousin spoke French and very little English and I very little of either, but what we lacked in ability to communicate we made up for in mutual goodwill and the desire to understand each other. Like all members of my father's family he was dark and of slight build. His pale complexion and glasses gave his appearance something scholarly. This was indeed what he was. At the time he was studying Sanskrit in Paris and later became a distinguished archaeologist.

At the station in Cairo my two aunts, both dressed in black as they were in mourning for my father, were waiting to meet us. A car driven by the family chauffeur took us home. The house, referred to in Cairo as the 'Villa Curiel' built in the style of an Italian palazzo with a large terrace and balconies could be considered a large mansion or a small palace. It stood, surrounded by palm trees, in a spacious garden on the northern end of the Island of Zamalek, between two branches of the Nile. It had no less than twelve bedrooms. My uncle, Daniel Curiel, though blind, was a passionate collector of antiques and the dining-room, library and reception rooms were furnished with furniture of various styles and periods. The walls were hung with paintings and tapestries and the floors covered with oriental carpets and rugs. These, I later discovered, were mostly part of my aunt's share in her father's inheritance.

I was at once taken to my uncle, who was lying on a sofa. Next to the sofa stood a large wireless set which played an important role in his life as he was an avid listener to the news in those years of the rise of national-socialism and anti-semitism in Germany and the ever-growing threat of war.

He was a small man with round shoulders and a rather flaccid body, due to lack of exercise. From a pale face protruded an aquiline nose and a thick reddish moustache. He always wore dark glasses which gave his appearance something mysterious. He had been blind since the age of ten months when a nurse accidentally dropped him. He was a great lover of music and played the piano beautifully.

My aunt led me to the sofa and I bent down to kiss him. As I did so, he felt my face with his fingers, a gesture to which I was to grow accustomed. In a soft voice he said some kind words of welcome to me.

Several guests arrived soon afterwards for lunch among whom were old friends of the family who had known my father in Constantinople and were curious to meet me. They were all very nice to me, but I felt rather bewildered in these new surroundings which were so different from what I was used to and much of what they were saying I couldn't understand. Lunch was a grand affair and consisted of six courses handed round by three Nubian servants in white gowns with red sashes.

My aunt Zephirah had married my uncle, who was some ten years her senior, when she was sixteen. By agreement between the two families she had been sent from Constantinople to Cairo to marry a blind man, whom she had never seen before and who would never see her at all. The marriage had turned out a very happy one. When I came to live with them she was about fifty. Of slender build, she was already grey, with well defined features and a great air of kindness. My aunt was very pious and much inclined to mysticism. I think marriage to a blind man was to her an offering and a fulfilment. She devoted much of her time to charities, both Jewish and Roman Catholic. There were many poor in the Jewish community in Cairo. Their families had been in Egypt since biblical times and they lived mostly in the Jewish quarter. They spoke Arabic and, religion apart, differed in no way from the Egyptian masses. My uncle and aunt gave much money to schools and orphanages. In particular an orphanage run by the nuns of the Order of Our Lady of Sion was an object of interest to my aunts. They frequently visited it and donated a lot of money to it. There was a reason for this. One of my father's sisters when still a young girl had been converted to Roman Catholicism and became a nun. She was now living in a convent of the Order in Constantinople.

My maiden aunt Marie, who was some five years younger than her sister and had jet black hair, bore a striking resemblance to my father. This made me feel very soon at home with her, although in the beginning I found it difficult to talk to her. She spent a lot of time knitting for her charities and always accompanied her elder sister on her tours of charitable institutions. She also looked after any member of the household who happened to be ill or just not feeling very well and knew an amazing amount of popular remedies. Thus she believed strongly in the effectiveness of cupping-glasses, which she very expertly fixed on the backs of her various relatives on the slightest pretext.

A rather colourful member of the family was uncle Max, the younger brother of my uncle Daniel. He was a tall, broad-shouldered man with handsome features. Being a sleeping partner in his brother's firm, he didn't do any work himself and led the life of a playboy. He had great charm and many mistresses. He used to get up late in the morning, spend a long time dressing and after lunch went out to play bridge, visit his many friends, and attend dinner parties. He usually ended the day in a fashionable nightclub. He took an amused, if somewhat detached, interest in me and was always very kind.

Although we were all related to each other, one way or another, all the inhabitants of the large house had different nationalities. The Curiel family, having originally come from Tuscany, my uncle and aunt had Italian nationality. Uncle Max however, for some reason or other, had an Egyptian passport. My aunt Marie had retained her Turkish nationality. My cousin Raoul was French, but his brother Henri, about whom more later, out of solidarity with the Egyptian masses had opted for Egyptian nationality. I was a British subject.

My uncle and aunt began by sending me to a French school so that I would learn to speak French fluently as soon as possible. In the years before the war French was the language used by educated people of the many national communities in the Middle East. They had intended to send me to the French Jesuit College in Cairo, where their two sons had been educated, but here I felt I had to put my foot down. I had been brought up in the Protestant tradition and the thought of going to a Catholic school and one run by Jesuits to boot, frankly shocked me. I told my aunt that my Dutch family would be very worried if they knew I was going to a Catholic school. She at once saw the point and decided to send me to the French Lycée, a secular establishment, instead. It had a very good reputation and ran special classes to teach French to the sons of well-to-do Egyptians. The year I spent at that school was not a very happy one, though I did learn to speak French pretty well. My class mates were mostly Egyptian, the spoilt sons of rich parents and several years older than myself. Outside the classroom they spoke Arabic with each other, a language I did not know at that time, so I had little contact with them. I made only one friend there and he was a Copt.

I have often wondered what would have happened if I had not

objected and had gone to the Jesuit College. I might well have ended up a Jesuit father myself.

My aunts and uncle were very kind to me and did everything they could to make me feel at home. Very soon I developed a great liking for my uncle and he for me. I started to accompany him on his walks or on visits to various Egyptian ministries where he frequently had appointments. From time to time he would take me with him to his office where I would sit in his room and listen to what was being transacted. He had given up all hope by that time that his sons, who both had strong left-wing views, would take over the family firm and I had a feeling that he began to look on me as a possible successor. I doubt whether I would have been suitable material. I had never felt attracted to business and had not felt in the least sorry that my father's firm had gone bankrupt. Be that as it may, violent upheavals were soon to occur which put an end to any such plans.

My uncle and aunt, in order to escape the heat of the Egyptian summer, every year spent a few months in Europe, mostly in France, where they had many relatives. I was given the choice of accompanying them or spending my school holidays in Holland. Without hesitation I opted for the latter. Although I was happy in Cairo, I missed my Dutch family very much and counted the days to the start of the summer holidays. On a small calendar over my bed I struck off the days as they passed.

A friend of ours in Rotterdam was a shipping agent and he secured a passage for me as a passenger on a Norwegian freighter, which plied regularly between Antwerp and Piraeus, calling at various Mediterranean ports. When, early in June, I climbed up the companion ladder of the SS *Bruse Jarl* as she lay at anchor off the Greek port of Patras an unforgettable period in my boyhood years began. For the next month I led the kind of life most boys at the age of fourteen dream of. At first I was simply a passenger, but gradually I became involved in the ship's life and by the end of the voyage I had become almost a full-blown member of the crew. I would regularly take my turn at the wheel and in between help with the chipping and painting or, if it was foggy, go up aloft in the crow's nest as a look-out.

The last port of call before Antwerp was London and so for the first time in my life I was to set foot on the land to which by nationality I belonged and for which the precepts of my father had filled me with deep respect and admiration. As we proceeded up the Channel a feeling of mounting excitement, as if before some great event, began to get hold of me, heightened by the general air of anticipation and bustle usual on board a ship approaching a big port after some time at sea. It was a beautiful summer morning with a slight haze when I got my first glimpse of England, the low shore line and white and black lighthouse of Dungeness where we picked up the pilot. I looked at him with interest for he seemed to me a rather special person, the first Englishman I saw who actually lived in England. Late that afternoon a small tug pulled us through the locks into East India Dock. As soon as the ship was tied up and the gangway had been lowered, I stepped ashore. As I was familiar with the atmosphere of Rotterdam, its dockland areas, its working-class houses, its pubs, warehouses, railway lines, disreputable cafés and seamen's clubs, my first walk in London along the Commercial Road brought nothing new except that everything seemed just that little bit grimier and shabbier than in my home town. What struck me most was the people. Did these often undersized, sharp featured, agile and wiry men belong to the same nation as those tall, good-looking, languid young officers I had seen playing polo at the Gezira Sporting Club? I had not then heard of Disraeli's two nations, but this was exactly the impression I got on that first visit. It was as if two nations inhabited England, different not only in habits, language and culture, but even in physical appearance.

Two days later I was reunited with my mother and sisters after our first long separation. There were to be many more in later life, some much longer and more painful, but always carrying with them the hope and joy of a reunion.

The summer passed quickly. In September I left again to join the *Bruse Jarl* in Antwerp for the return journey to Egypt and school.

Having learned to express myself freely in French, the language spoken at home, my uncle and aunt were of the opinion that the next step should be for me to learn to speak English fluently, all the more so as I was a British subject. There was an excellent English school in Cairo, for the children of British officials serving in Egypt, but attended by children from other communities as well. I was sent there to prepare for the London University matriculation examinations. I was much happier at this school than I had been at the French Lycée and felt more at home. The school was run on the lines of an English public school though most of the boys were day boys. The masters wore gowns, there were prefects, morning prayers and corporal punishment. I acquired several good friends there, among them an American boy of Dutch extraction. He loved English literature and under his influence I became a great fan of Dickens. I read nearly all his works, which I liked all the more at that time for the contrast they offered with the life around me in Egypt. Other friends I made were an Irish-American boy and girl who lived nearby, the children of the Greek Ambassador, who were cousins of my cousin Henri's best friend and through whom I met the children of the Dutch Ambassador, a boy and a girl of my age. We used to meet at each other's houses, listen to music, play games and talk. The wives of the representatives of Phillips also took an interest in me which enabled me to spend the occasional afternoon in a Dutch atmosphere.

Looking back now, I am sure that I lived through an identity crisis in those years. Where did I belong? A Jewish cosmopolitan home, an English school, which reflected the glory of British imperial power of which I also felt a part and in my heart, all the time, a longing for Holland and all things Dutch.

I was a very religious boy and always went to church on Sundays, sometimes even twice. The first year I spent in Egypt I was not able to do this because I could not follow the service, but the second year, when I began to speak English well, I started going to the American Reformed church, where the services were most like those in the Dutch Church. Later I also liked going to the Anglican cathedral, being much attracted by the beauty of the liturgy. In my uncle's library I had found a large French Bible which I took to my room and from which I read a chapter every morning and evening. My aunts did not put any obstacles in the way of my going to church. On the contrary, they rather welcomed it. They never tried to convert me to Judaism. Only once was the question raised in a rather casual way and when I politely declined it was never referred to again. I could not imagine, how, having known and recognised the Messiah, one could go back to not knowing and recognising Him. Otherwise the fact that I had Jewish blood did not worry me. On the contrary I was rather proud of it. It seemed to me that I was now twice elect; once by birth through the promise made to Abraham and once by grace through redemption by the blood of Christ.

My religious fervour was increased through my heated discussions with my cousin Henri. He was my aunt's youngest son and studying law at Cairo University. Tall and extremely thin he had at that age already a slight stoop. He had wavy black hair, a pale complexion and well defined features. Immense charm and a dazzling smile made him very attractive, not only to women, but to all who met him. His principal interest was politics and left-wing politics at that. It was the misery of the Egyptian people, which he had seen around him since his childhood, that motivated him. He had been introduced to the works of Marx and Lenin by his elder brother Raoul who himself, however, remained a social-democrat throughout his life and was at that time a young protégé of Leon Blum, the French Prime Minister, of the Front Populaire. Henri saw the only solution to Egypt's ills in Communism and used his considerable skills, acquired from his Jesuit schoolmasters, to propagate the faith. Later he became a co-founder of the Egyptian Communist Party and spent many years in prison. After being expelled from Egypt, he settled in France, where he became deeply involved in support for the Algerian war of liberation. He was also very active in seeking a rapprochement between the Israelis and the Palestine Liberation Movement. He was murdered in Paris in 1978 by right-wing extremists.

Although he was eight years older than me he liked talking to me and sometimes took me with him when he visited the peasants on his father's large estate fifty miles outside Cairo. Their living conditions were miserable. Most of them suffered from eye disease and bilharzia. Henri always took large quantities of eye lotion and medicines with him which he handed out to the peasants and their families. His father did not approve of this at all and, generally, disliked his left-wing views. It was not that he was not a kind man and he gave generously to Jewish charitable works, but his charity did not extend to the Egyptian fellah. Anyway that would have been a hopeless undertaking. Henri soon began to realise this himself. Handing out eye lotion wasn't the right remedy. It was necessary to change the whole system. Only political action was truly effective.

I liked him very much and got on very well with him, but his example and the discussions I had with him had little or no influence on me. On the contrary it called forth strong opposition. It was not that I was insensitive to the sufferings of the Egyptian poor, though I tended in those days to look upon this more as a traditional aspect of the oriental scene than as a great social evil which could be remedied. Nor could I deny that the Communist ideals were in many ways admirable. But there was for me one insurmountable obstacle to accepting his views. Communism was the declared enemy of God and wherever it had triumphed, be it in the Soviet Union or in the Spanish Republic (it was the time of the Spanish Civil War), it had relentlessly persecuted the Christian churches and their ministers. This alone was enough for me to condemn it utterly and doom it for ever. All my cousin's arguments in the end butted on this point. If, when I later joined the Secret Service, the check on my background ever revealed that I had been close to my Communist cousin, I have no idea. If it did, then the Service never raised it with me. And of course, in 1943, the enemy was Germany and not the Soviet Union, so it would have made no difference anyway.

Thus I lived for three years, spending the winters in Egypt and the summers partly at sea on the *Bruse Jarl*, which I always managed to catch, and partly with my mother and sisters in Holland. Then came the summer of 1939. I had passed my end-of-term exams well with prizes for History and Latin. I had moved up to the sixth form and was due to sit for the London University matriculation examination the following spring. I was sixteen and enjoying life. I had spent a pleasant summer staying with various relatives and was due to sail for Egypt again in a week's time. Then came the news that the German forces had entered Poland. Two days later on a Sunday morning, drinking a cup of coffee with my mother and sisters after church, I heard Mr Chamberlain announcing that war had been declared. I wondered then how its end would find us. Would I come out of it alive? At once it was decided that I should not return to Egypt. The times being so dangerous, the future so uncertain, my mother felt that we should all stay together. I did not offer much resistance. Deep in my heart I was pleased that it was now possible to resume what I thought was going to be my normal life.

Chapter Three

A new episode in my life started. Arrangements were made for me to go to school in Rotterdam for my last year. I would live with my grandmother and aunt and spend the weekends at home with my mother and sisters in The Hague. I was glad to be back in Holland. The curriculum at school was, of course, quite different from that of the English school in Cairo. In some subjects I was behind, in some ahead, especially in languages, but, on the whole, I did not find it too difficult to adjust myself. I made new friends and, naturally, I felt more integrated and part of the scene than I had done in Cairo. The winter of 1940 was cold and there was a lot of ice so that I was able to go for long skating trips on the canals around Rotterdam. There were still ample food supplies although a distribution system was being put in place. Of the war, which anyway had not yet started in earnest, we noticed very little. Occasionally a British or German aircraft was brought down which had violated Dutch neutrality. The members of the crew would be interned if they were alive or buried with military honours if they had been killed. Among the population there was, in general, a feeling of quiet confidence that Holland could manage to remain neutral, as it had done in the First World War, provided it took care not to offend either side, especially its more irascible Eastern neighbour. The German invasion of Norway and Denmark shook this confidence to its roots and the mood became more pessimistic. In spite of the strict neutrality, the sympathies of the vast majority of the Dutch people lay with the British and the French, especially the former. In spite of colonial rivalries, at times of great dangers in their history – the Eighty Years War and the French occupation under Napoleon – the Dutch had always looked to Britain for help. Since it was a constant of British policy on the continent that the Low Countries should remain independent, they never did so in vain. Also, being a commercial and seafaring nation, they felt closer in spirit to the British than to the Germans whose martial traditions were foreign to them and which they feared and disliked, especially in their recent national-socialist manifestation.

When I was woken in the early hours of Friday the 10th of May by the sound of an explosion, my first reaction was that a passing car must have burst a tyre. I turned over to go to sleep again when there was another explosion followed by machine-gun fire. My grandmother came into my room with a worried look asking me what I thought those explosions could be. 'Probably a German or Allied aircraft which has violated our neutrality,' I said, half believing this and half wanting to put her mind at rest.

Still, I got up and looked out of the window. People, most of them still half dressed, were standing in little groups in the street or leaning out of the windows. Some had even climbed on the roof tops. All were looking up at the sky where several aircraft were giving each other chase and firing bursts of machine-gun fire. From the direction of the port came the sound of heavy explosions. This was clearly more than an aircraft violating our neutrality. 'War, invasion, Germans' – these menacing words came drifting up to me from the excited groups in the street below. I switched on the radio. The announcer, his voice heavy with foreboding, kept on repeating the same news. In the early hours of the morning German troops had crossed the frontier and were now engaged in heavy fighting with the Dutch Army which had been ordered to resist. War had been declared, the Dutch Ambassador in Berlin recalled and the Allies asked for assistance.

That morning the atmosphere in the streets was reminiscent of a public holiday. The streets were full of people who, having had no experience of war, were quite heedless of the danger from the air. Their mood reflected patriotic fervour mingled with indignation at the treachery and meanness of this attack by a powerful neighbour on a small country which only wished to live in peace. There was no question of going to school and my friends and I made our way to the centre of the city from where the sound of battle came. We were all in a state of joyful excitement, most inappropriate to the occasion. This mood was heightened by one particular news item broadcast in the course of the morning. The government, as a gesture of hostility towards the enemy, had abolished the teaching of German in the schools. On reflection, this seemed a particularly irrelevant measure. One would have thought that, at that juncture, it would have had more important things to worry about. But as schoolboys we were, of course, delighted.

When we got near to the centre of the city, we were driven back by gunfire. As they crossed the frontier, the Germans had simultaneously dropped paratroops over Rotterdam to occupy the airfield and the bridges across the river Maas, which linked the Northern with the Southern Netherlands. These objectives were stubbornly defended by the Marines, garrisoned in Rotterdam, but they were suffering heavy casualties and the Germans kept dropping new waves of paratroops. In a few places, not far from our home, bombs had fallen and houses been hit.

In the course of the day the reality of war began to make itself felt and drove away the euphoria of the first hours. There was no question now of leaving for The Hague to join my mother and sisters. The Germans had also dropped paratroops on an airfield between Rotterdam and The Hague and were using the autobahn between the two cities as a landing strip. It would have been impossible to get through. In a few days when the situation might be clearer, I would attempt the journey.

In Rotterdam the fighting in the centre of the city continued over the next few days. Though the Germans had managed to establish a foothold there, the Marines were holding out. Elsewhere, the Dutch Army was retreating westwards on all fronts. Little or no help was forthcoming from France and Britain which were too busy stemming the German tide in Belgium and Northern France.

Then came the 14th of May. The sky was cloudless, as it had been all those four days of war. We were just sitting down to lunch when they came. The sirens sounded and their wailing merged with the heavy drone of aircraft. Wave after wave of enemy bombers came flying in and, turning almost overhead for their run in, dropped their bombs and incendiaries on the centre of the city. Time and time again came the sickening whine of the Stukas as they dived, followed by explosion after explosion and, time and time again, we thought our end had come. I don't think the attack lasted more than twenty minutes, but to us it seemed to be going on for ever as we sat under the table in the dining-room with kitchen pans on our heads, in accordance with instructions given over the radio. Gradually the noise died down like a thunderstorm drifting away. The high diminishing drone of a laggard enemy aircraft, a few explosions at ever longer intervals, then all was quiet until we became aware of a roar. At first it puzzled us, but soon we recognised it for the roar of flames. I looked out of the window. Our square was still standing but over it hung a thick pall of black smoke totally obscuring the sky. The entire old centre of the city was burning.

The streets were full of people fleeing from the burning hell. Some were half dressed, others were pushing prams and handcarts with the few belongings they had managed to snatch with them. Many were injured, dazed or crying. In a nearby church an emergency hospital was immediately set up to deal with the casualties. I worked there all night, together with many other people from our neighbourhood. We felt both grateful and guilty that we should still have a roof over our heads.

That same evening came another heavy blow. It was announced that Holland, threatened with similar attacks on other big cities, had surrendered. The Queen and the government, together with virtually the whole fleet, had left for England to continue the struggle from there. The next day the German Army entered the city. It was a bitter sight, but as I watched them in their tanks and armed vehicles, I felt an inner certainty that the day would come when British troops would march through these same streets to liberate us. I saw before my eyes a Scots regiment, their kilts swinging and pipes swirling coming down the road to our square, as I had seen them many times in Egypt. I saw it almost as if it was a vision.

Soon help began to arrive from all over the country which, recovering from the shock, found that so far the war had been too short to do much damage. Order was re-established, the dead were buried and a beginning made with clearing away the rubble. After a few days, things began to settle down and I decided to venture on my bike to The Hague to find out how my mother and sisters were.

When I arrived at our flat, I rang the bell, but nobody answered. I rang again, then opened the door with my key. Nobody was there. This was strange. Even stranger were some dirty teacups on the table. I had never known my mother go out without washing up first. I decided to enquire from the neighbours. When the woman next door saw me, she raised her hands in astonishment and said, 'What! You are still here? We thought you had gone to England with your mother and sisters.'

'To England?' I exclaimed in great surprise. 'I know nothing about that.' As British subjects we had been registered at the British Consulate. On the third day of the war my mother had been warned by telephone that if she wished to avail herself of the last opportunity to flee to England, she must report at the Consulate by five o'clock that afternoon. When she said that she would like to leave but did not want to go without me, she was told that, no doubt, I would also have been warned. My sisters at that time were two attractive teenagers and fearing the worst of the behaviour of the German soldiery, my mother felt that she should take them to safety, if she had the opportunity. In haste they had packed a few belongings and left in the hope of seeing me on the boat. This was all the neighbour could tell me.

Probably, because of the fighting, it had not been possible to warn every British subject in Rotterdam individually and, anyway, my grandmother did not have a telephone. Perhaps there had been an announcement on the radio, but I had not heard it. Anyway, that would have made no difference. In the frame of mind I was in, I would not have left even if I had received a warning. In my eyes that would have meant abandoning the sinking ship. Besides, I would not have left my grandmother alone in those dangerous times. That this was a very short-sighted point of view, I was soon to find out. Before the end of the year, I had come round to exactly the opposite.

If we schoolboys had hoped that the war would bring any changes in the old-established school routine, we were soon disappointed. A week after the invasion, my school, which was undamaged, opened its doors again and a month later, on the usual date, we sat for our exams. In spite of my secret hope that the war might deliver me from this ordeal, I had nothing to fear and passed with good marks to everyone's satisfaction.

To recover from all the shocks, it was arranged that my grandmother should spend the summer months with my uncle Tom, the grain merchant, who lived in a small village not far from the town of Zutphen and I would go with her. That part of Holland is very beautiful, hilly, with lots of forest, many old castles, fine country houses and small historic towns. I liked staying with my uncle, with whom I got on well, and who would take me with him in his car on his visits to farmers and millers with whom he had business to transact.

I had been there about a fortnight when one warm afternoon, as I was lazing in the garden with a book, the elderly village constable came to see us. Very apologetically he explained that he had just received instructions to arrest me as a British subject and take me to

Rotterdam. He was unable to tell me what would happen to me and kept on saying how sorry he was, but orders were orders. We had to leave early the next morning and his proper course was to lock me up in the local police station. In deference to my uncle, however, he would allow me to spend the night at home if we promised not to take advantage of this.

This totally unexpected development brought great consternation in the family. Looking back now, it seems astonishing that this event was so totally unexpected. On the contrary, we should have foreseen it and taken evasive action in time. The fact is that my family, and indeed I myself, were so used to regarding me as an ordinary Dutch boy that the thought that I might be interned as a British subject simply never occurred to us. As it was, since my uncle had promised the constable that I would be ready to accompany him the next morning, it was now too late to do anything. To my grandmother, especially, it was a big blow. I tried to console her and give myself courage by suggesting that it might be just a question of reporting and that when they realised I was just an ordinary schoolboy, they would let me go. The next morning the constable came to fetch me and, so as not to make it look as if I was some young hooligan who had been taken in custody, he had put on civilian clothes. On arrival in Rotterdam he took me straight to Police HQ. There I was told that, in accordance with instructions received from the German authorities, I was to be interned as a British subject.

In the course of the afternoon my aunt came to visit me. She was in tears. What seemed to shock her most was that, in accordance with the regulations, they had taken my tie away. She brought me cherries and a change of clothes and took the opportunity of giving the policemen present a good piece of her mind. She told them in no uncertain terms what she thought of Dutch officials who carried out German orders and locked up little boys, a category to which in her eyes I still belonged.

I spent the night in a police cell and the next morning was taken by two Dutch detectives by train to Schoorl, a small village on the coast, north of Amsterdam. At the station a sergeant of the German Security Police was waiting for us and took us in a police van to the nearby camp. There my passport was taken away from me, my small bag searched and my name registered in the books. I was then taken to a hut, already crowded with young Frenchmen and Englishmen, and assigned a bunk.

Though I soon became accustomed to my new circumstances, I felt at first quite apprehensive. The worst excesses had not yet taken place, but sufficient was known about German concentration camps to chill the heart of anyone who entered their gates as an inmate. The fact that this particular camp was guarded by Waffen SS, with the skull and crossbones on their caps, did nothing to reassure me. As it turned out life in the camp was not as bad as I had expected. All the inmates were French or British subjects. Those under twenty were put in a separate hut under a young and aggressively fit SS sergeant who made us do everything at the double. Much of the day was taken up by roll calls, scrubbing our hut, keeping the compound clean and peeling potatoes. The food was adequate. We were civilian internees and the Germans were well aware that thousands of their own nationals were interned by the British authorities in all parts of the world so they observed the rules of international law.

I had been in the camp about two weeks when the news came of the fall of France. Naturally this had a most depressing effect, though most of us, even among the French, felt that this was by no means the end and that Britain would go on fighting. The Germans, on the other hand, were convinced that all was over bar the shouting. In a few weeks, they boasted, they would land in England and quickly bring the war to a victorious end.

One evening in the fourth week of my internment, immediately after dinner, the sergeant called everyone in the youth hut out and lined us up in the courtyard. He then ordered those who were under eighteen years of age to take a step forward. About five of us, including myself, did so. He told us that as we were not yet of military age and the war was nearly over, it had been decided to release us. We could return home the next morning.

I was by now accustomed to camp life and had begun to make good friends among my fellow prisoners. Though thrilled at the unexpected prospect of freedom and of seeing my family again, I felt sad to leave my new friends behind to an uncertain fate. Much later I heard that a week or so after my release all French subjects had been set free. The British were kept. They stayed in the camp till the beginning of the winter when the Germans, realising no doubt that the war would not be over as soon as they had expected, moved them to another camp in Eastern Silesia where they remained until they were liberated by Russian troops in the spring of 1945.

The family was sitting in the garden drinking tea when quite out of the blue I walked in. I got a hero's welcome though I had done nothing heroic. Many neighbours and friends called to hear my experience which I had to tell over and over again. In those early days of the war, it was still something new among the Dutch to have been arrested by the Germans. Not much time would pass before it became a common occurrence and the tales of those who survived and returned differed tragically from mine.

The summer passed and the Germans were clearly making no headway with their invasion of England. The Battle of Britain had been fought and the RAF emerged victorious. Rumours were circulating in Holland that the Germans had concentrated large numbers of ships and landing craft in the estuary of the Scheldt. It was even said that an invasion attempt had actually been made, but that it had been foiled at sea by a wall of fire. Whatever the truth of all this was, one thing was certain: the Germans would not be able to land in England that autumn. On the BBC, to which it was forbidden to listen, we heard the stirring speeches of Churchill. These gave us hope and strengthened our resolution to resist.

There was thus every prospect that the war would not be over soon. There was also every prospect that when I became eighteen in November the Germans would intern me again. I was determined that this should not happen and I was fully backed in this resolve by my uncle. He had among his acquaintances a farmer who lived in a small hamlet called Hummelo, some 20 miles from Zutphen in the depth of the country. This man agreed to give me a small room in his house and let me live with his family in return for a small payment. Another friend of my uncle's, the burgomaster of the village where he lived, provided me with a real Dutch identity card in a fictitious name. If there were any enquiries about me from official quarters, he would report me as missing. With these precautions, we felt I stood a good chance of keeping out of the hands of the Germans who, anyway, were unlikely to waste much effort to find me.

From my mother and sisters I had no news. We heard that on the day of the surrender several British and Dutch destroyers had left the Hook of Holland with refugees on board. Some of these had been sunk. We could not, therefore, be certain that they had reached England safely.

Early in October, I moved to the farm. Though I gave a helping hand with the farmwork, my existence there would have been dull had it not been for certain developments which made that period of my life one of the more exciting ones and predetermined, to a considerable extent, the course it was going to take.

I continued to be a regular churchgoer and my religious opinions at that time put me firmly in what is called today the fundamentalist camp. Already I had decided for myself that, when the war was over, I would try to become a minister of the Dutch Reformed Church, a calling for which I felt strong attraction and for which, it seemed to me, apart from faith, I had certain abilities.

Meanwhile, when the first shock of defeat had worn off, the will to resist began to manifest itself among the Dutch people. As the war continued the food shortages became greater, the German terror and pressure to impose national-socialism on an unwilling nation increased and the persecution of the Jews started, and this will to resist began to spread to ever wider sections of the population. To the majority of the people Queen Wilhelmina became the symbol of freedom and a rallying point for resistance. She was a woman of considerable dignity and authority to whom people felt they still owed allegiance and who was directing affairs from a country which was continuing the struggle. That fact kept alive the hope that one day the tide would turn and the invader be driven out. This hope was an essential factor in the will to resist, giving it purpose and meaning.

I too hated the Germans, felt passionately pro-British and my thoughts also began to turn to resistance. It seemed to me that I was in an ideal position to do this kind of work. I had already gone underground, was living under a false identity, did not have to go to school or to work and did not have to give account of my movements to anyone. I began to look for ways to make contact with an underground organisation.

In Zutphen, I had become acquainted with Dominee Padt, a well-known local minister. I had attended his confirmation classes and on several occasions he had invited me to his house to have tea with his family. He was an inspiring preacher who, with subtle allusions to biblical figures and events, would castigate the enemy and keep alive the hope in his congregation, which was always vast, that one day he would be defeated and the country free again. Among his friends it was generally believed that he was in contact with people in the underground movement.

One day in the early spring of 1941 I decided to go and see him to talk to him of the possibility of offering my services to a resistance group.

He was a slender, ascetic looking man with very dark eyes and a soft voice which under the high vaults of his church, which before the Reformation had been a Catholic cathedral, acquired unexpected power and intensity. He listened to me with sympathy, but did not give a direct answer and asked me to come and see him again the following week. When I called again, he told me that he had spoken about me to a friend of his, who had expressed a wish to meet me. Could I accompany him to Deventer, a large provincial town some thirty miles north of Zutphen, in three days' time. I naturally agreed at once.

On the appointed day we travelled together to Deventer. There we made our way to the market square where we sat down on the terrace of a large café and ordered a cup of the concoction of barley and chicory which in those days passed for coffee. After about ten minutes, we were joined by a man who greeted Dominee Padt as an old friend. He had a pleasant, open face and, though his short grey beard indicated that he must have been well into middle age, his lively blue eyes, compact, well-knit body and quick movements gave his personality something young. He was introduced to me by the name of Max and that was all I ever knew about him.

He asked me to tell him about myself and listened attentively as I told him my story in broad outlines. I had brought my British passport with me which I showed him to convince him of my bona fides. He studied it carefully and then nodded, apparently satisfied. He said he needed an assistant; I would do. My job would be to act as a courier. I would have to visit various places all over Holland to collect and deliver parcels and messages. I was to travel the following Monday to the village of Heerden, north of Deventer. There I was to go to the local grocer, whose name and address he gave me, and say that I had come from 'Piet' to collect the groceries. I would then receive further instructions from the grocer.

Having settled this, we talked for a while about the war situation. Persistent rumours were going around that the Germans were preparing to attack the Soviet Union. Max had heard of several cases of German officers, stationed in Holland, who had been ordered to leave for Poland where large German forces were being concentrated. He added thoughtfully that if Hitler did attack the Soviet Union he would find that he had bitten off more than he could chew.

When the following Monday afternoon I entered the small grocer's in the village street not far from the station, there was nobody in the shop. In answer to the bell which rang as I opened the door, a man with silver grey hair, a high complexion and steel-rimmed spectacles, dressed in a white coat, emerged from a room behind the shop and asked me what I wanted. When I said I had come from Piet to collect the groceries, he at once asked me to follow him into the back room.

It was a cosily furnished living-room where his wife, a jolly looking, stout, middle-aged woman, was sitting at the table busy with
the administration of the coupons, an important element in a shop-
keeper's work in those days. When her husband told her I had come
from Piet, she expressed no surprise and at once got up and offered
me a cup of tea and a biscuit. I remember this well for it was real tea,
something rare in those times of shortages. The grocer told me that I
would have to spend the night in their house and the next morning
early take the train for Assen, a large town in the north of Holland,
where I had to deliver a parcel to a local dentist. I would be given an
envelope which I was to take back to them the same day. The grocer
and his wife turned out a very friendly, warm-hearted couple who had
no children of their own. They evidently took a liking to me, as I did
to them, and we spent a very pleasant evening together. I subsequently
stayed frequently in their hospitable house which served as a kind of
base where I received my instructions and to which I reported back.
My work consisted of travelling all over Holland, partly by train,
partly by bicycle, depending on the distance, carrying parcels with
illegal literature and delivering messages. If I could not return home
in time for the curfew, I would stay at the house of a member of the
group or at the grocer's. About once a month I would meet Max at
some pre-arranged place when he would give me new instructions and
some money for my travelling expenses. I look back on that time as
one of the most interesting periods of my life. I met many wonderful
people, whose names I do not remember and often did not know and
who did not know mine, but with whom I felt a strong bond forged by
the knowledge that we were doing a dangerous job in a cause in which
we all believed. By opposing the authority of the hated invader we had
set ourselves free from that authority and had become free men again,
even though we lived in occupied territory.

Although I was only a small cog in the organisation, about the
activities of which, quite properly, I knew very little, the journeys I
undertook involved some danger. In the first place, there was the ever
present risk that our organisation, which published the illegal
newspaper *Vrij Nederland*, might be penetrated by the German
security police and that one day, calling at an address with a parcel,
I might find the Gestapo waiting for me. Indeed, during the period I
worked for the group a number of its top organisers were arrested, but
some survived and managed to resume the publication comparatively
quickly. I was lucky that among the people with whom I was in
immediate contact no one was arrested.

Another ever present danger was the elaborate inspection system, set up by the occupation authorities with the assistance of the Dutch police, to combat the black market. Passengers on trains and other forms of public transport frequently had their luggage checked and on the roads cars and cyclists were stopped to see what goods they were carrying. I had, therefore, to be constantly on my guard for sudden checks and ready to take evasive action. I usually put my parcel or briefcase in a luggage rack some distance from where I was sitting so that if there was a check, I could always pretend that it did not belong to me. What helped also, I think, was that I looked extremely young for my age. When people saw me with my satchel, I don't think it occurred to them that I was anything else but a schoolboy on his way to or from school.

Once I was nearly caught through my own carelessness. It happened in the town of Assen where I called regularly at a café, the owner of which was a member of the organisation. In a backroom he gave me a parcel with newspapers. As I was in a hurry to catch the train so as to be able to return home that evening I hastily transferred the newspapers to my briefcase. There was no room for about six, so I stuffed them between my shirt and pullover under my raincoat and ran to catch the tram to the station. Just as I reached the tram stop the papers worked loose and scattered all around me. The only other person waiting for the tram was an elderly German officer. As I knelt down in a frantic attempt to collect the newspapers before he could see what they were, he also stooped down and began to help me to pick them up. He handed them to me without even looking at them. I thanked him profusely and boarded the tram. I didn't tell any of my friends about this adventure.

The illegal press fulfilled an important function in Holland in the years of the occupation when all political parties, except the Nazi party, were banned and the official press was completely under German control. Everything that the official press was not allowed to publish found expression in the illegal press: the hatred of national-socialism, indignation at the German terror, the thirst for freedom and the strong faith in the ultimate defeat of the enemy. It called for resistance, spiritual resistance always, resistance in deed whenever possible. Holland is a small, densely populated country, highly cultivated with no impenetrable forests or inaccessible mountains to give refuge to partisan bands, harassing the enemy. Here the battle had to be fought in a different, more secret and modest way, avoiding open confrontation with the enemy forces. The 'Vrij Nederland' group, like other similar groups, did not only publish and distribute an illegal newspaper, but tried to organise intelligence networks and set up radio transmitters to supply the Dutch government and our British allies with intelligence on enemy troop movements, fortifications, headquarters and airfields. It arranged for addresses where allied air crews who had been shot down and managed to bale out could be hidden, and organised escape routes to enable them to return to England. Of most of these activities I was not aware at the time and I learned about them only afterwards.

On my travels through the country, I increasingly had to pass through or visit towns and villages which had been put out of bounds for Jews by the German authorities. This was part of a carefully thought-out system of humiliating measures, designed to isolate and harass the Jewish population, to make life impossible for them, prior to deporting them to Poland for the 'final solution'. Although like the vast majority of the Dutch people, I loathed these measures, I did not feel myself directly affected by them. There were several reasons for this. In the first place I looked upon myself as a Christian and not a Jew. After all, I had not even known I had Jewish blood till I was thirteen. I had not had a Jewish upbringing, was not a member of any Jewish religious community or organisation and had no Jewish relatives in Holland. My name, which was then Behar, was a Jewish name – indeed, it is of Hebrew origin – but it was hardly known in northern Europe and not immediately associated with Jewishness, as are such names as Cohen, Rosenzweig or Goldstein. Besides, I was living under an assumed name. Although I am dark, I do not look particularly Jewish and it would not be immediately obvious that I have Jewish blood. If the Germans were looking for me at all, they were looking for me as a British subject and not as a Jew. The only way therefore the persecution of the Jews affected me was that it increased my hatred for the Nazis and all they stood for even more.

One Sunday morning in midsummer 1941, shortly after I had started work for Max, the news came that the German armies had crossed the frontiers of the Soviet Union. With fanfares of trumpets and much Wagnerian music, it was announced that the Führer had decided to rid Europe and the world once and for all of the Red Menace and put an end to the Jewish–Communist conspiracy to dominate the world. That day, posters appeared everywhere depicting the German eagle swooping down on the many-headed Red monster. In the evening we heard Churchill on the BBC welcome a mighty and valiant new ally to the common cause.

59

The news inspired new hope and generated a wave of optimism. Everyone thought this was the beginning of the end. What Napoleon couldn't do, Hitler would not be able to do either. The first months of the Russian campaign, however, brought nothing to cheer us. The German armies seemed indeed invincible as they swept along the entire front deep into Soviet territory and presently stood before the gates of Moscow and Leningrad. It was not until the Soviet winter offensive of 1941, which halted the German advance, that hope returned.

Whenever I happened to be in the neighbourhood, I visited my grandmother. Her health was deteriorating. Patriotically minded and of independent character, the defeat and occupation of Holland caused her much pain. She worried about the fate of my mother and sisters and found it difficult to cope with the increasing food shortages and the lack of fuel. Her strength began to give way and she died in the spring of 1942 on her seventy-seventh birthday. Her death was a big blow to me. Together with my mother, she was the person closest to me. Now that she was dead, I felt that I could leave the country with a quiet conscience and attempt what I had long dreamt of.

Like many other young people in Holland during the occupation, I had a strong wish to escape from the country and make my way to England. Especially since my involvement in resistance work this wish had become stronger. I had ambitious plans of reaching England, getting a proper training there and then returning to Holland as an agent to act as a link between the resistance movement and the intelligence services in Britain. In addition to this dream there was, of course, the hope of seeing my mother and sisters again.

My friends and I had often discussed the possibility of escape. We had explored ways of getting hold of a boat and crossing the North Sea. This proved very difficult. The Germans had forbidden private boats in any waters communicating with the sea and were keeping a strict watch all along the coast. From time to time we heard rumours about people who had got away by other routes. Some had reached Switzerland and Spain through France. Others had managed to reach Sweden. There were even stories that RAF aircraft had landed on one of the Dutch lakes and picked up people, but for that one obviously had to be an important person.

In the end I decided to talk to Max. He listened to me in his usual attentive and patient way. He could fully understand my desire to go to England, though he would be sorry to see me go. He knew nothing about escape routes himself, but he might be able to put me in touch with somebody in the south of the country, who, he thought, could help. Some weeks later I got a message to meet him in the station restaurant in Breda. I was to take my passport with me. When I arrived Max was waiting for me in the company of a young man of about thirty. He introduced himself as de Bie, a name well known in that part of the country, and turned out to be the owner of a large tree nursery in the village of Zundert, just on the Dutch side of the border with Belgium. He said that Max had told him about me and that he was willing to help. A small escape party was shortly leaving for Switzerland and he would try to have me included, but the decision did not rest with him. He suggested that I should wind up my affairs and come south to be ready to leave as soon as the word was given. He could put me up in his house while I was waiting.

I had been staying for nearly three weeks in the hospitable house of the de Bie family, where there were lots of young people and a jolly atmosphere reigned, when my host informed me that the escape organisation could not help me. They were only prepared to accept people who were of immediate use to the Allied war effort such as RAF pilots, Dutch army and naval officers or people with special skills. I did not fall into any of these categories. What should I do now? I felt that though I had not gone very far yet and was still in Holland, I had started on my journey and there was no question of going back. I would somehow manage to get across the Dutch–Belgian border and then I would see from there.

My host's two younger sisters, with whom I had become very friendly, immediately suggested that they should take me across the frontier themselves as they knew many of the footpaths used by smugglers. Once across, they would take me to their aunt in Antwerp who, they were sure, would be prepared to put me up for a few days.

We set out on a beautiful Sunday morning and were about a hundred yards from the border, which ran along the edge of a pinewood just ahead of us, when, suddenly, from behind a haystack, a German soldier stepped out and barred our route with his rifle. He was going to shout something at us when his face lit up as he recognised the two girls. 'What on earth are you doing here?' he said, half in Dutch, half in German. 'This is a forbidden zone!' The eldest girl hastily explained that we were cousins and wanted to visit an aunt who was in a nunnery just across the frontier in Belgium. The soldier smiled and nodded. 'All right, I'll let you through and pretend I have not seen you. If you return this way this evening between nine and

twelve, I shall be on duty again and let you back in. Good luck.'
He gave us a friendly wave as we walked on.

I had watched this scene at first with intense apprehension and then
with growing bewilderment. The explanation was simple. The girls,
like most people in the southern provinces, were Roman Catholics and
members of the local Catholic youth organisation. The soldier was an
Austrian and also a devout Roman Catholic, the only member of the
German garrison who regularly attended mass in the church and the
activities of the Catholic youth organisation in Zundert. It was there
that the girls had got to know him as a quiet, friendly man, homesick
for his Austrian mountains. Cheered by the almost miraculous
coincidence that this man should have been on duty at that point at
that time, we continued our journey without further incidents. In the
afternoon we reached Antwerp where the girls' aunt received us kindly
and agreed to put me up.

Once more I had to say goodbye that day and for the first time I
experienced a feeling which was often to recur in later life – a feeling of
the inadequacy of words to express gratitude and admiration to people
who, by assuming very considerable risks, had ensured my safety and
freedom.

The next day my new hostess gave me a letter of introduction to a
Dominican monk at the University of Louvain, whom she thought
might be able to help. When I went to see him he told me that there
wasn't anything he could do himself, but that he would give me an
introduction to a very good friend of his in Paris, also a Dominican,
who might be able to put me in touch with people who could help.

There was a regular train service between Antwerp and Paris. At
the frontier, so I was told, because Belgium and occupied France
formed one German military district, there was only a luggage check
by French and Belgian customs officers. I left for Paris the next day.
The train was so crowded that I had to stand in the corridor. As we
approached Mons, the last Belgian town before the French frontier,
I saw at the end of the corridor two German Feld Gendarmes
(a particularly awesome brand of German soldiery, who wore steel
breastplates on a heavy chain and a fierce-looking German eagle on
their helmets) advancing slowly but surely towards me, checking
identity papers. All I had was my British passport, concealed in a loaf
of bread. As they were approaching, the train began to slow down as it
entered Mons station. I jumped out, ran down the platform and
reached the exit before it had come fully to a halt. Outside the station,
I disappeared into the narrow streets behind it. I entered an old

church and sat down to recover from the emotion and think out what to do next. I decided to try and cross the frontier, which I knew could not be very far, on foot. I left the church and began to walk in a southerly direction. I must have gone the right way for presently I came upon a signpost pointing to Lille. A small steam tram passed along the road and I decided to board it. Eventually the tram stopped in a village square and everyone got out. It was the terminus. I continued walking in a southerly direction. After a while I found myself in a small hamlet, a few houses grouped along a quiet country road which was closed by a striped barrier. Two Belgian customs officers stood chatting near a sentry box at the side of the road. This was the frontier post. A German airman with a bicycle was leaning against the barrier smoking. He threw away his cigarette, got on his bicycle and muttered something that sounded like a salutation. The two Belgian officials appeared not to have heard this for they did not reply. When he had gone one of them made a remark which, though I could not hear it, must have been something disparaging to judge by the expression on his face. The other gave a contemptuous chuckle. I had lived long enough in occupied territory to know instinctively from the reaction I had just witnessed that these two men did not like the Germans. I decided to risk it.

I walked up to the barrier as if I expected to be let through. One of them wanted to see what I had in my briefcase. That was all right. Could he see my identity card? 'I haven't got one,' I said. 'I am an Englishman on my way to France.' The reaction was remarkable. They both looked at me and smiled. 'Why didn't you say so at once. Come with us into the office and we'll see what we can do.' They took me into a small office on the side of the road and offered me a chair. I took the loaf of bread out of my briefcase, removed the passport and handed it to them. They studied it carefully. It was quite an impressive passport as it happened. In the five years I had had it, I had travelled a great deal and it was full of visas and stamps. It satisfied them completely. They discussed what should be done. It was decided that one of them would take me home for a meal while the other would try to find me accommodation for the night. To this day I remember the homely scene round the table with the customs officer's two little girls and his plump friendly wife. At the end of the meal my host produced a bottle of brandy which he kept for a special occasion. We drank to Allied victory. I spent the night on a nearby farm and early the next morning one of the customs officers came to fetch me to take me himself into France. After about an hour's walk, we arrived in

the small town of Maubeuge. There we went straight to the house of
the local chief of customs. He had evidently been warned and was
waiting for us with breakfast. An hour later, I walked with the French
customs chief, now in full uniform, to the market square where the
bus for Lille was waiting.

At six o'clock that evening, I stood outside the Gare du Nord,
thrilled to be in Paris for the first time in my life. In those days of
petrol shortage, there were no taxis in Paris and some enterprising
people had started a taxiped service – a small carriage with seating for
two, drawn by a man on a bicycle. I took one of these and gave the
driver the address on the letter the Dominican monk in Louvain had
given me.

I was deposited in front of a typical Parisian apartment house.
It turned out that the monk to whom I had an introduction was a
member of a small religious community engaged in social studies and
housed in two adjoining flats. An elderly housekeeper showed me into
a book-lined study. A tall, slender monk of about thirty-five rose from
behind a desk. His face was pale and finely chiselled and had
something very engaging. In his intelligent, grey eyes I noticed that
slightly mocking expression one frequently encounters in well-
educated Frenchmen. I showed him my letter and told him who I
was. Could he help me in any way? A worried look crossed his face as
I told him my story. He explained that he was in a difficult position.
Not long ago, the Abbot of the Dominicans in Paris had issued strict
instructions that no shelter should be given by his monks to anyone
hiding from the Germans as this might seriously endanger the work of
the whole Order in France. He was, of course, bound to obey his
Abbot's orders. I said that I fully understood the situation and would
go away immediately. He begged me, however, to stay while he looked
for a solution. He had to give a lecture that evening, but would be
back in two hours. He hoped to have hit on something by then.
Meanwhile I was not to leave the room.

When he had gone, I looked at the books on the shelves and then
saw a monk's white habit hanging on a hook on the door. Knowing
that I would not be disturbed I could not withstand the temptation to
try it on. I looked at myself in the mirror and thought it suited me
rather well. It might be a good disguise for my journey through
France.

When the monk returned, he was not alone. With him was a middle-
aged couple whom he introduced as very good friends. They had
attended his lecture and afterwards he had told them about his

predicament. They had at once offered to put me up until I could continue my journey.

My new host and hostess lived not far away in a side street of the Boulevard St Germain, in a small but elegantly furnished flat. He was the owner of a private security firm which provided night-watchmen and other security measures for factories and large shops. The couple was childless and devout Roman Catholic. For several years they had been members of the third order of St Dominic. They were also fervent French patriots, supporters of General de Gaulle, with connections in the resistance movement. One of their contacts, who went under the pseudonym of 'the Belgian', was the leader of an escape organisation. It took some time to get hold of him as he was frequently away on business. At last one afternoon, when I had been in Paris about a fortnight, 'the Belgian' called. He was a tall, broad-shouldered man in his late forties who listened to my story and studied my passport. Then he explained to me that it was doubtful whether his organisation would get permission from London to organise my journey to England. I was not an airman, an important member of the resistance or a person of particular interest: in short, the same arguments I had encountered in Holland a month earlier. But he thought that even if that turned out to be the case, he might still be able to help me in some other way.

Two years later, when I was working for the British Secret Service, I discovered that he had indeed reported my case to London and had received instructions not to concern himself with me. This was entirely understandable. Nevertheless, partly out of kindness, partly out of consideration for my hosts, he managed to help me without involving his organisation. Through him, I was provided with a French identity card, in the name of a schoolboy from Amiens, and the address of a person in Salis de Bearn, a small health resort in the south-west of France, just inside the occupied zone, who could arrange for me to be smuggled into unoccupied France. He also gave me an address in Lyon, then still in the unoccupied zone, to where I could turn for further assistance.

Thus provided, I was ready to continue my journey. All of a sudden it looked as if most of the obstacles lay behind me. There was only one more hurdle to cross, the demarcation line. After that I would be out of reach of the Germans and the rest should be comparatively plain sailing.

One evening, at the end of August, my friends saw me off at the station as I boarded the train for Bordeaux. I had lived almost a month in their hospitable flat and had accumulated a lot of new impressions. With them as guides, I had seen a lot of Paris and they had introduced me to the austere services in the Dominican Abbey near Paris and to the beauty of Gregorian plainchant. I had done a lot of reading in their well-stocked library and we had long discussions on politics and religion. I began to take a less prejudiced and narrow-minded view of Catholicism. Although they were Gaullists and fervently prayed for an Allied victory, they, like many French people, harboured a grievance against England and thought it had not done enough in the summer of 1940 to avoid the disaster. I thought this was an unfair assessment and, naturally, our different positions sometimes gave rise to heated discussions. I was sad to leave them, but eager to continue my journey.

Salis de Bearn is a small town, pleasantly situated among low green hills, the waters of which are said to be especially beneficial to women. The demarcation line ran just along its outer edge. The man who would arrange the crossing owned a small boarding house. When I told him who had sent me and gave him the password, he at once agreed to take me. A small party would be crossing that very evening. Once we were safely across, we would be taken to a farm where we could spend the night. Vichy gendarmes would collect us there the next day and put us in a refugee camp. I had heard enough of the Vichy French not to relish the idea of spending the rest of the war in one of their camps. I had not come all the way for that. I talked to the boarding house owner who advised me not to go with the party to the farm, but to continue walking all night. I might succeed in getting sufficiently deep into the country and avoid patrols. This I resolved to do.

Just after nightfall, two young Basques, looking agile and tough in their black berets, came to the house to collect the crossing party which consisted of three Jewish ladies of various ages and myself. The two men had brought a small dog with them whose function it was, as they explained, to give timely warning by barking at the approach of German patrols who always had dogs with them.

Through narrow back lanes we reached the edge of the town. The atmosphere was tense. We were now in the immediate danger zone and expecting the German dogs to set on us any moment. Thus we continued for about twenty minutes, scrambling across ditches and crawling through fields. Then we saw, not far ahead, on the top of a gentle slope, a brightly lit house. It was the farm. We had arrived safely in unoccupied France. Reaching the crest of the hill, we

66

suddenly saw lights twinkling everywhere like a promise of peace and security, while behind us the land lay dark. It was as if an immense burden of fear and gloom was lifted from me. I was out of the hands of the enemy. But I did not have much time to indulge in these emotions. I had to go on and chance my luck. I walked on all through the night and met no one. Occasionally a dog barked as I passed a cottage or farm. A few times I sat on a stone to rest, but never for long. I had to get as far away from the frontier as possible.

When the first streaks of dawn began to light up the sky, there suddenly rose up before me the dark outlines of what looked like a medieval castle with battlements, towers and turrets. The road led up to a huge gateway. I had come to the old town of Argagnon. In the market square a bus was waiting to leave for Lourdes. I got in. There were only a few passengers. Just as the bus was going to leave, a gendarme came in to check identity papers. I gave him mine from Amiens. He looked at it and handed it back without saying anything. I reached Lourdes safely and that same evening boarded the train for Lyon.

On arrival the next morning, I went straight to the address given to me by 'the Belgian'. His friend in Lyon was a French colonel with an aristocratic, Breton name which was extremely difficult to pronounce. He lived with his wife in a suite in a big, fashionable hotel. Both were active members of the French resistance movement which had its branches in the unoccupied zone. When they heard that I had been sent by 'the Belgian', they received me most kindly. The colonel appeared to be especially pleased that I could pronounce his name correctly, a feat which, apparently, few people managed the first time. He advised me to report without delay to the American consulate which was looking after British interests. He knew the young man dealing with British subjects there and would give me a note of introduction. That might be helpful. In the mean time, he would try and find somewhere for me to live.

At the American consulate, I was called into the office of a young man who was obviously English. Two years later I was to run into him in a corridor in Head Office in London and discover that he was, in fact, a member of the Secret Service. I showed him my passport and the colonel's note. This satisfied him. He suggested that the best way would be to issue me with a travel document instead of my passport. This would certify that I was a British subject and be true in all particulars except that my age would be given as sixteen instead of nineteen. I would thus not be of military age and the Vichy authorities would grant me an exit visa. At the same time, the American consulate would apply on my behalf for Spanish and Portuguese transit visas. Once all the permits had been obtained, I could travel to England legally. It would take about a fortnight for him to get permission from London to make these arrangements. After that, it might take anything from two to three months to get the necessary visas. The Vichy authorities would require me to live during this period in a place designated by them, which I would not be allowed to leave without permission. This was called *residence forcée*.

That afternoon I called on the colonel again and told him about the very satisfactory outcome of my visit to the American consulate. He had with him a young man who, he said, would look after me while I was in Lyon. They had found accommodation for me and the young man would take me there.

My new quarters were in a very old house, dating from the Middle Ages, and reached through a long dark passage and a winding stone staircase. Two sisters kept an eating house there, open only for lunch and dinner with a fixed menu and regular customers. They were good acquaintances of the colonel, who often ate there and used the premises for clandestine meetings. They had agreed to put me up in a small room at the back of the dining-room. The two sisters, one in her early forties and the other somewhat younger, were friendly, cheerful women and excellent cooks. I stayed with them for more than three weeks and extremely pleasant and interesting weeks they were. Most afternoons I spent at a small, clandestine printing shop located in a nearby cellar. There the colonel's friend, a medical student, and some other members of their group printed a weekly Gaullist newspaper, which was published under the colonel's direction. I would help them with the work. When the newspapers were printed, they had to be taken to distribution centres located in factory stores or wine cellars. This was done fairly openly. Three or four of us pushed a handcart through the streets with several thousand copies concealed under the canvas cover. This was, of course, before the Germans were in Lyon.

After about three weeks, I was told by the American consulate that permission had been received from London to arrange my onward journey. I was issued with a travel document, given some money and could now report to the Vichy authorities and apply for an exit visa. A letter from the colonel to an acquaintance in the Lyon prefecture helped to smooth the process. During the period that I was waiting for my travel documents I was to live in a small inn in a village a few kilometres outside Grenoble.

I had been there for about a month when one day, as I entered the small restaurant in Grenoble where I usually had my frugal lunch, I at once noticed that something unusual had happened. People were talking excitedly and shouting comments from table to table. I gathered that Allied troops had landed in North Africa and as a counter-measure the Germans had entered unoccupied France and might arrive in Grenoble at any moment.

I realised that I had to act at once. I decided to leave my *residence forcée* that very day and try to reach the Spanish frontier before the German troops could start to patrol it. I quickly finished my lunch and hurried back to the inn. I picked up my few belongings and left unnoticed. At Lyon I stopped off to contact my friend the colonel. He gave me some money and the address of a friend in Toulouse who might assist me in crossing the frontier with Spain. That same evening I continued my way south.

Coming out of the station in Toulouse the first thing I saw was a column of German armoured vehicles. I was back at square one. My onward journey, England, Christmas with my family, these hopeful visions had once more receded to a distant and uncertain future.

The man whose address I had been given turned out to be a local journalist. He was at once ready to help and said he would put me in touch with a *passeur*, as the people who smuggled refugees across the frontier were called. Meanwhile, I could stay at his flat, where he lived with his wife, his mother and a teenaged sister.

Two days later, this charming girl, with whom I had become good friends, took me to the *passeur*. The room in which he lived was mainly remarkable for an enormous bed which filled it almost entirely. A dark, elegantly dressed young man, who said his name was Fernandez, and an attractive young woman, a trifle too heavily made up, whom he introduced as his 'assistant' were sitting on it when we entered.

The young man was rather self-important and garrulous which did not inspire much confidence. He told me that I was to be at the station that evening in time to catch the train for Pau. He would be on the platform, but I was to pretend not to know him and travel separately. In Pau he would join me outside the station.

I acted as instructed and on arrival in Pau I was joined before long by the couple under whose, what seemed to me, dubious auspices I was now travelling. They were accompanied by another person who must have been on the same train. He was middle-aged, fat and flabby and obviously Jewish. Later that evening, when I had to share a bed with him in a shabby hotel, I learned that he was a Portuguese Jew who had been on a business trip to unoccupied France where he had been caught by the German invasion. He was now trying to get back to his wife and children in Portugal. To be taken across the Spanish frontier, he had had to pay Fernandez a large sum of money. In the course of the journey, it turned out that this was not all for it was he who had to pay for the lavish dinners which Fernandez ordered whenever we stopped on our way. Through his contacts in the hotel trade he ensured, however, that we did not have to register in any of the hotels where we stayed.

The next morning, the four of us boarded a bus which took us further south. I had seen no evidence of any Germans in Pau or on the road. It looked as if the only opponents we had to outwit were the French frontier guards. So we moved on from place to place, a rather ill-assorted company, with my Portuguese friend getting more and more sore at what he considered Fernandez's extravagant spending but afraid to say anything for fear of being left stranded in France. I also disliked the way in which Fernandez exploited my travel companion and I would have certainly taken him for a swindler, had he not been introduced to me by my friend in the resistance movement and not asked me for more than the normal travelling expenses.

At the end of the third day, after another bus journey, we reached a village high up in the mountains, dominated by the ruins of a castle. From here we would continue on foot.

When darkness had fallen, Fernandez took us to a house on the edge of the village. Here he handed us over to two young men who would actually take us across into Spain. The journey would take two days. We set out straightaway and started climbing the slope which rose steeply above the village. Soon we were panting and sweating. It was not so bad for me. I was young and used to plenty of exercise, but my middle-aged companion was having a difficult time. All I could do to help him was to carry his bag for him. Our guides kept urging us on. This was a dangerous stretch as it was important to get away from the village unnoticed. Once we had reached the crest the going would be easier. Towards dawn we reached a mountain hut where we had something to eat and slept a few hours. The roasted meat and fresh bread, which the guides had brought with them, tasted delicious.

The sun was already high in the sky when we continued our march, climbing on and on towards the snow-clad peaks which we had to cross before reaching the frontier on the other side. I was now carrying two briefcases all the time for my companion was getting more and more short-winded as we climbed higher. Our two guides, though friendly, kept rather aloof as if to underline that they had been paid only to show us the way and that it was our business to keep up with them.

We spent the night in another mountain hut, well above the snow-line. We lay huddled together to keep warm as we could not make a fire for fear of attracting the attention of mountain patrols. As soon as it was daylight, we set out again. The snow got deeper as we climbed and we made slow progress towards the Pic du Midi, the highest point on our route. I remember it as a narrow track from which the mountain fell away sharply on either side so that I had the feeling of walking on a knife's edge. Then we started to descend and the going got easier.

It was about three o'clock when we came to a meadow which sloped down to a mule track running along a gorge at the bottom of which gurgled a mountain stream. Here our guides stopped and informed us that we were now in Spain and this was as far as they would take us. If we followed the mule track, we would get to a farmhouse where we could spend the night. Tired though we were, we felt elated at the thought that we had reached safety at last. In celebration, we all took a deep draught of wine out of the goatskin. Then our guides shook hands and soon disappeared among the trees of the oakwood out of which we had just come.

We got down to the track and began to follow it in the direction our guides had indicated. We walked on for about two hours, but saw no sign of a farmhouse. My companion, exhausted from the strain of the last two days, began to express strong doubts that we were moving in the right direction. He now became convinced that we had lost our way and insisted that we should retrace our steps. I myself had no doubt that we were going the right way. My companion was not to be persuaded and insisted on going back. This was a matter of life and death for both of us. The one who was wrong would be returning to German-occupied France. There could be no compromise, therefore, and with the sun already setting behind the mountain tops we parted, each going the way he thought was right.

I had walked on for about ten minutes when I heard the tinkling of little bells. Round a bend in the track came a flock of sheep, followed by a shepherd, the first human being I had encountered since I left the village. He spoke no French but from his mixture of Spanish and Basque I understood that I was going in the right direction but I was still in France and the actual frontier still lay a little way ahead.

I felt very angry with the guides who had let us down at what seemed the most dangerous point of our journey. I had to go back now and find my travelling companion to tell him what I had learned.

I started back at a trot and had not got far beyond the point where we had parted when I found him leaning despondently against a rock. I told him of my encounter with the shepherd and that we were still in France. The sense of danger and the knowledge that the goal was near lent him wings and we hurriedly retraced my steps. Suddenly the track descended steeply into a deep gully through which a watercourse ran into the stream we had followed. We clambered down and waded through, not realising that in doing so we were actually crossing the frontier. The track again rose steeply and when we got to the top a small valley spread before us. On the bank of the stream stood a large farmhouse from which the sound of voices reached us. The figures of soldiers and mules moved among the trees. We hastily withdrew behind a rock, but it was too late. We had been spotted. A warning shot rang out and the soldiers, who, to judge by their uniforms, were neither French nor German, motioned us to come down. When we got to the stream they surrounded us. We were in Spain, but no longer free.

In the farmhouse we found a small group of refugees who had arrived earlier by the same route. We were given bread and a nourishing soup and spent the night in a large barn. The following morning the luggage was loaded on a mule and another provided for one of the women who had a small child. Then we set out, escorted by a few soldiers. Late in the afternoon we arrived in a village where we were put up in the local inn. The next morning we had to appear before the commander of the Guardia Civil who asked us our reasons for coming to Spain and took down our particulars. My travel companion was able to establish that he was Portuguese and that he had enough money to travel on his own, so he was allowed to go. The refugee family and myself were taken by bus to Irun, a well-known crossing point on the French–Spanish border. The small hotel, where we spent the night, was already full of refugees. It stood not far from the customs barrier on the Spanish side. From the windows we could see the French barrier, some fifty yards away, guarded by helmeted German soldiers. This was an unpleasant enough sight in itself, but what made it worse was the strong rumour going around that we had been brought to Irun to be handed back to the Germans.

The attitude of the Spanish government in the war, so far, made such a move not at all unlikely. It had openly sympathised with the

Germans and Italians and described its position not as 'neutral', but as 'non-belligerent'. The Allied landings in North Africa, however, had brought about a subtle change in this attitude, which became less openly pro-German. Finding themselves suddenly inundated with refugees, as a result of the occupation by the Germans of the whole of France, they had not quite made up their minds what to do. The policy of handing back refugees was now, evidently, thought too risky, for the next morning we were all herded into a bus which, to our great relief, headed south, away from the dreaded barrier. Although it would not have been very difficult to run away, it needed not much imagination to realise that one would soon be caught. Without knowledge of the language, without money and above all without being able to count on the help of the local population, as one could in the occupied part of Europe, it would not be long before one ran into the arms of the ubiquitous Guardia Civil.

The bus took us to Pamplona, the capital of the province. There it stopped in front of a crenellated gateway, flanked by two turrets. The gates swung open and the bus drove slowly into what was unmistakably a prison courtyard. We were ordered to get out and taken into a high, glass-domed central hall. Here the men were separated from the women and children. We were crowded seven into a cell and given two blankets between us. The cells were unheated and the nights at the end of November in that part of Spain pretty cold. We spread one of the blankets on the concrete floor and huddled together, covering ourselves with the other as best we could. The next morning breakfast was served through a hatch in the door. It consisted of a lukewarm, brown liquid in which floated a few crusts of bread. Of one accord we put it down after the first spoonful or two – it tasted so horrible that none of us would eat it.

After a while our cell door was unlocked and we were taken down to the courtyard. In the middle stood a stool on which we had to sit in turn while a Spanish prisoner shaved our heads completely bald. After that we were taken back to our cells. Our position seemed suddenly pretty desperate. If they shaved our hair off, they meant to keep us for a long time. Nobody knew we were there, nobody could claim us, and, if the Spanish authorities felt so inclined, they could keep us in prison indefinitely.

At about four o'clock the rattling of tins on the landing heralded the second and last meal of the day. This time it was another brownish liquid in which floated a few potato peelings. This first day set the pattern for the next three weeks. Kept completely in ignorance of

73

what our fate would be, we sat huddled together all day, numbed by cold and hunger, until at eight o'clock in the evening we were allowed to lie down on the floor. With me in the cell were two young Poles, who had succeeded in making their way from Poland, and four Frenchmen of various ages, who wanted to join the French forces in North Africa. We were too cold and hungry to talk very much, but as soon as we heard the rattling of tins on the landing, we would crowd round the little hatch like wild animals to receive our ration, which never varied from day to day. We gulped it hastily down and sank back again in silent apathy.

Early one morning we were all taken out of our cells. In the central hall we were lined up in fours and handcuffed together. Under escort of armed Guardia Civil in their shining black Napoleonic hats and wide capes, we were marched through the streets of Pamplona to the station. There we were hustled into the reserved carriages of a waiting train.

It was already late when we arrived at the camp of Miranda del Ebro, where the citizens of Allied nations who had entered Spain illegally, were interned during the war. We were put in a long, bare hut, where the only furniture consisted of two tiers of bunks, and given some tattered blankets. The next morning I wandered out in the cold drizzle in search of breakfast which was served in the main square. The rain had turned the paths between the huts into a soggy mess of heavy, sticky mud. Long queues were slowly advancing towards a number of large, black pots, from which prisoners were ladling the same brownish liquid with which I was already familiar from Pamplona prison. I joined one of the queues, but well before I got near the pot, it was already empty.

I walked round rather disconsolately and wondered how I was to survive in this place where one apparently only got food if one managed to be first in the queue. The Spanish authorities limited their ministrations to guarding us and providing twice a day the brownish liquid which passed for food. Apart from this, they left us completely to our own resources. These, as I learned later that morning, when I struck up acquaintance with two French Air Force cadets who had arrived a week earlier in the camp, were not inconsiderable. They also told me that each nationality had a representative in the camp, an internee, who represented the interests of his fellow countrymen with the camp authorities and was in touch with his consulate. I found the British representative in a small room made of jute and the wood of tea cases. I had no difficulty in establishing my identity as, to my great surprise, he turned out to be none other than the young man in the American consulate in Lyon who had issued me with my travel document. He had arrived in the camp the week before and just taken over as British representative. I at once became eligible for a very generous food ration, supplied by the British Embassy in Madrid. I was given packets of biscuits, tins of sardines, tea, coffee, milk, sugar, cigarettes and bars of chocolate. The vision of death by starvation, which had haunted me that morning, vanished as by magic and suddenly life had become quite bearable again. In a much more cheerful mood I went back to my new French friends and shared my unexpected riches with them. We not only were no longer dependent on the food supplied by the Spaniards but could now purchase all sorts of things, such as a primus stove, a tea kettle and a frying pan which helped to vary our menu. Later we obtained some wood from packing cases and built ourselves a little room.

People of some twenty-six different nationalities were detained in the camp and formed a very colourful community indeed. Several enterprising people had opened little restaurants and coffee shops so that, when one entered some of the huts, one had the impression of being in an Eastern bazaar. A brisk black-market trade flourished in foodstuffs and other commodities. These reached the camp in two ways: through the embassies of the wealthier nations which sent parcels for their nationals and through people who had money and could purchase things outside the camp. The largest national contingent were the Poles who formed a closed and well-disciplined community. In many ways they ran the camp for they had been there the longest. The stronger nations could bring some pressure to bear on the Spanish government to release their citizens. The weaker nations could not.

In the middle of January 1943, when I had been nearly two months in the camp, the lingering discontent and bitterness against the Spanish authorities, who kept the refugees indefinitely in the most squalid conditions, burst into open resistance. The movement started among the Poles and spread rapidly to the other nationalities. It was decided that we should all go on a hunger strike. This, it was hoped, would alert the international community to our plight and force the Spanish authorities to change their release policy and improve conditions in the camp.

The strike lasted a whole week. It was organised by the Poles, who formed the pickets and made sure that nobody accepted any food. To demonstrate that the strike was in earnest, the national representatives were not allowed to distribute any food to their nationals and all purchases outside the camp were stopped. Anyone who broke the strike ran the risk of a nasty beating-up at the hands of a gang of tough Poles. Already after the first few days, the camp administration began to try to lure the inmates back to eating by improving the daily fare. We were ordered to queue up and walk past the pots, even if we refused any food.

Exactly a week after the strike had started, a four-member team of the diplomatic corps, among whom was a British diplomat, visited the camp and talked with the strike committee. They advised the inmates to start eating again as they had received assurances from the Spanish authorities that conditions in the camp would be improved and releases speeded up. This was accepted.

I cannot say that I felt the worse for this experience. In the beginning I suffered from headaches, but after a few days my body seemed to get used to doing without food. The feeling of hunger disappeared and gave way to a strange feeling of elation, lightness and energy. I found this so pleasant that in later life I have frequently practised fasting for some days in order to recapture this feeling of euphoria. One result is that I can easily skip several meals, if circumstances require this, without experiencing any inconvenience.

A few days after the strike ended, I and several others were suddenly released. I don't know on what basis the group of about fifteen inmates was formed. All I know is that a young Dutchman and myself were included because we were minors. A man from the British Embassy came to collect us and took us by train to Madrid. There we were put up in a hotel which we were not allowed to leave. Two days later, we boarded a train for Gibraltar, escorted by two members of the British Embassy. We arrived at La Linea the next afternoon. A few short formalities at the Spanish customs post and the barrier was lifted. We walked through to the other side. Here British soldiers were standing guard and we were met by blue-uniformed policemen. I had reached my destination. I stood on British territory.

Waiting buses took us straight to the quayside where naval launches transferred us to a passenger liner, the *Empress of Australia*, lying with a great number and variety of other ships at anchor in the roadstead. A convoy had been formed and would leave in a few hours for England. The voyage was uneventful, though the tension, created by the lurking danger of U-boats and enemy aircraft, never quite left us.

As soon as the ship was alongside in Greenock, immigration officers came on board. We had to queue up and were questioned in turn. I showed them my travel document and told them that my mother and sisters were living in England, but I did not know where. Later in the day, we were taken by train to London under an escort of soldiers. From King's Cross station buses took us to a place called the 'Royal Victorian Patriotic School'. This name rather baffled me. I imagined it to be some kind of special school where one attended lessons in patriotism and if one passed the examination, one was released. I was wrong, of course, but not all that much for the school was an interrogation centre for refugees, the purpose of which was to weed out German spies and other security risks. The name had nothing to do with the centre, but was that of a requisitioned girls' school on the premises.

After a few days there, I was called up for interrogation. It was conducted by a sharp-featured, dark, young captain in the Intelligence Corps whose manner was polite, but distant. I told him my life story and, especially, the details of my escape from occupied territory. He took everything down in longhand and, as he frequently interrupted to ask probing questions, it took two full days before I had finished. On the third day, he called me again and went over certain parts of my story which needed elucidation. I repeated everything in a straightforward way, exactly as it had been.

The following day I was not called for by him. In the afternoon there was a film show, 'The Dictator' with Charlie Chaplin, but I never saw it. The film had just started when I was called out to see the CO of the establishment. A tall, grey-haired colonel told me that he had succeeded in locating my mother and that I would be allowed to go. He then picked up the telephone and dialled a number. At the other end my mother answered. He told her she was speaking to an immigration officer and asked her if she had a son in Holland. She confirmed this and he then asked her to give a short description. Satisfied, he said, 'Well, I have good news for you. He is here with me now and I'll hand the receiver to him so that you can speak to him yourself.'

I don't remember what we said to each other, but the outcome was that she would meet me in an hour's time on the platform of the station in Northwood, where she lived. The colonel then gave me half a crown for the fare and shook hands. I was free to go. An hour later, after several changes and much asking, I got out at Northwood station. It was dark and raining, but at the end of the platform I recognised at once the waiting figure of my mother. I was home.

Chapter Four

The first few days after my return passed in a whirl. My sisters, who were both working as nurses in London hospitals, came home for the weekend to see me and it was one of those occasions, very rare in our later life, when we were all home together. My sudden and un-expected arrival from the enemy-occupied continent aroused much interest among my mother's friends and I had to tell my story many times. When the first excitement had died down, I had plenty of time to take a good look at England at war and begin to explore London. What struck me at once was the tremendous sense of solidarity among the people, their friendliness and their desire to help each other. The 'we are all in this together' spirit; the quiet discipline, which manifested itself in such things as people forming up in orderly queues outside shops or the strict observance by everybody of the black-out regulations and the civil defence rules; the stern sense of duty, which made people anxious to do their bit and inspired elderly ladies to drive mobile canteens and ambulances or serve in hospitals for the troops, while others, less agile, formed groups to make camouflage material; the cheerful courage shown under enemy air attack and the stoicism with which those who had close relatives killed bore their loss; all these things I found most impressive. I thought the English women and the cheerfulness and competence with which they undertook heavy and frequently dangerous work, normally done by men, especially admirable. Seeing them at work, often with a cigarette stuck between their lips, I drew at first an entirely wrong conclusion. Holland before the war was a rather puritanical country and very few women wore lipstick or make-up and they certainly did not smoke. As far as I knew, only women of easy virtue did these things. I was therefore surprised when I went about London in the first days after my arrival to see so many women apparently belonging to that profession. It was a little while before I realised that in England even women with the highest moral standards smoked and made-up.

There seemed to be also a relative absence of black-market activities, so marked a feature of life in Europe at that time. Most people considered it unpatriotic, unfair and beneath their dignity to have anything to do with it. It is true that the food situation was far better than in the occupied territories. With bread and potatoes off the ration, nobody need ever go hungry. On my walks, I used to enjoy stopping for tea in one of the small tea-shops kept by two elderly spinsters in an old cottage where one got delicious home-made scones and jam. It was something typically English, very pleasant, that I believe has now almost completely disappeared.

I confidently expected that I would be called up very soon. But the weeks passed and still I did not receive the expected notification. I began to miss the excitement and tension to which two years of illegal existence had accustomed me and my thoughts began to turn increasingly to the possibility of returning.

Tired of waiting for the call-up which did not come, I decided to volunteer for the Navy. In those days there was a recruiting office for the Royal Naval Volunteer Reserve in Trafalgar Square and it was there that I applied for the necessary forms. Two weeks later I was summoned for an interview. Together with several other young men I was first given a written examination, consisting of a mathematics paper, a general knowledge paper and an intelligence test. This was followed by an interview. A few weeks later I received a letter, informing me that I had been accepted and would in due course receive instructions where and when to join.

Meanwhile time began to drag and I felt that I could not go on sitting at home doing nothing. A friend of ours in the Dutch government was quite prepared to help and arranged for me to get a temporary job in the Dutch Ministry of Economic Affairs. It had its offices in Arlington House, St James's, and for nearly five months throughout that summer of 1943 I commuted every day like a civil servant between Northwood and the West End. It taught me something I had already suspected; I was not made for a nine-to-five office job.

My call-up finally came in October. I was to report for my initial naval training to HMS *Collingwood*, a large camp not far from Portsmouth. I was there for ten interesting but exhausting weeks. We were kept going all the time and at the end I was a great deal fitter than at the beginning. Those of us who had volunteered for the Naval Reserve and had been earmarked for a commission received special attention; we had to remain constantly on the mark.

I passed out with high marks, getting a so-called Commodore's recommendation to the next part of the course, a spell on a training cruiser based at Rosyth. I can only explain this recommendation by the fact that my final interview went well.

Late one evening in early January, our draft arrived in Rosyth and we were taken by tender to the cruiser *Diomede*, at anchor in the middle of the Firth of Forth. It was pitch dark and bitterly cold and we had difficulty in climbing the ice-covered rope ladder. This introduction to life at sea was in keeping with the whole period that we served afloat. If the initial training course had been hectic, this part was not only hectic but uncomfortable to a degree bordering on hardship. I believe that the guiding idea behind this part of the training was to create as close an imitation of life at sea in the eighteenth century as it was possible to achieve in the twentieth, and thus to recapture and instil in us the 'Nelson spirit'.

Six weeks on the cruiser were followed by two months at Lancing College, the well-known public school, with its cathedral-like chapel rising high on the downs. It had been taken over by the Navy as an officers' training establishment. The accent on the training at Lancing was on polish, to make sure that we would not only be officers but also gentlemen. Although we were still ordinary seamen and dressed as such, we now had our meals together with the officers on the staff in the high, wainscoted hall and were served by Royal Marines. Once a week there was a guest-night dinner at which the traditional protocol reserved for this occasion was meticulously observed. Usually these guest nights were preceded by a talk or lecture, given by the guest of honour.

The commander-in-charge of our training had somehow heard about my journey from occupied Europe. One day he called me to his office and asked me to give a talk about it on one of the guest nights. I had had no previous experience of speaking in public and the prospect frightened me.

One Thursday evening, the traditional night for guest nights, I found myself being led to the podium by the commander through a large assembly hall, where the whole ship's company was waiting. I was feeling nervous and saw with apprehension the moment approaching when he would finish his short introduction and I would have to launch forth on my talk. Fortunately I had prepared my opening sentences. By the time I was through these most of my nervousness had gone. The lecture was a success and I was rewarded with loud applause.

For the last part of the course we were transferred to yet another establishment, HMS *King Alfred*, in nearby Hove. In contrast to Lancing, all Gothic and pseudo-medieval, *King Alfred* was all glass and steel and very modern. It had been a Lido before the war with restaurants and swimming pools, now used as drill halls and lecture rooms. It was here that we had to sit our final examination before being commissioned.

The tension never let up. Indeed, it seemed to be considered an essential part of this course. It was sustained by an elaborate system of examinations and weekly tests, which in the event of failure, resulted in immediate dismissal from the course. Now with the passing-out exam just a few weeks ahead the tension mounted to an almost unbearable pitch.

When the lists with the results were put up, I found myself among the lucky ones and was able to go to collect my uniform.

The commissioning ceremony the next day was performed by an old admiral, recalled from retirement for this sort of thing, and was accompanied by a complicated and confusing piece of drill. One had to walk up to the admiral, stand to attention, salute, take off one's cap, put it under one's arm, accept the commission, put it with the cap, shake hands with the admiral, put on one's cap, without dropping the commission, salute again and turn smartly away. We rehearsed this procedure several times beforehand, but even so I remained worried that in the excitement of the moment I would put the commission on my head and hand my cap to the admiral.

However, all passed off well and that evening I, together with many other happy and at last carefree young officers, crowded into the first class compartments of the London train on our way home to show ourselves off for a few days to proud parents, sisters and girl friends.

At the end of our leave we had to return for a further fortnight's post-graduate training to *King Alfred*. It was during this period that a man came down from the Admiralty to lecture to us on the various branches of naval service open to us. Starting with a short description of life on battleships, the lecturer worked his way through cruisers, destroyers and submarines down to MTBs, minesweepers and landing-craft. Right at the end of his talk he added, 'There is one other branch, which I should mention. It is called "Special Service" and I cannot tell you very much about it because it is secret and, as far as we are concerned, the people who join it vanish.'

I at once pricked up my ears. This sounded exactly what I wanted. Special Service, secret, people not heard of again. It must be intelligence work, the landing of agents on the enemy coast. That same day I put my name down for Special Service, with destroyers as second choice. I suppose the reason was simply a hunger for adventure. I wanted to be a real member of the Dutch underground. I wanted to be dropped into Holland to do secret, important work and I thought Special Service would provide this opportunity.

I had done well in navigation and, before getting a final appointment, I was sent with a few others to the Royal Naval College in Greenwich, on a three-week navigation course. It was an appointment which had many advantages. The course itself was not arduous, compared to what we had been through, and every evening we were free to go up to town.

At the end of my navigation course, I was given a short leave. While I was home I received a letter instructing me to report to HMS *Dolphin*, the Submarine Headquarters in Portsmouth for Special Service. I was much dismayed when I read this. The last thing I had thought of was submarines to which I did not feel particularly attracted. When the lecturer had enumerated the various possibilities, he had given no indication that Special Service was in any way connected with this weapon. I had signed on, however, for whatever it was; there was no going back now. I had made a blind date and I had to keep it.

HMS *Dolphin* was located in a large fort built by French prisoners of war in Napoleonic times. It guards the western bank of the entrance to Portsmouth harbour. On arrival, I was informed that I was to be a member of a small mixed group of officers and other ranks who were to be trained as divers for midget submarines.

Our training group, which was small and consisted of some twelve men only, had two unusual features. It was mixed. That is to say officers and other ranks trained together, with no distinction between them during working hours; and it was commanded by a medical officer. The reason was that in the initial period the training was more a question of endurance than of acquisition of special skills. Continuous medical supervision was required to find out how the trainees were reacting to long periods under water.

After a few weeks' training in the deep tank that towers above HMS *Dolphin*, and in a lonely creek nearby, we were to be transferred to a base on one of the islands off the west coast of Scotland, to start training on actual midget submarines. Before this there was one hurdle to pass. Below a certain depth the pressure of the water is such that it affects the oxygen in the containers and slightly alters its substance. Certain people are allergic to this altered oxygen and if they breathe it they lose consciousness.

It was essential therefore that we should be tested in this respect before being sent on the next part of the course. I have never quite understood why this test could not be carried out in artificial conditions at the beginning of the training period and why it was necessary to wait till the trainee had acquired sufficient practice to be able to dive to such a depth. Be that as it may, the outcome of the test as far as I was concerned was negative. When I descended to the required depth I lost consciousness and was quickly hauled back to the surface.

Removed from the course, I was given the job of officer of the watch on HMS *Dolphin*, pending a new appointment. I now spent my hours of duty walking up and down the landing stage with a long telescope under my arm and exchanging pleasantries with the attractive Wrens who manned the motor launches linking the various Naval establishments and ships in the harbour. I had to see to it that the flag was hoisted and lowered at the right time, that bugles were sounded when it was required, and the bosun's whistle blown when officers in command of ships arrived at or left the landing stage. One day the captain of HMS *Dolphin* called me into his office and asked me if I would be interested in fast boats and plenty of action. This was just the sort of thing that appealed to me. I was therefore told I was to go to London early the next day and report to an address in Palace Street, just off Victoria Street.

When I got there, the doorkeeper gave me a pass to fill in and took me to the first floor, where a young lieutenant RNVR showed me into a room. At a large desk near the window sat a captain RN. He was small and slender with a sallow complexion and dark, thinning hair. He spoke abruptly but his manner was friendly enough.

He asked many questions about my background, my escape from Holland and my schooling. He then told me to write my biography in considerable detail. When I had finished I handed it in and was asked to come back after lunch.

When I returned the captain put his cap on, picked up a black ebony stick with silver knob and asked me to accompany him. We walked to a tall, narrow building, just opposite the entrance to St James's tube station.

Here again I had to fill in a pass, and the captain took me to a small room on the top floor. It had an attic window and was almost filled by two large desks placed against each other. At one of these sat a major in his shirt-sleeves, a handsome man with very thick, glossy blond hair. Without his uniform jacket on I could not tell his regiment so I took him to be a Royal Marine. After all, I was being interviewed for service in fast boats, so I presumed that this must be a branch of the Admiralty.

The major, it turned out, spoke fluent Dutch, albeit with a marked English accent, and interviewed me in that language. The questions he asked were much the same as I had already answered that morning, but he dwelt rather longer on my work for the Dutch underground.

When the interview was finished the captain took me to a small, bare room on the first floor, where I had to fill in a four-page printed form with a number of questions about my parents, my schooling, my hobbies and other personal information.

About a week later I was summoned once more to London. I had to be in Palace Street at exactly two o'clock in the afternoon. On arrival there, I found the captain already waiting for me. He took me straight to the same building we had visited the week before. This time we went up to the fourth floor and, as soon as I stepped out of the lift, I realised that I was in a much more important part of the building than on the previous occasion. The corridor, where I was asked to wait, was covered with a thick red carpet and the captain told me to sit down in one of two Chippendale armchairs, standing at each side of a narrow mahogany table covered with copies of *Tatler* and *Country Life*.

The captain left me for a while and, when he came back, invited me rather solemnly to follow him. At the end of the carpeted corridor we entered a large boardroom, the centre of which was occupied by a long polished table. At one side of this sat five men. Two of these were civilians, one wore the uniform of an air vice-marshal, and two that of a brigadier-general. The captain took a seat at one end of the table and I was invited by the air vice-marshal to take the chair facing the board. He had in front of him my biography, the form I had filled in and several minute-sheets.

For the next half hour I faced a barrage of questions about myself. They were fired at me, apparently at random, by the various members of the board. I answered them as best I could, quietly and in a straightforward way. I cannot say that I was particularly nervous, I had by now come to the conclusion that it was probably more than just a question of service in fast boats, probably something in Naval intelligence, or liaison work with Allied Navies. Certainly, the questions I was asked gave me no clue. When they had finished, the air vice-marshal, who acted as chairman, asked me to wait outside.

I had sat there for about ten minutes looking at *Tatler* when the captain came out. He put his hand on my shoulder and said that I had been accepted and would have to report for duty at ten o'clock on the following Monday morning. On arrival I should ask for Major Seymour. I was pleased as I was getting bored with the dull existence of officer of the watch at HMS *Dolphin*.

When I reported for duty at 54 Broadway Buildings, I was taken up by the ground-floor watchman to the small attic room on the eighth floor where I had been before. Major Seymour turned out to be the officer who had interviewed me in Dutch. He wore his uniform jacket now and I could see that he was not a Royal Marine, as I had thought, but in the General Service Corps. This somewhat mystified me. The first thing he did was to take me along to see Colonel Cordeaux who, he said, was the head of the department to which I had been appointed and who wanted to see me before I started. Colonel Cordeaux's office was a large room at the other end of the corridor and was guarded by three secretaries, two of them young and pretty, the third a tall, extremely thin, middle-aged woman with glasses and buck teeth. She looked like a caricature of the prim spinster, but turned out later to be very nice and to have quite a lot of life in her.

Colonel Cordeaux himself was a short thick-set man, with pale blue eyes and a bristle moustache. He spoke in a brisk, military manner and walked with a marked limp, caused by arthritis from which he suffered badly. He actually was a Royal Marine, so I thought this must be the Admiralty after all. The Colonel motioned me to sit down and began to address me. What he said, I must confess, made a deep impression on me.

He informed me that I was now an officer of the British Secret Service and that the building in which we were was its Headquarters. I would be attached to the Dutch Section, which bore the symbol P8 and was headed by Major Seymour. This section was part of a larger department called the Northern Area, of which he himself was the

Controller and which, apart from Holland, covered the Scandinavian countries and the Soviet Union. My actual duties would be explained to me by the major, but before I started work I would be sent on a parachute jumping course at Ringway near Manchester. Before dismissing me, the colonel impressed on me the responsibility of my new position and what an honour it was to have been selected.

I don't know if the colonel himself meant what he said – he was an old man after all and had seen much of what went on behind the scenes – but I, a twenty-one-year-old sub-lieutenant in the RNVR, who had just been commissioned, certainly looked upon it as an honour and an extraordinary piece of good luck. In fact, I could hardly believe that it was true. I had of late suspected and hoped that the job for which I was being interviewed had something to do with 'Intelligence'. But that I would actually become an officer in the British Secret Service, this legendary centre of hidden power, commonly believed to have a decisive influence on the great events of this world, was something that far exceeded my wildest expectations.

Before the war each controller had under him a number of Production or 'P' sections, as they were called. These were not large. They were usually staffed by one or at most two officers and a number of secretaries. Each P section was denoted by a number indicating the country in which it operated. Thus P8 was Holland, P1 France and P4 Germany

The 'P' sections were the London desks of the SIS stations abroad, which carried out the actual work of recruiting and running agents.

The war and the rapid occupation of most European countries changed all this. The SIS stations in the countries overrun by the enemy had to be closed down and their personnel withdrawn. With operations now being mounted from England the 'P' sections took over their functions and from the very start developed a particularly effective way of operating, made possible by the very triumphs of the Germans. Hatred for the occupying power had turned the populations of Western and Northern Europe into a vast reservoir of potential agents and, what is more, agents working for one of the most powerful of motives, patriotism.

Rather than trying to recruit and run agents in the occupied countries themselves, the chief policy-makers in the Secret Service decided that the most effective way of doing this was through their governments in exile in England. This step was not only imposed by logical reasoning and correct psychology, but even more by the catastrophic situation which faced the Secret Service as a result of the

German victories in the first years of the war. The state of muddle and unpreparedness in which England found herself after Dunkirk in the military field was faithfully reflected in the intelligence field. It was surmounted with the same resourcefulness and pragmatism and, here too, victory was snatched from the teeth of defeat.

The pre-war principle was to operate against a target country from an adjoining country. Thus the SIS station in The Hague had been working against Germany, not against Holland. On the further principle that every war is fought on the pattern of the previous one, the station in The Hague had not organised any agent networks in Holland. Therefore, when the Germans invaded Holland and The Hague station was hastily withdrawn, SIS found itself without a single agent in occupied Holland itself.

The first thing that had to be done, therefore, was to organise, with the help and advice of SIS, a Dutch Secret Service in London. This service, the 'Bureau Inlichtingen' (BI), established, at first with considerable difficulty, permanent contact with the Dutch underground. Quite early on, an agreement had been reached between the British and the Dutch Secret Services which laid down the principles on which the two services would co-operate, and delineated their respective spheres of activity. The Dutch were responsible for the recruiting of agents among Dutch nationals in England, while the British, with their infinitely vaster resources, would train and equip them, take care of their transport to Holland and maintain W/T communication with them. They would be briefed jointly by the two services in accordance with requirements of the customer departments, which were in fact mostly British. The intelligence obtained would be shared, though again, of course, only the British were in a position to make operational use of it.

By the time I joined P8, this arrangement had been working for more than two years and a great number of agents had been trained and sent to Holland. Several of them had been arrested by the Germans and shot or sent to concentration camps, but new ones were constantly being recruited and despatched to replace them. They were usually sent in teams of two, a so-called organiser and his radio operator. It was the task of the organiser to set up intelligence networks with the help of contacts in the Dutch underground. The radio operator ensured communication with Headquarters in London.

One of the stipulations in the agreement between the two intelligence services was that no British nationals should be sent to Holland as agents. Many of the resistance groups were linked, one way or another, to political groupings or personalities and both services were anxious to avoid suspicions, easily aroused, that the British were in any way trying to influence the post-war political settlement in the Netherlands.

This stipulation dashed my hopes of being sent back to Holland as an agent. Instead, as Major Seymour explained, I was to act as conducting officer to the young Dutch agents during their training period. I would accompany them on their parachute course which was why it was important that I should be able to jump myself. I was to look after them during their training course in London, see to it that they were happy, had all they required, take them out from time to time to a restaurant or show and generally act as a friend. Finally I would be responsible for checking that they had all their equipment and the necessary false documents and accompany them to the airfield on the night that they were dropped over Holland. As I spoke perfect Dutch, had just come from Holland and been through similar experiences as the boys I was to look after, Seymour thought I should be well suited for the job.

Major Seymour took me to an adjoining room, equally small and attic like, to meet his second-in-command, Lieutenant-Commander Child RNVR. This officer, an old hand at Secret Service work, was in charge of the agents' training programme and also looked after supplies and equipment. I was to work directly under him. He was big, burly and coarse-featured. In his crumpled uniform he looked remarkably like the American film actor of the Thirties, Wallace Beery, who generally played the rough diamond with the heart of gold. Later, I discovered that under his rough exterior Commander Child did indeed hide a kind disposition and a readiness to help others, as well as an extremely astute business head. Whe he got up to shake hands with me, I noticed that he had a wooden leg.

Unlike most SIS officers, who come from an upper-middle-class background, Commander Child was the son of a Deal fisherman, and went to sea before the mast when he was fifteen. After years of service in the Merchant Navy, during which he got his master's certificate, he found himself in the years of the great slump as a skipper of private yachts, taking their wealthy owners along the Dutch waterways and up the Rhine. In this way, he got to know Holland and Germany well, learned to speak Dutch and above all established a wide acquaintance-ship among Dutch and German bargees. This made him a valuable contact for the SIS station in The Hague in the years when Germany was rearming.

At the outbreak of war, being a member of the Royal Naval Reserve, he joined the staff of the station under cover of a lieutenant-commander in the Naval Attaché's office. While carrying out a mission in the first days of the invasion of Holland, his car was attacked by German parachutists who had landed between The Hague and the Hook of Holland. He was seriously wounded and was taken to hospital where his leg had to be amputated. Enjoying diplomatic cover, he was interned after his recovery by the Germans, together with other British diplomats who had been caught by the sudden German onslaught. For two years they lived in a hotel somewhere in the Harz mountains and then were exchanged, via the Portuguese territory of Lourenço Marques, for German diplomats whom the outbreak of war had stranded in various parts of the British Empire.

My first job that day was to accompany Commander Child to Hans Place, where in a large flat the wireless training school was housed, to collect two transmitters. The agents who had been practising on them were to be dropped over Holland during the coming new moon period. Their set had to be packed in containers to be despatched with them. In my zeal as a neophyte I nearly dropped one, and I remember the Commander saying to me, 'Take it easy, son. We are not over Holland yet.' From then on he would frequently call me 'son', strengthening the Wallace Beery impression.

Next day I left for the Parachute Training School at Ringway with three young Dutch agents for a week's course in parachute training. Agents of different nationalities were trained at Ringway and the various groups had to be kept strictly apart. One of the duties of the conducting officers was to see that they did not mix.

When our initial training was completed three of us, including myself, who had never flown before, were taken up for a short preliminary flight. This by itself I found quite exciting. But then we were taken up for the actual jump. With an air of deliberate unconcern we installed ourselves in the long narrow cabin of the Lancaster and had our parachutes hooked on to the wire which ran along it. Soon after that the voice of the pilot on the intercom warned us that we were circling over the dropping ground and that he was about to start running-in.

The first man to jump was our trainer. I was next. I looked down at my feet dangling in the hole and saw the earth rush past deep down underneath them. I gripped the edge more firmly, afraid that I might fall too soon, and kept my eyes fixed on the red light.

Suddenly it was no longer red but green. At the same moment I heard the voice of the despatcher loud in my ear, shouting 'Go', I felt a push as I lifted myself off and closed my eyes. I expected the sinking feeling of a long drop, but it was nothing like that. Instead, there was a strong push backwards as the slipstream under the aircraft caught me, followed almost immediately by a sharp pull upwards, caused by the opening of the parachute. Then I felt myself gently rocking in the air. It was an unforgettable moment. The relief that the parachute had opened, the light, floating feeling as if I was without weight, the country stretching far away in all directions, all this blended into a unique sensation. I thought this is what angels must feel like when they fly through the heavens. I did not have long to enjoy my descent, for suddenly the earth seemed to rush up towards me. I braced myself for the fall, and the next instant hit the ground with a fair thud. I had done it. It was one of the most exhilarating experiences of my life.

In the evenings we were free and would go to the nearby village where there was a cinema and a dance hall. I got on well with my three companions. They had arrived in England not very long before by various routes and had passed through many adventures. In a few months from now they would be sent to an underground organisation as W/T operators to replace those who had been arrested. Having reached freedom, they had opted to return to the gloom and oppression, to the hardship and privations of occupied Holland. They would lead a life of constant danger. They would not be able to contact their parents or their friends but live a restricted existence in hiding, passed on, together with their equipment, from safe house to safe house in an attempt to evade the prowling radio-location vans ever searching for clandestine operators. Every time they went on the air to pass intelligence or receive instructions, they were drawing the enemy's attention to themselves as surely as a hidden machine-gun post when it opens fire. And then when they had tempted their luck too long, when the sinister grey vans had closed in around them and pin-pointed their hideout, when the SS had surrounded the house and there was no escape, what bitter fate awaited them? Torture to force them to give away their comrades, followed by death at the hands of a firing squad or, worse perhaps, the slow agony of a concentration camp. Yet now, preparing for such a life they were carefree and happy, dating the rosy-cheeked Lancashire girls, determined to enjoy life while it lasted.

Our first jump was followed by others under differing conditions, such as jumping with a heavy pack, jumping at night and coming down in the water. This was especially important for people to be dropped over Holland, so much of which is water. It required a special technique in that one had to get out of one's harness while still in the air and remain hanging on to it by one's hands until letting go just before hitting the water.

I returned to London, looking back with satisfaction on the ten days at Ringway. Parachute jumping had been an exciting interlude. Contrary to expectations, however, I soon found myself immersed in desk work to a far greater extent than had originally been intended. The reason was shortage of staff.

Very shortly after I joined the section, two officers had to be detached to set up an advance station in the Southern Netherlands. The Allied armies, pushing up through France and Belgium after the D-Day landings, had now reached the estuary of the Rhine and Meuse, which separates the Northern from the Southern Netherlands. Here their advance had been halted by this formidable natural barrier, made even more formidable by large areas flooded by the Germans. P8 took advantage of this situation to set up a field station in the liberated part of the Netherlands, with the task of sending agents across the rivers into the territory still occupied by the enemy. This reduced the London staff to Major Seymour, Commander Child and myself. Day and night a flow of telegrams poured in from our agents in Holland, containing urgent and valuable information on German troop dispositions and the locations of headquarters and other military objects. In fact about 80 per cent of the intelligence produced by P8 was received in this way. Only bulky material such as maps, plans and statistics were sent by courier routes, mostly via Switzerland or Sweden.

These telegrams were sent in code and received at the large W/T transmitting and deciphering centre at Bletchley, where they were decoded and sent to SIS Headquarters by teleprinter. The reception was often bad due to atmospherics. They had been written, encoded and transmitted in a hurry, under dangerous conditions and as a result the text was frequently badly mutilated, with words and even whole strings of words missing. It needed a lot of time and patience and a thorough knowledge of Dutch to try and restore these mutilated messages so that they made sense. I was given this job.

Any time of the day or night an important telegram might arrive requiring immediate action. It might be a message reporting that a German general had just set up his HQ in some castle or country house in Eastern Holland. Its location had to be pinpointed on the map and the information together with co-ordinates and other relevant details, telephoned to the Air Ministry, for inclusion as a target in the next day's operations of the Tactical Air Force. Or it might be a message informing us that an important member of one of our networks had just been arrested. A warning would have to be sent immediately to several agents in the field to keep away from certain addresses which had become compromised by the arrest. So it was that I spent most nights on a camp bed in the office, on call to go to the teleprinter room as soon as something urgent came in.

Commander Child had a small flat in Petty France, about three minutes' walk from the office. He suggested that I should leave my lodgings and come and live with him. I would be more comfortable and within easy reach of the teleprinter room. It worked very well, especially as we led a kind of Box and Cox existence and were seldom at home together. He was frequently away supervising the training courses, and organising dropping operations of agents and stores. I now helped in this as much as my office work allowed, rather than the other way round as had originally been intended. We were especially busy at the period of the new moon. Conditions were most favourable then for dropping and landing operations and we tried as much as possible to concentrate all operations in this short period.

Major Seymour was also away from the office a great deal. Much of his time was taken up with consultations with his chiefs and conferences with the Dutch Secret Service and other intelligence organisations. The regular conferences with SOE, the wartime organisation responsible for organising sabotage and guerilla activities in the enemy occupied countries, were of especial importance. Constant care had to be taken that there would be no line-crossing, i.e. that an underground group working for one organisation should not become involved in the work of a group working for the other. In a country as small as Holland this was a real danger and SIS was most anxious to avoid it.

Apart from these general considerations, which made SIS squeamish of contact with SOE in the field, there was another more weighty reason. This was the tragic disaster of operation 'Nordpol' which made a deep and lasting impression on all who were concerned with clandestine operations in Holland during the war. It started in March 1942 with the arrest by the Germans of an agent and his W/T operator, who had been sent to Holland by SOE to set up sabotage networks.

It was accepted by the British intelligence services that too heavy a burden would be put on agents if they were given instructions never to give anything away under interrogation. It was well known that the Gestapo used torture methods under which virtually no one could hold out. Agents were therefore permitted, when forced, to give away their personal code and transmitting schedule. This being so, it was considered likely that the Germans would use their knowledge to make the arrested W/T operator continue to transmit to London as if nothing had happened. Such a game or 'Spiel', as it was called by the Germans, represented serious dangers. If it was not noticed, radio contact with the arrested agent would be continued with the result that all information or material sent to him would fall into German hands; if the W/T contact was used to make arrangements for new agents to be dropped, these would either immediately be arrested or allowed to operate for a while under surveillance so as to discover their contacts in the underground. Thus entire resistance organisations might be rolled up. Finally, the Germans could use this radio contact to pass on misleading information.

It was in order to guard against this danger that so-called security checks were devised. These consisted of the intentional inclusion in the text of a coded telegram of certain, pre-arranged, small mistakes, syllables or words. As long as the agent continued to include the pre-arranged mistakes in his telegrams all was well. Under pressure the arrested SOE agent and his W/T operator agreed to continue sending telegrams to London, but omitted the pre-arranged security checks as a warning that they were under enemy control.

Although the Dutch section of SOE noticed the absence of the security checks it refused to draw the obvious conclusions, attributing this fact to bad atmospherics. It continued radio contact with the arrested agents under the impression that all was well. The Germans, hardly believing their luck, then mounted a cleverly executed deception operation to which they gave the code name 'Nordpol'. They proposed new sabotage operations and asked London for more agents and supplies. These were duly despatched and naturally fell straight into the hands of the Germans. At one point the Gestapo was in contact with London through no less than eighteen W/T transmitters. The 'Spiel' lasted till November 1943, when two of the arrested agents managed to escape from prison and make their way to Switzerland where they warned the Dutch and British authorities of what was going on.

Official Dutch sources estimate that as a result of the 'Nordpol Spiel' some 49 agents and 430 of their contacts in the Dutch resistance were arrested and a vast quantity of weapons, sabotage equipment, radio transmitters, as well as large sums of money fell into German hands. In addition, twelve British bombers, used for dropping agents and stores, were shot down.

To put the record straight, it should be pointed out that the successes achieved by the Germans with the 'Nordpol Spiel' were never more than tactical. The British Double-cross Committee booked real strategic successes against the Abwehr by managing to arrest and turn virtually all German agents sent to Great Britain during the war and using them in 'Spiele' which far exceeded the 'Nordpol Spiel' both in scope and duration. I have read everything on 'Nordpol', including the voluminous Dutch work and although my personal knowledge of the operation is limited because I came in only on the tail end of it, I feel that it went wrong as a result of genuine mistakes rather than a conspiracy.

SOE, this time with an entirely new team in charge of their Dutch section, had to start building up its organisation in Holland again from scratch. Fortunately, partly because its networks there were still very small and partly because of the innate caution with which it had always approached anything to do with sabotage, SIS activities were little affected by this disaster.

The officers in P8 were assisted in their work by four secretaries. One, as in many SIS sections, was a middle-aged spinster, the other three were young girls of my age.

If most SIS officers were of middle-class or upper-middle-class origin, many of the secretaries were decidedly upper class and belonged to the higher strata of the establishment. There were among them daughters of Tory MPs and ministers, of bishops, of a Viceroy of India, of court dignitaries and some were even related to the Royal Family. Though often scatterbrained, they worked hard because they were very conscious of their patriotic duty, instinctively equating the interests of England with those of their own class. They had joined mostly on the recommendation of friends or relatives who had contacts in the Service. It was considered a good way for them to do their national service for it enabled them to stay in London and join the social round without exposing them to too intimate a contact with the lower classes, inevitable if they had joined one of the Armed Services. They were mostly pretty, some very beautiful, but inclined to be vague and incompetent in varying degrees, though to this there were exceptions. They were pleasant to work with and helped to create a cheerful, friendly atmosphere in the office. I was a beneficiary of this as I spent most of my time there.

The war was now in its last bitter months. For us in London they were marked by the constant menace of V1 and V2 rockets.

One Saturday morning I was working in my small attic room in Broadway Buildings when a shattering explosion shook the whole building to its foundations. We rushed out of our rooms to find out what had happened. A V2 had come down only some hundred yards away, across Queen Anne's Gate, destroying the Guards Chapel at Wellington Barracks where a wedding service was just in progress, killing and maiming many of those present.

I remember being on duty one Sunday afternoon in September. Before he left, Major Seymour had given me the text of telegrams which I was to despatch immediately upon receipt of a telephone call from SHAPE. It contained instructions to our underground organisations in Holland, especially those in the Arnhem–Nymegen area, to render every assistance to the Allied troops about to land and to keep us constantly informed of enemy troop movements. It was a tense afternoon waiting for this call. I realised that an important operation was afoot, which, if successful, would bring about the liberation of Holland within a matter of days. Then the call came and I at once sent off the telegrams. I felt as if a spring had been released inside me. We were very busy the next few days dealing with the greatly increased flow of traffic, processing it and passing it on, much of it by telephone. It soon revealed that the enemy was succeeding rapidly in bringing up vastly superior forces, including a whole Panzer Division, and that the main body of our troops stood little chance of linking up with the parachute troops which had landed north of the river. The operation miscarried. Thousands of lives were sacrificed in vain and Holland faced the most bitter and cruel winter of its war.

Occasionally, to give me a break from office work, Commander Child would suggest that I accompany an agent to the airfield on the night of a dropping operation. We usually set out in the early afternoon in a large car, driven by a girl in one of the Women's Services, to an airfield in Essex. On the way we would stop, first for tea and then for drinks in some cosy old pub. We all three did our best to keep the mood gay and carefree and usually succeeded in this. At the airfield we always had supper with the crew of the aircraft which was to drop the agent. Just before departure the agent changed into clothes of Dutch origin and I had to check carefully that he had no English coins, letters, bus or cinema tickets or anything else on his person, which might give him away. Then I gave him his false Dutch identity documents, his money, his codes and transmitting schedules and, if he wished, a lethal pill.

After that he put on his jumping suit and his parachute and was ready to start out on his dangerous mission. We got into a jeep and drove to the waiting aircraft. There I checked that the right containers with supplies and equipment were on board and then came the moment to say goodbye. A brief handshake, muttered good wishes and he climbed into the aircraft turning round once more to give the thumbs up sign before the door closed behind him. A final wave as the aircraft rolled out to the runway and then the wait as it gathered speed, lifted itself in the air and with its light winking disappeared into the night. The drive back to London in the dark was usually a silent one. Neither the driver nor I felt much like indulging in small talk. Our thoughts were with that aircraft flying eastward into enemy territory. Would the dropping operation be successful and our companion of an hour ago come down alive and well among his comrades of the underground? Would the crew with whom we had just supped and who had been so cheerful and matter-of-fact return to base safely?

One such journey has remained deeply impressed on my mind. The agent I accompanied was a nice, fair boy, just turned eighteen, who was going out to one of our groups in the Amsterdam area as a W/T operator. Just before take-off there was a last minute hitch. But, after a longish wait the aircraft took off after all. Two days later we received a telegram from the group to which the young agent had been dropped. He was dead. The dropping ground had been laid out not far from a large lake. He must have jumped a little too soon and came down over the lake. Probably not realising this in time, he did not release his harness before he hit the surface. There had been a fairly strong wind and his parachute had dragged him under water. His body was found the next day. Although we did not know it then, he was the last agent to be dropped over Holland. Before the next new moon period came round, the Germans had surrendered unconditionally.

VE day found me alone, in charge of P8, now reduced to a mere shadow of a section. A week before, the German armies in the Netherlands had surrendered and Major Seymour, promoted to the rank of Lieutenant-Colonel, had gone to The Hague to open a SIS station there. Commander Child, with no more agents to train and supplies to drop, had taken up an Intelligence appointment with Naval HQ in Germany.

Two things remain in my memory of that day. The long wail of the sirens, giving the All Clear after the surrender of the German armed forces had been announced and the streets that evening lit up again for the first time. Although I was on duty, there was now no radio traffic and I went out in the streets for a while to join the festive crowd. I found myself pushed in the direction of Buckingham Palace where a surging mass of people kept on chanting: 'We want the King! We want the King!' and then, when he and the Royal Family came out on the balcony, started singing 'For he's a jolly good fellow'. The war was over, we had won.

Chapter Five

A week after the armistice, I left for Holland to join the newly set up SIS in The Hague. I was accompanied by three of our secretaries, who had donned a kind of pseudo-military uniform so as not to attract attention to themselves in the vast military camp which liberated Europe then was. We took with us a lot of files and stores and travelled out on a Naval MTB belonging to the Secret Service flotilla. It was a beautiful spring afternoon when we sailed up the New Waterway to Rotterdam. I was back in Holland, once more free of enemy occupation.

We arrived in Rotterdam in the early evening. As soon as we were alongside, I went ashore to find out what had become of my aunt. She lived a fair distance away from the port and there was no transport. A kind workman, to whom I explained the situation, lent me his bicycle. It had wooden wheels and it took me some time to get to the house which I had last seen on the day of my grandmother's funeral. I rang the bell and my aunt opened the door. She had become very thin, but otherwise was well. It was a tearful reunion and we talked till deep into the night when I had to get back to my ship. The next time I came, I drove up in my own requisitioned car and brought with me ample supplies of food. My aunt needed these badly after the winter of famine she had just lived through.

The station was housed in two large villas in Wassenaar, a

fashionable garden suburb of The Hague. The largest one, which was used as living quarters for the staff, had belonged to a wealthy Dutch Nazi, who only two weeks previously had been taken to a prison camp to await trail for his wartime activities. The other was used as the office. The day after my arrival, I was already engaged on my new job. Assisted by a secretary, I had to go through our files and collect facts to be used in support of citations, which I had to draft, recommending our agents for various British decorations. The station's mission at that time was to wind up our wartime organisations and commitments. The fate of agents who had disappeared had to be investigated; the relatives of those killed had to be cared for; those who had survived prison and concentration camp had to be rehabilitated; most had to be settled in a peacetime career and all had to be recommended for awards, many posthumously. All this was done, of course, in close co-operation with our colleagues in the Dutch Service, who had installed themselves in a large country house not far away. The officers of that service, who had worked in London, were also awarded British decorations while the officers of P8, including myself, received the Order of Orange-Nassau for our work during the war.

I must admit, however, that I do not remember this first summer of peace primarily for the work we did. Rather it has remained fixed in my memory for the almost unbroken round of parties, drinking sessions and high living into which I was flung. It was as if the sudden release from danger, from suffering and privation, from strain and excessive work, from gloom and misery had gone to people's heads so that they lost for a while all sense of measure, and with dizzy abandon threw themselves into a whirlpool of pleasure. Those in the first place affected by this passing madness were the military, who at that time held all power and controlled all supplies and facilities. Requisitioned cars, luxurious villas, stocks of champagne and brandy (hoarded by the defeated Wehrmacht) clubs located in the most expensive restaurants or the most picturesquely situated country houses, luxury hotels in famous spas and holiday resorts, attractive girls avid for a good time after the gloom of the occupation years, all these privileges normally enjoyed only by the very rich were now available to every officer.

I too found myself irresistibly drawn into this maelstrom of pleasure. In the words of the well-known hymn 'the world, the flesh and Satan dwelt around the path I trod'. To my shame, I must admit that my strong religious convictions, although I had not lost them, proved no safeguard against the temptations which surrounded me.

By September most of the winding-up work had been done in spite of all these distractions. I was recalled to London to look after P8 once more.

It was a period of reorganisation and of adjustment to new conditions, to a new style and tempo for the Service, as a whole, and every individual in it. The past was coming to an end, the future had not yet begun. Many people were leaving, returning to their old professions and occupations, some to the City, some to the Bar, others to schools and universities. Several former officers of the Service stood for Parliament in the 1945 General Election which put a Labour Government in power. Colonel Cordeaux was elected Conservative MP for Grimsby and became a regular speaker on intelligence affairs in succeeding Parliaments. Lt-Col Seymour left to return to his old job as the representative in Holland of a large tobacco company.

Meanwhile, in the higher echelons of the Service a good look was being taken at the new distribution of power in the world, brought about by the war, and the framework of a new service, designed to meet the new challenges, hammered out. It was clear already then that the main target of the future would be the Soviet Union, the new socialist countries of Eastern Europe and the world Communist movement.

The pre-war Secret Service had been very much a kind of club of enthusiastic amateurs, autocratically ruled by the Chief, who could take them on, sack them and pay them as he deemed fit, not bound by any Civil Service rules and regulations. The new SIS, which emerged after the big post-war reorganisation was a properly established Government Department with a personnel department, gradings, regular promotions, pension schemes and annual increments. There were many old hands who shook their heads at all this new-fangled bureaucratic paraphernalia, predicting that the new organisation would be too cumbersome, too hidebound, not flexible enough for such a subtle and delicate business as spying.

At the beginning of 1946, Commander Child paid a visit to Head Office to put forward a proposal which involved me. A certain Naval Intelligence unit was in process of being wound up. During the war it had specialised in commando-type operations against enemy shore establishments with the purpose of capturing personnel and documents of intelligence interest. The last remnants of it were still stationed in Hamburg, and Commander Child suggested that I should be appointed its nominal CO as a convenient cover for secret service operations in Germany. There was already a large SIS station in

Hamburg, but, as CO of the Royal Naval Forward Intelligence Unit, as it was called, I might be better placed to carry out certain operations, especially those with a naval angle.

The proposal was accepted and in March of that year I went to Hamburg to succeed from the unit's last real CO, Captain Charles Wheeler, Royal Marines, who later became well known as a BBC correspondent in Washington.

The unit was located in an attractive villa with a garden sloping down to the river Elbe. This house I now took over, together with a naval writer, who spoke excellent German, a station wagon with a Royal Marine driver and an ample store of food, cigarettes and drink to be used for operational purposes.

My assignment was an interesting one. Immediately after the surrender of the German fleet in Kiel, the unit had been engaged in the interrogation of U-boat commanders and senior naval officers. In two wars the U-boats had been a serious menace to Britain's lines of communication, the struggle against them long and bitter and it was natural that the British naval authorities should look upon the German submarine service, and especially its ace commanders, as among the most fanatic and militaristic elements in the German nation. They were, therefore, the object of special attention. Those known or suspected of having committed war crimes were sent to prison camps to await trial, the others were released and demobilized. Through their work, the officers of the RNFIU had established contact with a large number of U-boat officers, contacts which could perhaps, in certain cases, be developed for intelligence purposes. I was to take over the most promising of these contacts with a view to selecting among them people who could help me to organise intelligence networks in the Soviet zone of Germany. These would be briefed to collect information on the order of battle of the Soviet armed forces and on political and economic developments in the Soviet zone. It was thought that the strong anti-Communist sentiments and traditional hatred of the Russians among the German military would make them amenable to co-operation and that supplies of food, drink and cigarettes would do the rest. At the same time, through my contacts in former naval circles, I might be also in a position to receive early warning if fanatical elements among the former U-boat officers were to contemplate any action hostile to the British occupation authorities, a possibility which in those early years of the occupation had to be taken into account.

I set out on this assignment with enthusiasm and in a relatively short period acquired a wide acquaintanceship in German naval circles. This was not so difficult as it may sound when one bears in mind that at that time the Germans had very little and we had everything, that we were the fount of all facilities, privileges and even justice and that a couple of thousand cigarettes represented a small fortune.

By the spring of 1947, I had succeeded with the help of so-called talent scouts among my naval contacts to build up two intelligence networks in East Germany, the members of which were nearly all former naval and Wehrmacht officers.

The easiest way, at that time, of sending agents into the Soviet zone was through Berlin where movement between the Eastern and Western sectors was still virtually free. To get my agents to Berlin through the Soviet zone, I used to dress them up in a Royal Marine uniform, issue them with a movement order in a fictitious English name and service number and take them myself in my station wagon through the Soviet control posts at Helmstedt and Berlin. Once in Berlin, they made their own way across the boundary into the Eastern sector and from there to various towns in the Soviet zone.

As to the second part of my mission, I was able to report, that in my considered opinion, there were no elements in German naval circles who were contemplating any hostile action against the British occupation authorities. Like all Germans at that time they were fully absorbed with the problems of daily existence. Moreover, it seemed to me, they had, quite rightly, come to the conclusion that any kind of resistance, active or passive, would not only be futile, but contrary to the long-term interests of Germany.

How did I feel about having to establish contact with the officers of the German armed forces whom, not so long ago, I had loathed and hated? Well, in the first place, I realised that they had been defeated and no longer represented a danger to our interests. At the same time, it was clear that they constituted promising material for use in the struggle against Communism and the Soviet Union which now, according to the conventional view, which I shared, constituted the new enemy and the principal menace to Western civilisation and our way of life. More generally speaking, this is a problem with which an intelligence officer is often faced. If he limits his contacts exclusively to people of the highest moral standards and of whom he personally approves, he will not get very far. He has to work with the tools at his disposal. Besides, it is wrong, in my opinion, to look upon some nations as inherently virtuous and others as inherently evil. All nations are capable of the highest virtue and courage, all are capable of evil and cruelty. This applies to the English, the Dutch or the Jews as much as to the Germans, the Japanese or any other nation. There is no nation which has not committed atrocities, though the magnitude may vary. It all depends on the particular historical circumstances in which it finds itself. It seems to me, therefore, that it behoves no nation to point an accusing finger at another, but only humbly to bow its head and say: 'There but for the grace of God go I.' Nobody knows what he will do tomorrow.

The life I was leading in Hamburg was very much a continuation of life in the first months after the war in liberated Holland. The same large villas, requisitioned cars, luxury hotels and country clubs with French chefs formed the background to a busy life filled with meetings, business lunches, report-writing and frequent journeys to follow up new leads. All this gave me a feeling of importance and did nothing for my humility. In addition, my social life was fairly intense. The Naval Headquarters had moved to Hamburg which meant a lot of entertainment and parties. Charles Wheeler, before he left, had introduced me to some of his personal friends, many of whom were members of the high German aristocracy. Their circumstances much reduced by the war and irked by the shortages, they were glad of any pretext for a party. Of these there were many, lasting till the early hours of the morning. Beautiful women and champagne, in high-ceilinged rooms stuffed with antique furniture and portraits of ancestors looking down from the walls. All this was, inevitably, accompanied by a fair amount of drinking. This, however, has never been a problem for me. I am very lucky in that my system simply rejects alcohol. Otherwise, I might well have become an alcoholic. I just happen not to like whisky, gin, vodka or brandy, though I do enjoy, occasionally, a glass of wine. On the rare occasions when I have been the worse for drink, I have had to pay for it with such a dreadful hangover that I have always been very wary of repeating the experience. It's as simple as that and there is no virtue in it.

There was, I must admit, a side to my character which very much enjoyed the kind of life I have just described, but there was another, what I call my Calvinistic side, which strongly disapproved and thought it all rather dissolute. The inner battle which ensued had one important consequence. I felt that I was no longer worthy of becoming a minister of the Church as I feared that I might not be able to live up to the high standards that calling demanded. I abandoned therefore all thought of going to a theological college after my return to civilian life. Shortly afterwards, I was offered a permanent career in SIS. I accepted without much hesitation. I found intelligence work fascinating and liked travelling. The thought of having to serve perhaps in far-flung and wild countries did not worry me and, indeed, rather attracted me. Besides, having abandoned the idea of going into the Church, I had no other definite prospects which appealed to me. Commander Child, who had been demobilised from the Navy, was in the process of setting up a company organising pleasure cruises on the Rhine and the Dutch waterways and wanted me as his assistant. A friend of my mother's who was the owner of a large fashion house offered me a job as a buyer. Neither prospect held out much attraction for me and, anyway, I was sure that I had no head for business.

After I had accepted and become a permanent SIS officer, Head Office suggested that I should be sent on a special Russian language course for officers of the Armed Services run by Cambridge University. The idea appealed to me and I agreed at once.

The course was to start in October, the beginning of the university year, and I returned to Hamburg for a short time to hand over my agents and most valuable contacts to officers of the SIS station there.

At Cambridge the officers who took this course were fully integrated into the life of the University. We lived as ordinary undergraduates, were attached to colleges – I was at Downing because of its naval connections – wore gowns and followed the curriculum of the Slavonic faculty, with some extra coaching thrown in.

The Slavonic faculty in Cambridge was headed in those years by Dr Elizabeth Hill who has trained several generations of Russian scholars and done much to spread the teaching of the Russian language in England. She had a striking personality, a rather unconventional approach, and an enthusiasm for her subject, which she had the ability to communicate to her students. I was fortunate to have her as my tutor. She also was descended from a long line of English merchants from St Petersburg, had a Russian mother and looked typically Russian with her rather stocky build, broad features and hair severely drawn back into a bun. During her tutorials she managed to inspire many of her students, including myself, with a love for all things Russian. I must stress here 'Russian' and not 'Soviet' for she had little time for the Soviet régime. She was devoutly Orthodox and sometimes took some of her favourite pupils in her car to London to attend the services in the Russian Orthodox church there. We not only learned the language, but also followed lectures in history and literature. Already by the Christmas holidays, I attempted to read my first Russian novel, Tolstoy's *Anna Karenina*. I do not pretend that I understood every word, but, with the aid of a dictionary, I managed to follow the story with interest. I had a real sense of achievement when I finished it and at once began on *Resurrection*, another book by the same author.

I look back upon my time in Cambridge as one of the watersheds in my life. It opened up new horizons to me. I acquired the key to the rich storehouse of Russian literature. I began to get a better understanding of the Russian people and develop an interest and liking for their customs and traditions. Until then I had made little distinction between the notions 'Russian' and 'Soviet' and regarded the Russians as semi-barbarians, oppressed by a ruthless, atheistic dictatorship which relentlessly persecuted all Christians. During the war I had, of course, looked towards the Soviet Union with hope, admired its fighting spirit and welcomed its victories, realising that the fighting on the Eastern front would have a decisive influence on the outcome of the war. But these sentiments were mixed with fear and dislike for Communism and devoid of any particular affection for the Russian people. This attitude, which, I think, I shared with many, is perhaps best illustrated by an anecdote which circulated in Holland during the height of the Soviet counter offensive in the winter of 1942. It was said that at that time a poster was erected on the Dutch–German border, facing Germany and bearing in large letters the words: 'Halt, Timoshenko! Holland begins here'. In other words, the Soviets could do with the Germans what they liked, but their presence in Holland was not welcome.

Now, gradually, under the influence of my reading and the inspired teaching of Dr Hill, much of this changed. My interest in all things Russian was awakened and this developed into a real affection and admiration for the Russian people, their warm-hearted and generous nature, their great courage in their struggle against cruel invaders from East and West and tyranny at home, their infinite patience in adversity and suffering. Little did I think then that life would offer me ample opportunity to put these sentiments to the test.

During my first term in Cambridge, I lived in rooms in the town, but soon discovered that it was very difficult to settle down to hard work. My fellow students on the course were all Army, Air Force or Naval officers, mostly convivial people used to the companionship of the officers' mess. Some had their wives with them and there was always something going on. People frequently dropped in or invited one to come round to their rooms for tea. If one went out one invariably met someone in the street one knew who would suggest going to a coffee shop or a pub for a drink. I realised that I would not get very far with my Russian studies if I went on with that kind of life. By chance, I heard of an elderly lady, the widow of a vicar, who lived in a large house in Madingley, about five miles outside Cambridge, and was looking for a lodger not so much because she needed the money, but because she did not like being alone in the house. I went to see her and she agreed to let me have a bedroom and sitting-room in a wing of her house for a relatively modest sum. She also provided meals which I shared with her. She was a good cook and as I was an appreciative guest this encouraged her to try even harder. For the last two terms I lived very comfortably and was able to concentrate on my studies without being distracted. I only went to Cambridge when it was strictly necessary to attend lectures while seldom was anybody tempted to cycle all the way to Madingley to come and see me.

I loved Cambridge, its old buildings and churches, its narrow streets and medieval atmosphere. I considered it a great privilege to be able to study there. I particularly enjoyed going to evensong in King's College chapel. I used to stay behind after the service when the candles were extinguished, but the organ went on playing, the sound filling every space. Sitting there in the darkness it was as if I no longer existed but had become one with the sound of the music. It was a mystical experience.

In the religious system to which I adhered the doctrine of predestination occupied a central position and I had given this doctrine much thought. I found no difficulty in accepting it as it fitted in completely with my concept of God as the Creator of Heaven and Earth, All-powerful, All-knowing, the King of the Universe, without whom not one sparrow falls to the ground and by whom the very hairs of our head are numbered (Matthew 10- 29, 30). There was no room in this system for such a thing as casualty or accident and, even less, free will on the part of a human being. The whole creation, from the heavenly bodies to the indivisible particle, is subject to the Supreme Will and under special observation, government and direction of the Omnipotent Mind. To imagine that human beings possessed of a free will could constantly interfere and change God's plans according to their whim seemed to me to subvert every notion of the Deity. Free will despoils the Divine Being of his unlimited supremacy, his infinite knowledge, his infallible wisdom, his absolute independence and eternal immutability by exempting some things from the providence of God. The whole of human history, for instance, which is made up of an infinite number of decisions by human beings, apparently exercising their 'free' will, would thus be exempt. Very few believers would agree with this.

If everything is pre-ordained by God then, whatever is, at any given time, is right and cannot be otherwise. From this it follows, I argued, that both what we call good and what we call evil proceed from God and are necessary elements in the working out of His purposes. Good and evil, it seemed to me, are relative notions applicable only to relations between human beings, to relations within human societies, but have no meaning as applied to the Supreme Being. Much of what we call evil and suffering in the world anyway is directly attributable to God and can in no way be ascribed to deliberate human action. Take earthquakes and natural disasters, incurable diseases and children being born handicapped and mentally retarded. Even where human action is directly involved, we see the hand of God. It is generally accepted by all believers, whether they hold the doctrine of predestination or free will, that our births and deaths are in the hand of God. But if the time, the place, the circumstances of our birth, the man and woman who are our parents are determined by God then he must have willed all the circumstances in which they conceived us, irrespective of whether this was in wedlock or as the result of a licentious relationship. If our death, its time and manner is pre-ordained by God, it follows that, if I am murdered, it is He who directs the hand of the murderer, if I am killed in an accident, it is He who wills the circumstances of the accident, if I die in hospital from a painful disease it is He who visits it upon me. These are facts we cannot get away from. It is often objected that this view of mankind makes us into mere robots and deprives us of our human dignity. But what, I ask, is humiliating in being a robot who is programmed, not by another human being, but by the Most High, the Creator of Heaven and Earth, the King of the Universe who set the heavenly bodies on their courses?

It is no good interposing Satan to get out of the dilemma. Satan, if he exists, is, after all, only the instrument of God who has been given power to do evil, a power which he exercises under the full authority of God and with His foreknowledge of how it will be used.

But if all depends on the will of God, it follows that he has made every individual exactly as he is with all his virtues and all his faults, some with more virtues, and others with less, in accordance with His own inscrutable purposes. As St Paul says in Romans 9, 15–21:

> For he saith to Moses, I will have mercy on whom I will have mercy, and I will have compassion on whom I will have compassion.
>
> So then it is not of him that willeth, nor of him that runneth, but of God that sheweth mercy.
>
> For the scripture saith unto Pharaoh. Even for this same purpose have I raised thee up, that I might shew my power in thee, and that my name might be declared throughout the earth.
>
> Thou wilt say then unto me, Why doth he yet find fault? For who hath resisted his will?
>
> Nay but, O man, who art thou that repliest against God? Shall the thing formed say to him that formed it. Why hast thou made me thus?
>
> Hath not the potter power over the clay, of the same lump to make one vessel unto honour, and another unto dishonour?

The truth of these verses seemed to me confirmed by life, by the realities which I saw every day around me. But if this is so, and I believed it to be so, then there can be no sin in the sight of God, let alone original sin, for sin is as necessary an element as virtue in the working out of this purpose. From this it follows that He being just, cannot hold us responsible and require our punishment for sins of which He himself is the author. Would it be just to condemn a creature to everlasting misery for sins which he cannot but commit? God cannot wish this. But if there is no sin and no punishment then there is also no need for atonement and justification through Christ's sacrifice. Would God play an elaborate game with Himself and, having implanted sin in man and using it to work out His eternal purposes, find it necessary to come into the world Himself and be crucified to atone for this sin? This, in my view, was highly unlikely, all the more so as man, after the coming of Christ, remained as sinful as he had been before. If God had really been among us in this way, we should have known the difference.

From this reasoning I was led to the inescapable conclusion, however reluctant I was to face it, that Christ was not God, that he had not by his sacrifice atoned for our sins and, indeed, that there was no need for any atonement. Having come to this conclusion, I realised that I no longer believed in the central doctrine of the Christian religion. However much I might continue to respect and admire the person of Christ as a human being, the most perfect of human beings, perhaps, and an example most worthy of imitation, but still a human being, I found I had argued myself out of the Christian religion and could no longer call myself a Christian. I am not certain that there is any label to describe what I then became. Some people say that I am a fatalist, and then ask me if that is so then why didn't I accept my imprisonment as my fate and sit quietly in Wormwood Scrubs. The answer to that is that I believe our reaction to events is also pre-destined. If it was my fate to be sentenced to forty-two years imprisonment, it was also my fate to act and organise my escape. Fatalism is not sitting back and accepting what has occurred. It is also the impulses which force you to act in a particular way. That is why I believe it is justified for someone to say, 'You cannot punish me for my sins because my sins were put inside me and are not my fault.'

I finished the course with top marks and left Cambridge at once after the exams, not waiting for the May Balls, to spend three weeks, together with a naval friend on the course, at the house of Russian émigrés who lived in a small village not far from Dublin. In those days there were no exchange programmes for language students. If one wanted to get practice in speaking one had to go and live for a while with a family of Russian émigrés, either in England or abroad. Our host was a prince who made a living by growing mushrooms, which he sold to Dublin restaurants, and by having Russian language students staying at his house. His wife was a tall, stately woman, the daughter of the last Russian viceroy of Poland, who tried against all odds to maintain an air of bygone splendour. This was not easy in her modest circumstances. Nothing could conceal, for instance, that her drawing-room sofas were made of vegetable crates covered with chintz. I found this spirit admirable. While we were there an old Cossack general with thick, grey whiskers called on our hosts and crossed himself before the icons in the corner as he came into the room. This impressed us much and we imagined we were somewhere in old Russia.

We had to speak Russian during all the meals and whenever we were with the family. This was, at first, very tiring, but gradually became easier. The main benefit of our stay, apart from the long walks in the beautiful Irish countryside, was that we acquired a certain assurance from the fact that people actually understood our spoken Russian and that we got the hang of most of what they were saying.

When I returned to London to report for duty at SIS Head Office, I was told that I would be sent to the British Consulate-General in Urumchi in Western China, near the border with Soviet Kazachstan, as an assistant to the SIS representative there. Though I welcomed this appointment, I would have preferred to be sent to Afghanistan, a country I have wanted to visit all my life, and which to this day has retained a strong attraction for me in spite of the cruel war which is being fought there. A few weeks later, without being given any reasons, the assignment was changed and I was informed that I had been appointed Head of a new station which was to be opened in Seoul, the capital of South Korea. Frankly, the prospect of going to the Far East did not enchant me. I had never felt much interest in Far Eastern culture, whether Chinese or Japanese and was much more attracted to the world of Islam. This feeling of disappointment was outweighed, however, by the satisfaction of being put in charge of a station, albeit a small one. Also, Korea was considered a critical area where a lot of trouble was expected, so it promised to be an interesting appointment which had plenty to offer in the way of excitement and responsibility. As it turned out, I got more than I bargained for.

For the rest of that summer of 1948, I was attached to the Far Eastern Department in order to acquaint myself with the background to the situation in Korea and the tasks and problems which awaited me. I read a lot of papers and had an interview with Mr Kermode, the outgoing Consul-General in Seoul, who was home on leave, and who gave me much valuable advice on life in that city and what clothing and equipment to take with me. Among the papers which I was given to read was a small handbook on Marxism prepared by section IX, the section in Head Office concerned with Communist affairs. Entitled the 'Theory and Practice of Communism', its purpose was to acquaint SIS officers with the main tenets of Marxism on the sound principle 'Know your enemy'. Its author was Carew Hunt, the senior SIS theoretician on Marxism, whose works on this subject are also well known to the general public. This booklet, written by a scholar not for propaganda purposes, but in order to inform, set out in lucid and objective terms the philosophical, economic and political teachings of Marxism and explained why it held such attraction for millions of people the world over.

The booklet turned out to be an eye-opener to me. Up to then I had read very little about Marxism and what I had read was negative. After reading the 'Theory and Practice of Communism', I was left with the feeling that the theory of Communism sounded convincing, that its explanation of history made sense and that its objectives seemed wholly desirable and did not differ all that much from Christian ideals even though the methods to attain them did. I began to ask myself whether Communism was really the terrible evil it was made out to be.

In October I flew out to Korea. There was such a hurry to get me there that I could not travel the longer and more interesting way by sea, which I would have much preferred. As it was, I went by sea-plane and the whole journey to Japan took a week. Every night was spent in a different staging post. The third day we arrived in Cairo where the passengers were put up in Shepherd's Hotel for the night. I at once tried to telephone my aunt, but there was no reply, however often I tried. I then took a taxi to the house. Ahmed, the old principal servant, opened the door, but everything else had sadly changed. My uncle and two aunts now lived alone in difficult circumstances. As a result of the creation of the state of Israel, the old harmony between the Jewish community and the Arabs had been destroyed. As Jews, they had become the target of all kinds of petty restrictions and humiliations. Their telephone had been cut off and it was difficult for my uncle to conduct his banking business. My cousin Henri was in prison as a Communist and my other cousin Raoul was living abroad. All this had affected the health of my uncle and aunts. They were glad to see me after all those years of war and we had a lot to tell each other, but it was a sad reunion. I left at midnight as I had to resume my journey in the early morning. With a heavy heart I said goodbye to these three aged and lonely people who had done so much for me. I never saw them again. They died, as I later heard, one after the other, at short intervals, before I returned from Korea.

On arrival in Seoul, I was at first put up in the Consulate-General. This consisted of two houses in the Victorian style, one large and one smaller, standing in a large garden which had once been part of the park surrounding the former royal palace. The large house was occupied by Captain Vyvyan Holt, the Consul-General, who a few months later, when Britain recognised the newly proclaimed Republic of South Korea, was elevated to the rank of Minister Plenipotentiary. In the smaller house the ground floor was occupied by the chancery and the first floor by the living quarters of Mr Faithful, the Consul, who was also a bachelor. He very kindly made a room available for me until I could find my own accommodation. A few weeks later I was joined by Norman Owen who was to be my assistant and who, though married, had left his wife and child behind in England. I had succeeded by that time in renting a large Japanese-style house in the commercial district of the town where Norman Owen and I installed ourselves. Later I invited the newly arrived French Vice-Consul, Jean Meadmore, who had difficulty in finding accommodation, to occupy two of our spare rooms. He proved an amusing and convivial addition to our household.

At weekends I would often go with friends on picnics in the mountains. We would drive in our jeeps – the only vehicle suitable for Korean roads – to some beautiful spot. This was usually near the site of an old temple on the banks of a fast mountain stream, with bare, craggy peaks rising all around us into a deep-blue sky. Especially in autumn, these outings were a delight, for at that season both Korea and its climate are at their most beautiful. Vivid colours against extraordinarily blue skies in an absolutely still, warm air. Soon my initial dislike turned into a deep attachment to this beautiful, wild country and its ruggedly independent, often maddeningly awkward people, who, when one got to know them, revealed an unexpected and therefore all the more disarming charm.

The war, though it eventually came, did not come as soon as expected. Instead of a few months, which was all the time it was thought I would have to entrench myself, I had a full year and a half before it broke out. During this period I had ample opportunity to get acquainted with the Korean scene and to lay the groundwork for my intelligence activities. My first and most important task was to try and establish an intelligence network in the Soviet Maritime Provinces, and, in the first place, the Vladivostok area. This turned out to be far from easy, not to say impossible. Seoul was, indeed, the nearest point on the map to the Soviet Maritime Provinces where there was a British diplomatic mission and this had probably been the chief consideration when it was decided to open an SIS station there. I had not been installed very long in my new post, however, when it became clear to me that although, as the bird flies, I was as close to the Soviet Far East as it was possible to get, in reality there existed no communications whatsoever between South Korea and that area. There were neither trade nor any other links which could be exploited. In those circumstances I decided to concentrate my efforts on widening as much as possible my contacts among the Korean population in preparation for my second assignment which was to function as a monitoring station if and when the Communist forces of the North occupied the whole country. By doing so I might be lucky and, perchance, come upon leads which could also assist me in my principal task. The fact that I knew Russian turned out to be completely irrelevant in the situation in which I found myself. It would have been far better to have sent a man who knew Korean.

There was in Korea, and had been ever since that country was opened up to foreigners at the end of the last century, a large number of missionaries of various denominations from Roman Catholic to the Salvation Army. The Protestants among them were nearly all American or English and the Catholics French or Irish. They had over the years made many Korean converts and there were now sizeable Christian communities among the population. Adjoining the Legation compound stood the large Anglican Cathedral which had been built in the years between the wars. The Anglican community in Korea was led by Bishop Cooper, a kindly old man, well into his seventies, and his Vicar General, Father Hunt, a rather fat, jolly priest in his early fifties. Both were celibate and very High Church, especially Father Hunt whose only point of difference with the Roman Catholics, as far as I could make out, was the fact that the latter did not consider him a proper priest. Close neighbourly relations were maintained between the Legation and the Cathedral and before long I was on friendly terms with Father Hunt, a witty and amusing raconteur, who spoke with a plum in his mouth, was not averse to a drink and knew Korea extremely well.

On Sundays it became my habit to attend morning service in the Cathedral crypt, where the congregation consisted mainly of American Episcopalians from the Embassy and where there was no incense and genuflections. For the evening service I went to the American United Reformed Church where I had the opportunity of meeting the missionaries of the non-conformist camp. It may be asked why, if I had ceased to believe in the Christian religion, I continued to go to church. The reasons were twofold. Firstly, I was used to going to church and old habits die hard and, secondly and more importantly, I hoped that by extending and strengthening my links with the missionary community I might be introduced to Koreans who could assist me in my intelligence work. Thus I became friendly with several missionary families among whom were Commissioner Lord of the Salvation Army and his wife and Mr and Mrs Ferguson of the British and Foreign Bible Society. With the latter I had a problem in common. Both of us faced the daunting task of establishing contact with the Soviet troops in North Korea, though for different reasons. The Bible Society had sent him a consignment of 10,000 Russian Bibles for distribution among the Soviet troops. How he was to do this, when there was absolutely no communication between the two Koreas, was left to him. The minds of the people who sent him these Russian Bibles, for which he had difficulty in finding storage, must have worked along much the same track as those of the people who had sent me to South Korea to collect intelligence on the Soviet Far East.

The issuing of visas for Hong Kong was part of my cover duties as Vice-Consul. This provided me with another means of increasing my contacts, particularly among the Korean business community which was interested in exploring the possibilities of trade with that colony. When they applied for a visa, they had to provide a certain amount of personal information and this process offered me an opportunity to establish personal contact with them and, where I thought this might be useful, provided pretexts for continuing it.

Another side of my work was social. Starting with the people to whom Captain Holt introduced me in the first weeks after my arrival, I began to build up systematically a wide circle of acquaintances among officials and politicians and among members of the American Embassy and the large economic and military missions attached to it. In my kind of work it is advisable not to neglect any contacts. One never knows who one day may be useful. Incidentally, the US Embassy in Seoul could boast, at that time, of being the largest US diplomatic mission in the world. All this kept me very busy.

The only other foreign mission in Seoul was the French Consulate. We maintained extremely friendly relations with them, strengthened, subsequently, by three years common imprisonment in North Korea. At that time a United Nations Commission on Korea was meeting regularly in the former royal palace in Seoul to discuss reunification. A Turkish representative, notorious for his amorous exploits, represented his country on the Commission, the president of which was a prim Australian diplomat. North Korea refused to attend the meetings. M Perruche, the French Consul-General, who represented his country on the Commission, used to characterise its work in the following terms: 'C'est du cirque et nous sommes les clowns.'

In 1945, after the surrender of Japan, by common agreement, a Soviet military government was established in North Korea and an American in South Korea, with the 38th parallel as the demarcation line. The avowed aim was to set up, as soon as possible, a Korean government and give the country its independence. Since the Soviets in their zone set up a system which was almost an exact replica of their own and the Americans did the same in their zone, it was not surprising that no progress was made to the formation of a single government for the whole country. Each zone became totally isolated from the other and began to develop along its own lines. When it became quite obvious that no agreement could be reached, the US government set up the independent Republic of South Korea and withdrew its troops, leaving a strong contingent of military, political and economic advisers to guide the first steps of the young republic. Shortly afterwards the Soviets did exactly the same in their zone and set up the People's Republic of North Korea, also withdrew their troops and also left behind a strong contingent of military, political and economic advisers.

In the wake of the American army which had landed in Korea after the Japanese surrender, a host of Koreans returned who during the Japanese occupation had lived in exile in Hawaii and the western coast of the United States. Many of them had acquired American citizenship, all spoke English and had absorbed over the years a strong dose of American culture.

Since virtually none of the officers of the American Military Government could speak Korean or knew anything about Korea, they came to rely heavily on these ex-émigrés. Nearly all the interpreters were recruited from among them and many were placed in key-positions in local government. In this way they became the sole link between the military government and the population which it administered and acquired considerable influence and power.

When in 1948 South Korea became an independent republic, these people became the senior officials and in many cases the ministers in the new administration. Syngman Rhee, the first President of South Korea was himself an ex-émigré who had lived many years in the US and Hawaii.

Unfortunately, close and prolonged contact with the American way of life, has, as I have frequently observed, a most detrimental effect on the character and manners of Orientals. They seem to take especially to the less admirable aspects of that way of life, lose entirely their inborn dignity and refinement, which often distinguishes them favourably from the white man, and turn into loud-mouthed go-getters. The Korean ex-émigrés were no exception to this sad phenomenon and to these people it now fell to administer the millions of dollars which the US government poured into the country in the form of economic and military aid. It was not surprising therefore that much of this money found its way into their own pockets and into those of the handful of businessmen, speculators and unscrupulous politicians in league with them. The population benefited very little or not at all, and the poverty remained appalling.

In the countryside next to nothing was done to curb the feudal power of the landlords and the lot of the majority of the peasantry was wretched. Even aid in kind, such as large consignments of powdered milk and canned meat sent to relieve the poor, ended up for the most part on the black market. Never before had I encountered such a contrast between rich and poor.

Often at dusk I would go out into the streets, savouring the smells from the eating houses, looking at the coppersmiths patiently hammering out their vessels, watching the beautiful Kisang girls, the professional entertainers, in their brightly coloured silks and brocades hastening to an assignment. Flashy American cars would pull up in front of the large Chinese restaurants. Out of them emerged well-dressed businessmen and politicians who would spend the evening there carousing with their favourite entertainers. A little further on I would have to push my way through a clamouring crowd of beggars, clad in filthy rags and displaying their festering sores and maimed limbs. There were thousands of them in Seoul. Many of them were children who slept out at night under bridges or in the shelter of gates and porches.

Private charity, however generous, was quite inadequate to deal with poverty on such a scale as I saw here. Even the best intentioned efforts of such dedicated missionaries as the Commissioner of the Salvation Army and his wife, who had devoted their whole lives to helping the needy in Korea, were but a drop in the ocean. For every one they helped many thousands were left in wretched and hopeless conditions. Only a complete change of system, it seemed to me, could solve the problem.

The more I saw of the Rhee régime, the more I disliked it. This old dictator, for that is what he was, brooked no opposition. If the Korean National Assembly showed any signs of having a mind of its own, it was disbanded and the elections for a new one were thoroughly rigged. Opposition leaders were intimidated or arrested as suspected Communists. Anyone who held views no more extreme than those daily canvassed in England at that time in the *Herald* or the *Daily Mirror* was branded as a dangerous red and attracted the unwelcome attention of an extremely ruthless security police.

It was indeed so loathsome that I could not help but feel sympathy with anyone who opposed this régime. It was difficult to withhold admiration from the bands of partisans who had taken to the mountains, from which they were harassing the government forces, or from the Communist underground movement operating in extremely dangerous conditions. They seemed to me not unlike our own resistance fighters in Europe during the war and moved by the same noble motives. It was all the easier to draw this parallel as the Rhee régime bore marked fascist characteristics. Its Minister of Education was an open Nazi sympathiser and even had a photograph of Hitler in his room.

As to the methods used by the police, they bore a striking resemblance to those of the Gestapo.

The police posts in Seoul were mostly wooden pavilions with one open side so that it was easy to look in. Often I saw people being beaten up with rifle butts or knocked about. One of my contacts was a young police captain who acted as ADC to the Seoul Chief of Police. He was a cocky and rather boastful young man who spoke excellent English, having been brought up in Hawaii. He was a useful source of information and in order to cultivate him, I used to invite him from time to time to dinner. On these occasions one of his favourite topics of conversation was to relate in detail how he interrogated Communist suspects. In order to obtain confessions he would hang them by their feet and pour boiling coffee into their mouths or hold them under water in a bath tub till they nearly drowned. When they came round he would start again until they spoke. Such things as applying burning cigarette ends or electric current to sensitive parts of their bodies were, in his opinion, comparatively light forms of pressure, while the beating up of suspects was simply routine. I found these stories disgusting, and what made it worse was that I had to listen patiently and hide my true feelings. I was after all supposed to be on his side and the purpose of the dinner was to butter him up.

But as I have had occasion to remark before, in intelligence work one cannot always be choosy as regards the people with whom one has to collaborate.

A man whose company I came to enjoy very much and to whose memory I remain grateful for having given me much sound advice from which I was able to benefit in later life was Captain Holt, the British Minister in Seoul.

He was a man of great charm but, as anyone who knew him will be able to confirm, also a great eccentric. He was tall and almost painfully thin. A lifetime spent in the Middle East, much of it in the open air to which he was much addicted, had given his skin the consistency and colour of wrinkled brown leather. This, together with almost complete baldness and rather sharp bird-like features, gave him a striking likeness to Mahatma Gandhi, especially when he wore his glasses without which he could not read. He was, like Gandhi, an ascetic and lived by preference on boiled vegetables, fruit and curds.

His official position, which required both that he extended and received a certain amount of hospitality, did not always make it possible for him to stick to this diet. In consequence, he hated cocktail and dinner parties, which he invariably referred to as 'hot meals'. Learning of the arrival of some new official at the American Embassy, he would give a weary sigh and mutter, 'Ah, well, I suppose I shall have to give the man a hot meal.'

At first my relations with Captain Holt had been rather distant. Like many members of the Foreign Service he had an innate distrust of SIS and its officers, fostered in his case by long experience in the Middle East as an expert on Arab affairs. But being a bachelor and living alone in his large house, he often felt rather lonely. He liked to work in the morning and when the weather was fine take the afternoon off to be as much as possible in the fresh air. Soon he began to ask me to accompany him on his walks. We would make our way through the narrow streets of old Seoul to the orchards on the lower mountain slopes which rose gently from the outskirts of the town. I enjoyed these walks and enjoyed our conversations. Captain Holt was a good story-teller and would describe many amusing incidents in his diplomatic career involving such well-known figures on the Middle Eastern scene between the two wars as Sir Percy Cox, Gertrude Bell, Freya Stark, Lord Killearn and King Feisal I.

Once he was suffering badly from mumps. He walked about with a white cloth round his head, looking more Gandhi-like than ever. Being a most considerate man, especially for his small staff, he insisted that nobody should come near him or enter his house while the illness lasted, for fear of infection. The work of the Legation had to go on, however, and certain documents had to be shown to him for action. For this purpose he devised a complicated procedure which avoided all personal contact and which he insisted we should strictly adhere to. If we had to hand him a document, we telephoned him. As he felt well enough to be up and about, he would appear on the big, sloping lawn which separated his house from ours and one of us would then take up position on the opposite side. At a given signal, we would advance to the middle of the lawn, deposit the paper on the grass, turn round and walk smartly back to our starting-point. When we had reached our original position, and not a moment earlier, Captain Holt would advance in turn, pick up the paper and return to his end of the lawn, where he would sit down on the grass and deal with it as required. When he was ready the whole manoeuvre would be repeated in reverse. All the time curious and laughing faces of servants and members of the staff, half hidden by the curtains of the windows overlooking the lawn, would be watching this bizarre scene.

He was very house-proud and had little faith in the cleanliness of his Korean servants so he was constantly supervising them. If he thought they had not cleaned the rooms thoroughly enough, he would do it himself to show them how it should be done. The windows he invariably cleaned himself. It was the custom for callers to come to the Chancery first as it stood nearest to the gate. As we never knew whether he was on a ladder with a sponge-cloth, or streaked with soot from tinkering with the oil-heating which often went wrong, we always had to make sure that he was in a fit state to receive visitors before sending them on to his house.

At the beginning of June, the Legation gave the traditional reception for the King's official birthday. For many members of the American mission, and especially their wives, this was regarded as an important social event, about as near as they could get to a garden party at Buckingham Palace. Accordingly, it was preceded by much discussion on what to wear and how to behave and the occasion was looked forward to with a certain excitement. Unfortunately there was one snag. June is the beginning of the rainy season in Korea and one could never be sure whether on the day it was going to rain or the weather would be fine. The simple solution would have been to make preparations to have the party in the garden if the weather was good, and in the house if it rained. Captain Holt, however, was adamant. The party must be held in the garden whatever the weather. He was not going to have drunken American colonels being sick all over his drawing-room as had happened the previous year.

When the day arrived, the weather, at first, promised to be good. The tables with the food and drink were all set out on the lawn. By four o'clock the sky became overcast and by five o'clock it was raining hard. I had been posted at the main door not, as they no doubt expected, to usher the guests in, but with express instructions to direct them towards the wicket gate leading on to the lawn. There Captain Holt in gumboots was standing holding an umbrella and welcoming his guests with his most charming smile. Knowing him well by now, I was sure he was chuckling to himself at what he thought was a good practical joke. I felt extremely embarrassed having to direct the ladies in their fineries, who had just hurried out of their cars into the porch, back into the pouring rain. Many guests left immediately in a huff, others, with more sense of humour perhaps, stayed a while to watch the amazing scene.

Captain Holt had his way and the party became the talk of the town. It might have led to a serious cooling off in Anglo-American relations, at least on a local level, had it not been for grave events which swept away all bad feeling left by this bizarre incident. A storm broke loose about our heads which brought far-reaching changes in many lives, including my own. In the early hours of Sunday the 25th of June, like a death which had long been expected, but still takes everyone by surprise, the war broke out.

Chapter Six

Sunday the 24th of June was the feast of St John the Baptist and the name day of my friend, Jean Meadmore, the French Vice-Consul, who shared our house. To celebrate this event, on the eve he had invited about thirty people, colleagues from the American Embassy and the UN Commission with their wives and girlfriends and some Korean friends. The party had been a great success from the start and the guests did not begin to leave till the dawn was breaking. I had been able to snatch a few hours sleep, but by 9.30 was already on my way to church. In the streets I noticed nothing unusual, though, I must admit that after the night before, I was not at my most alert. The service in the Cathedral crypt had just started when an American officer came in and approached several members of the congregation belonging to the Embassy and the military mission, and whispered something in their ear. One by one they tiptoed out, leaving their wives behind. Clearly something unusual had happened, but, as we did not know what, Captain Holt and I remained till the end of the service. Outside the church, people stood around in small groups talking excitedly. The wife of an American colonel, whom we both knew, told us that her husband had been called away because early that morning North Korean troops had crossed the 38th parallel and heavy fighting was in progress all along the line.

During the week preceding the outbreak of war, persistent rumours had reached us of massive troop movements on both sides. On Captain Holt's instructions, I had called on the G2 in the American military mission, whom I knew well, and asked him what the truth of these rumours was. He confirmed that there had been, indeed, large troop concentrations on both sides of the border and that the number of skirmishes had significantly increased. But this was not the first time this had happened and it was difficult to attach any particular significance to it. Asked what the US would do if the North were to attack, he answered quite categorically that, as far as the US was concerned, its line of defence was the Japan Sea, separating Japan from Korea, and that there was no question of the American armed forces intervening.

The first day of the war was one of confusion and conflicting reports. Nobody seemed to know exactly what was happening. One version had it that North Korean troops had penetrated deeply into South Korean territory and were advancing towards Seoul. Another that South Korean troops had occupied the Northern town of Haeju.

I was not on the 38th parallel at the time, so I cannot say who started the war. The overwhelming evidence points to the North. I cannot entirely dismiss the theory, however, that it was the South which provoked the attack. I do not put it past the old fox, Syngman Rhee, to have tricked the Americans into intervening on his side. Knowing that South Korea was militarily weaker, he may well have counted on the US not leaving him in the lurch and sending in its troops as soon as he got into difficulties. This is what actually happened. Be that as it may, of one thing I am quite certain in my own mind, the Americans on the spot were not privy to this plot, if such there was, and quite taken by surprise.

After church, I accompanied Captain Holt to his office where we were joined by Mr Faithful, the first secretary. I suggested that I should get in touch with my contacts in the American military mission to find out what exactly was happening, but Captain Holt did not want me to do this. He also did not want to ring the American Ambassador. He thought it was an unsuitable moment to trouble them, as, no doubt, they were all extremely busy. Later in the afternoon, the counsellor in the American Embassy himself rang Captain Holt. He told him that the situation was grave. The North Koreans were advancing rapidly in the direction of the capital. The Ambassador had given orders for all American dependants to be evacuated to Japan forthwith. He advised Captain Holt to warn the small British community to do the same and offered American facilities for the evacuation. As to what action the American government proposed to take in the Korean conflict, he had no idea and could not tell us.

I immediately went out in the jeep to call on the few British families who all lived in Seoul. They were a handful of missionaries and two or three representatives of Hong Kong business firms. I told them they had to assemble at the Legation with their personal belongings at 8 o'clock that evening and that if they stayed, they did so at their own risk. They all decided to leave with the exception of three missionaries who did not want to abandon their flock. They were Bishop Cooper of the Anglican community and his Vicar General, Father Hunt, and Commissioner Lord of the Salvation Army who sent his wife home, much against her will.

That evening the small, rather bedraggled and distressed group of refugees, clutching the few belongings they could take with them, assembled at the lower house in the Legation compound from which an American army bus took them to nearby Kimpo airfield. With them went Mr Faithful who would look after them till they could be shipped to England.

In the course of the day Captain Holt had sent an immediate telegram to London to ask for instructions as to what he should do if Seoul were occupied by Communist forces. Although this war had long been expected, he had never had any precise instructions from the Foreign Office as to what action he should take in such an event. We did not have our own wireless station at the Legation and were dependent for our communications on the Cable and Wireless Company. He would not get a reply till Wednesday at the earliest.

The next day, Monday, the news was bad. The South Korean troops were in full retreat and it was estimated, our American colleagues informed us, that the vanguard of the North Korean army would reach Seoul by nightfall the next day. General MacArthur was sending fighter squadrons to harass the advancing Communist troops, but the official attitude of the US government was not yet known. The South Korean government had left the city in haste for an unknown destination and the American Embassy staff and all American service personnel had received orders to proceed to Tokyo at once. If we wanted to leave, we had only a few hours to decide.

Captain Holt called us over to his house for a council of war. He explained the situation to us and added that by the time an answer from London could arrive, it would probably be too late. We would have to decide for ourselves what to do. As far as he was concerned, he would stay. Strictly speaking, he should follow the South Korean government, to which he was accredited, to wherever it went. But it had left in flight and had not informed him that it was going or where to. To take to the road, with fighting all around, and without a clear idea where to go, would be sheer folly. It would be better if the North Korean troops found us in our Legation, where there could be no doubt who we were, than if they found us stranded on some mountain road. As for the American offer to evacuate us to Tokyo, there was no justification for closing down the Legation. Britain was not involved in the war and there was no reason why we should leave. He asked me what I wanted to do. I told him that my instructions were clear. Head Office wanted me to continue to operate under a North Korean occupation as long as the Legation, or at any rate the Consulate, was able to function and I had been specially sent out for that purpose. I would stay therefore. Norman Owen also agreed to stay. That settled the question.

Later in the day we heard that our colleagues in the French Consulate had come to the same decision.

Having been told that we would not avail ourselves of their offer, the Americans kindly suggested that we go to their Commissary and stock up with as much food and petrol supplies as we could manage to move. We would probably need it. They were leaving everything behind, anyway, so we could have it for nothing. We accepted this offer gratefully and spent all the next day laying in stores for what might become a long state of siege.

Towards dusk, when we made our last journey back to the compound in the jeep, piled with tins, tea cases and canisters an eerie silence had descended on the city, broken only by the low rumble of guns in the distance. The streets were almost deserted, except for an occasional lorry loaded with soldiers. The Americans had left. Only hundreds of typewritten sheets with the US letter-head, which had escaped hasty burning, whirled and rustled in the dry warm wind, littering the pavements like dead leaves. This was all that was now left in this city of the impressive tokens of American power and influence, which two days earlier had still reigned supreme. The Cable and Wireless Company had also left and even if London had sent us instructions these could no longer reach us.

That evening we were joined by the three English missionaries who had elected to stay behind. Captain Holt had suggested that, for the time being, they would be safer in the Legation and invited them to stay in his house. Norman Owen and I had moved to the lower house.

The gunfire had come closer and was interspersed, now and then, by the ominous sound of machine-gun fire. Just before midnight, there were a couple of loud explosions and flashes of fire in the direction of the river. The railway and road bridges had been blown up. Even had we wanted to leave, our last escape route was now cut.

We did not go to bed that night. All around us was the sound of street fighting. At one point a party of retreating South Korean soldiers entered the grounds where they took up positions, but soon left again without having fired a shot. Towards the morning the fighting died down and the city lay silent. Our servants, who kept coming and going, informed us that it was now in the hands of the North Korean troops. A large number of them were installed in the broadcasting station overlooking our compound. We decided that for the time being it was wiser not to venture out in the streets and relied on our servants for information on what was happening in the town. Just outside the gate, in the narrow road which led up to it, lay the body of a soldier. In the heat of the day it was beginning to swell and gave off an unbearable smell. We had no choice but to remove it and bury it in a corner of the garden. It was an unpleasant and depressing task.

That evening we all had dinner together in Captain Holt's large dining-room. Afterwards we listened to the BBC news. What we heard came as a great shock and surprise. Mr Attlee had launched a bitter attack on North Korea in Parliament, branding it as the aggressor, and announced that Britain was sending troops to assist the United States in its intervention in support of the South Korean government, under the flag of the United Nations. We had been caught. Instead of being neutrals, as we thought, we were now belligerents in enemy territory. I did not blame SIS for what had gone wrong. I am certain that the British government had not intended to join in the war but had been drawn into it by the United States. In fact, I don't think that the Americans originally planned to get involved either, but General MacArthur had pushed them into it.

We spent that night burning our codes and secret documents in a sheltered corner of the garden in the hope that the bonfire would not attract the attention of the North Korean military. All passed off well. The next morning we were equally busy pouring our liquor stores down the bath. We had to reckon with the possibility that a mob might loot the Legation and if they got hold of the drink there was no saying what might happen. Then we settled down to our new existence. There was nothing more to do but await events. The weather was fine and we spent most of the day sitting on the lawn, reading, talking and drinking tea.

Around us the city lay quiet and silent. High on its tall flagpole the Union Jack was flapping lazily in the light breeze. It was a peaceful scene. Nobody who could have seen us would have believed that we were at the very heart of a dangerous world conflict.

The next morning a North Korean officer and two soldiers rang at the gate. Through a servant they asked politely if we would mind hauling down the flag as it might attract aircraft. Captain Holt immediately gave orders to have this done. The North Koreans left again. It had been our first contact with them and it seemed reassuring. Sunday came, the war had been on a week. In the morning the Bishop conducted a short service in the dining-room and the rest of the day we spent lazing in the garden. Just after tea, three jeeps with armed soldiers drove up to the gate and demanded to be let in. They drove on to the upper house where we were all made to assemble. They then indicated to us that we should get into the jeeps. Without time to collect any personal belongings, we were driven off to the Seoul police headquarters, of sinister repute. There we were questioned by an English-speaking officer who wanted to know who we were. We had not been able to take any documents with us, so Captain Holt and myself were allowed to return to the Legation under escort to collect everybody's passport. We were then taken back to the Police Headquarters. While I was sitting at a narrow desk opposite the officer who was questioning me, somebody in a room below us fired off a rifle. The bullet passed through the floor and the desk at which we were sitting, shattering the inkpot that was standing between us and covering us with ink, then whizzed past our foreheads and disappeared in the ceiling. This caused a certain commotion which was interrupted when two other foreigners were brought in. One was an American civilian engineer who had got blind drunk on the weekend the war broke out. By the time he sobered up the Americans had gone and the North Koreans had taken the city. The other was an elderly White-Russian, a diver by profession, to whom only a few weeks earlier I had had to refuse an entry visa for Hong Kong.

In the course of the evening, each of us was given some rice packed tight into a ball. Towards midnight we were all bundled into the back of a lorry on to which jumped armed soldiers. We were driven out of the city and then the lorry stopped in a small valley in the surrounding hills. We all had the same thought. We had been taken to this remote spot to be summarily executed. After all we had heard about the

Communists, this seemed to us the only explanation which fitted the circumstances. Even the reserve barrel of petrol we took as confirmation. It was to be used to burn our bodies afterwards.

However, after a longish wait, a jeep with two officers drove up and our journey was resumed. Throughout the night and all the following day the lorry drove steadily northward. We did not stop off for food. It was a nightmare journey through burnt-out villages, barely avoiding bomb-craters and the smell of rotting corpses hardly ever leaving our nostrils. Towards the evening we arrived, shaken and exhausted, in the Northern capital, Pyongyang. Here we were taken to a disused school-building, just outside the city.

In the course of the next few weeks we were joined there by various other foreign nationals. About a week after our arrival our colleagues from the French Consulate were marched in. The party consisted of M Perruche, the Consul-General, my friend, Jean Meadmore, M Martel, another Vice-Consul, together with his aged mother and sister, and M Chanteloup, a French newspaper correspondent who had been caught by events in Seoul. Eventually our group swelled to about seventy people. There were French and Irish Catholic missionaries, several French Carmelite nuns, one Anglican nun, Sister Mary Clare, some American Presbyterian women-missionaries, three White-Russian families, one Tartar family and the Swiss manager of the Chosen hotel, the only European-style hotel in Seoul. The last to join us was the colourful figure of Philip Dean, the war correspondent of the *Observer*, his arm in a sling and leaning heavily on a stick. He had been wounded on the front and captured before he could get back to the American lines.

To my certain knowledge at least two books have been written on the experiences of our small group of civilian internees during the three years of Korean captivity, one notably by my companion in misfortune, Philip Dean. I shall therefore not repeat the story here except for such details as had a direct bearing on the further course of my life.

We spent two months in the school in Pyongyang. The food was adequate, though monotonous – three times a day a bowl of rice and a small bowl of cooked cabbage. What we suffered most from were mosquitoes, fleas and lice and we became experts at picking the lice off each other. We were guarded by Korean soldiers, who otherwise did not interfere with us.

At the end of August we were moved. We were joined to a group of some seven hundred American POWs, captured at the front in the first weeks of the war, and taken by train to Mampo, a small town in the far North on the Yalu river, which forms the border between Korea and Manchuria. There we were put up in some derelict army huts, but our living conditions were reasonable. The most beautiful season in Korea is the autumn and the weather was fine. We were taken regularly for a swim in the river and sometimes for walks in the countryside. From time to time we were given the choice between a kilogram of apples or a small tobacco ration. Korean apples are delicious and I chose them in preference to the tobacco. Since then I have never smoked again.

This not unpleasant existence came dramatically to an end when General MacArthur's forces crossed the 38th parallel and, routing the North Korean army, rapidly advanced towards the Yalu river in a bid to unify the whole country under American auspices. This attempt would have succeeded and nearly did, were it not for the intervention of the so-called Chinese volunteers who moved in en masse and drove the UN forces equally rapidly back again to the 38th parallel. The whole country was turned into a gigantic battlefield and the destruction exceeded by far anything that I had seen in Germany.

During this period of chaos and heavy fighting, just before the intervention of the Chinese 'volunteers', it became clear to us by many signs of dissolution that the North Korean régime was collapsing and the army disintegrating. We had been moved from one derelict building to another, all in the neighbourhood of Mampo, and again been separated from the American POWs. It was at this point that the plan was conceived that some of us, with the help of two of our Korean guards, should make an attempt to reach the American lines and organise a rescue operation of the civilian internees. I don't remember who put forward the original idea, whether M Martel and M Chanteloup who both spoke fluent Japanese and conducted the negotiations with our guards, or the guards themselves who, in return for guiding us, demanded that we should intercede on their behalf with the American army authorities.

A small group was formed, consisting of the three French diplomats and M Chanteloup, on the one hand, and Captain Holt, Mr Dean and myself on the other, which would make the attempt. Accompanied by two of our Korean guards, who took us along narrow mountain paths, we set out one morning in a southerly direction, away from the Yalu river. We walked all day, avoiding villages and houses and spent the night in a small valley. The next morning we continued our journey. It must have been about midday when we met three Korean soldiers coming the other way. They stopped and engaged our guards in conversation. They sat down together some distance away from us so that we could not hear what was being said. The conversation lasted a long time and we got a distinct impression that something was amiss. At last the soldiers got up and went their way while our two guards continued in earnest conversation. When they rejoined us we at once noticed a change in their demeanour. They told us that the situation had changed completely in the last twenty-four hours and that the Chinese volunteers had come to the rescue of the North Korean army and were now engaged in heavy fighting with the Americans. It was now too dangerous, indeed impossible, to get through to the American lines and there was nothing for it but to return to the camp. With heavy hearts we started on the return journey. Freedom had seemed so near and had now receded indefinitely. On our return our fellow internees greeted us, partly with relief that we were safely back, partly with disappointment that our mission had not succeeded. The day after our return to the camp, we were moved once more to Mampo where we camped in a field between the road and the river. While we were there a tall, thin Korean major with a surly expression on his face and an ungainly gait, took over command of the camp.

I felt a terrible disappointment that our attempt to get through had failed. I was not sure that what our guides had told us was the truth. Perhaps they had simply got cold feet? Surely the Americans could not be far off? If one continued in a southerly direction through the mountains, walking at night, lying up in the day time, avoiding roads and villages, one was bound to get to the American lines, even if it took a week. It was September and one could feed on berries and maize.

I discussed my plan with Meadmore and Dean and suggested that we should make another attempt. They agreed and we decided to set out that same night when everybody was asleep. Later in the day, Meadmore told me that he had thought things over and that he had decided not to join us. It was too dangerous and most unlikely that we could get through to the front line. If we were caught we might be shot out of hand as spies. Dean and I decided to go together.

It must have been about eleven o'clock when I crawled to the hole in the ground where Dean had installed himself for the night. The soldiers who were guarding us were sitting round a camp fire, some distance away. I whispered to him that I was ready. Was he coming? He answered that he too had thought things over, that it was too dangerous and that he had decided to stay. I said I was going to try anyway and he wished me good luck. I then started to crawl in the direction of the road and when I thought I was far enough away not to be seen, I got up and started walking. Before long, I reached the road which I quickly crossed and started climbing the mountain on the other side. It must have been at least two hours, if not more, before I reached the top and started descending into the valley on the other side. I don't know how long I had been walking down, perhaps an hour or so, when suddenly from behind a bush stepped a Korean soldier who barred my way with his rifle. He shone a torch in my face and asked me something. In the vague hope that he would believe me and let me continue my way, I told him I was a Russian. He evidently did not believe me or, if he did, felt that I should establish my identity to his superiors for he ordered me to follow him. After a short walk we came to what looked to me like the entrance to a cave in which a fire was burning. About ten soldiers were sitting in a circle round it. One of them turned out to be a captain who was in command. He told me to sit down and started to ask me in Korean who I was. Although I couldn't speak Korean, I understood sufficiently to know what he was asking me. At first I tried to maintain that I was a Russian who had lost his way. When he asked me for my papers, I realised that that line wasn't going to get me anywhere so I told him who I was, a British Vice-Consul who had absconded from a camp near Mampo. He appeared to be aware of the existence of a camp. The conversation was carried on mostly in Korean of which I understood a few words, but with the occasional Russian word thrown in. When he and his soldiers, who looked at me with great curiosity as if they had never seen a white man and who joined freely in the questioning, seemed to be satisfied as to who I was and where I came from I was told to sit down at some distance from the fire, with my back to the wall of the cave. Thus I spent the night, dozing off from time to time, feeling weary and despondent that I had been caught so soon and wondering what was in store. When morning came I was taken outside and made to sit on a small mound not far from the entrance of the cave. I now saw that I was in a small valley of great beauty and in the warm sunshine my spirits rose somewhat. Meanwhile the soldiers went about their business, washing themselves in a nearby mountain stream and preparing breakfast. I remained an object of great curiosity, however, and from time to time they would crowd round me making remarks which I did not understand but which were no doubt rude as they called forth much laughter. After they had had their breakfast of which there was clearly not enough to spare for me, the captain mustered them and gave them a long talk which ended in what sounded like a long series of instructions. When he had finished, he indicated that I should follow him. Accompanied by an armed soldier, we set off along a narrow mountain track. About two hours later we arrived in Mampo where I was taken straight to the camp and was handed over to the surly major. All my fellow inmates crowded around, anxious to know what had happened to me. The major then ordered everybody, men, women and children, to form a large circle. I was made to stand in the middle. Commissioner Lord of the Salvation Army, who was a fluent Korean speaker, was called out to act as interpreter. For nearly twenty minutes the major harangued us, pointing repeatedly at me and getting at times very angry. I do not remember exactly what he said, but it boiled down to me being a very bad man, who had broken the rules of the camp and the laws of North Korea and who, instead of being an example to his fellow inmates as behoved one of my rank, was a bad influence. He ended up with the warning that if I ever tried to escape again I would be shot there and then and so would anybody who tried to emulate me. The internees were then dismissed. I was allowed to join them and no further punishment was inflicted on me. This was a bit of an anti-climax and I have often wondered why I was let off so lightly, all the more so as, a few days later, when we were on what became known as the death march, the major had no compunction in shooting any stragglers among the American POWs who were too weak to follow the column. My feeling is that he did not dare to take upon himself the responsibility of shooting a British diplomat who was, in a way, held hostage by his government without the consent of Pyongyang which, of course, in the circumstances he could not obtain.

I have dealt with this incident in some detail as later it gave rise to the theory that when I was caught in the mountains I was threatened with summary execution and, in order to save my life, I revealed that I was an MI6 officer and offered to work for the Soviets who, subsequently, blackmailed me into continuing. There are several factors which invalidate this theory.

First, it presupposes a modicum of communication between me and the Korean captain to begin to explain all this to him. This was almost totally lacking. Second, I could hardly have been recruited without the presence of a Soviet intelligence officer. Where could he be found at such short notice? The cave was situated at least two hours walking distance from Mampo and could only be reached on foot along a narrow mountain path. The confession, interrogation and subsequent recruitment would have taken several hours, at the least. All this could simply not have been done in the time I was away from the camp which was not more than twelve hours at the most. Of these at least five hours were taken up with my walk from Mampo to the cave and back. Third, about two days after my return to the camp, we set out on what became known as the death march, northward along the Yalu river, followed by three months of extreme hardship in a deserted mountain village. During this period I might well have died of privation and illness as did nearly half the American POWs and several of our civilian internees. If the Soviets had just succeeded in recruiting a potentially very valuable agent, would they have allowed him to be exposed to such hardships and run the risk of him dying on their hands? Surely they would have taken steps to keep me and my fellow diplomats in reasonable conditions so as to ensure my survival?

Fourth, if indeed I had been recruited by the Soviets in this way and had in fact been working for them under duress and against my will, would I have been as zealous as I was and supplied so much information? I could have given far less and the Soviet intelligence service would still have been well pleased with me. Surely also, if I had been working under duress, I would have accepted some money from them on the principle that as I had no choice, I might as well benefit from it. Fifth, when in April 1961 I was interrogated by my colleagues in MI6 and accused of spying for the Soviet intelligence service would I not have been glad to be able to plead in mitigation that I had done so under duress and against my will? Instead, once I felt sure that my interrogators knew that I was a Soviet agent, I confessed for the very reason that I wanted them and everybody else to know exactly why I had done so; that I had done so out of conviction and not because I had been forced to as they suggested. Finally, would the Soviet government, knowing that I had been working for them under duress and against my will, have bestowed on me the highest orders of chivalry in its gift: the Order of Lenin, the Military Order of the Red Banner, the Order of the Patriotic War in Gold, the Military Order of Merit and other medals and insignia? I should hardly imagine so.

The very next day after my escape and return to the camp our group of about seventy civilian internees was once again joined to the column of seven hundred and fifty or so American POWs. Then started what was to be the darkest and most dramatic period in our captivity. In long marches we were moved further north along the Yalu river. We walked all day through wild mountain country, stopping at night in deserted villages where we sometimes found only burnt-out shells instead of houses. The only food we got was a ball of half-cooked maize which was difficult to digest. Sometimes our column was attacked by American fighters which, sweeping down low, machine-gunned us so that we had to scatter hastily in ditches and fields. People who couldn't keep up and fell behind were shot by the Korean guards, so we tried to help each other as best we could. This may appear merciless on the part of the Koreans, but, if the stragglers had been left behind, they would have been doomed to a slow but certain death from hunger and cold. The winter, which is severe in those parts, had set in quite suddenly with hardly any transition from the fine autumn weather. Most of us had only the summer clothes we were wearing at the time of our arrest and a thin blanket with which we had been issued. Thus we walked on for nearly three weeks till we came to our final destination, a small, deserted hamlet. It was a period of great hardship and suffering. Food supplies were insufficient as communications were disrupted because of the heavy American bombing. There was little fuel. Many died of dysentry and pneumonia. Captain Holt and Norman Owen were taken seriously ill and we nursed them as best we could. They recovered only slowly. The only medicine available was penicillin of which the North Koreans seemed to have had large supplies. This was occasionally administered by two small Korean nurses who appeared to be mere schoolgirls. Father Hunt and Sister Mary Clare, exhausted by the long march, died shortly after arrival in the hamlet, the name of which I never learned. It was difficult to bury the dead because the ground was frozen and we had no tools. All we could do was cover the bodies with snow and stones.

Like many others, I too suffered badly from dysentry, which was eventually cured, I think, by the penicillin injected under much giggling by the two Korean nurses. On one occasion, I had to fetch water from the well. This was a chore we all had to take in turns. In normal conditions it was not a very arduous task. One had to carry two buckets on a yoke across one's shoulder and empty them into a large barrel. In the freezing temperatures of the North Korean winter this turned into a real ordeal, however. The rope with which the bucket was hauled up turned into a rod of ice and the sides of the well into ice walls. Going to and from the well, we were accompanied by an armed soldier. I had been hauling up many buckets and the barrel was nearly full. My hands were so cold that I had no longer any feeling in them so that I could not pull up the bucket. I told the soldier that I thought we had enough water, but he said I should fetch more. I refused, saying that I wouldn't and couldn't. He got very angry, shouted at me and starting hitting me in the chest with his rifle butt which was very painful. He then took me to the yard outside the peasant hut in which we lived and made me kneel in the snow with my hands behind my back and my head bowed. He called to the others so that I should be an example to them of what happened to anyone who disobeyed. I don't know how long I remained in that position, but it was certainly more than an hour before he told me that I could go inside. I was completely numbed and it took a long time before I got warm again.

I have often subsequently been asked how it was that, having witnessed and experienced on my own person the harsh treatment meted out by the North Koreans to us prisoners, I could ever join the Communist side. My answer is this. In the first place, a war was going on and war always begets violence and harshness on both sides. In the second place the bad treatment lasted only for the three months that the heavy fighting was going on and the country was in a state of disruption. As soon as the frontline stabilised and the war became static, conditions improved considerably and our lives were no longer in danger. Finally, I should like to make this point. I joined the Communist side not because I was well or badly treated. That had nothing to do with it. I joined because of its ideals. Just as the truth or otherwise of the doctrines of the Catholic Church is not affected by the fact that Joan of Arc or Giordano Bruno were burnt at the stake by the servants of that Church so the truth or otherwise of the Communist doctrine is not affected by the fact that George Blake was, on occasions, badly treated by his North Korean guards.

During this period I witnessed an interesting phenomenon, which gave me much food for thought. Of the group of American POWs, more than half died during the four months we lived in that hamlet. In contrast, of the group of civilian internees less than ten succumbed. This, in spite of the fact that many of them were in their seventies and some even in their eighties. The conditions in which we all lived were exactly the same. What then accounted for the high death rate among the American soldiers and the relatively low rate among the civilians? I ascribe this to the great difference in standard of living to which each group was used. These young American boys had been serving in the army of occupation in Japan. There they had been used to the hygienically prepared food in the army canteens, to their doughnuts and Coca-Cola. They had been pampered with army clubs, PXes and Commissaries. Many had owned their own cars and lived with Japanese girls. Overnight they were transported from this paradise to the wild mountains of Korea where they had to fight against overwhelming forces and to suffer the bitter experience of defeat and capture. Their organism and mental make-up could not cope with the lack of hygiene, the bad food, the cold, the hardships, the separation from their loved ones. They were so miserable they just didn't want to live any more and gave up the struggle for survival. Thus they became an easy prey to disease and deprivation. The civilian group was made of sterner stuff. Many of them were missionaries, who had lived most of their adult life in Korea, often in small towns and villages, without the comforts of Western civilisation. They were used to the climate, to frugal food and a simple existence. They had deliberately chosen to remain behind to be with their flock and both their bodies and their minds were able to adapt themselves much better to the conditions of captivity. Bishop Cooper, Commissioner Lord, most of the Irish and French priests, the French Carmelite nuns, the American women-missionaries, not to speak of the White-Russian and Tartar families survived while the young American servicemen died by the hundreds. The lesson I draw from this is that, though it is natural in man to do so, we should not aspire too much to the good life and, if it is good, we should deliberately impose restrictions on ourselves. A certain amount of deprivation is not necessarily a bad thing. It makes it easier to cope with evil times when they come, for as a wise old Russian saying has it: 'Nobody is guaranteed against prison and the beggar's staff.' One should bear this constantly in mind. I know not many will share this view, but it remains mine to this day.

By February 1951, the front had stabilised roughly along the 38th parallel, the old demarcation line between the two Koreas, and our conditions began to improve. We were given padded winter clothing and the food became more plentiful. We were also split up. The surviving POWs were taken to a large POW camp to join others already there. The main group of civilian internees were moved back to Mampo where they settled in some farmhouses. A small separate group was formed of the British and French diplomats and the two newspaper correspondents and put in a small farmhouse in a valley north of Mampo. From then on we had no more contact with the other civilians and did not even realise that, in fact, they were living quite near us.

We now suffered no longer from the cold, and the food, though monotonous, was sufficient to keep body and soul together. A long period of calm followed. We were guarded by a group of soldiers under a major and confined to the house and its small yard. Later, the soldiers tacitly allowed us to wander into the adjoining fields or walk along a nearby stretch of road. The French group lived in one room. The British party, consisting of us three and Philip Dean, had the second room and the guards occupied the other remaining one. There was no furniture and we slept on the floor, which, as in all Korean houses, was heated.

More than anything we suffered from boredom. With no work to do and nothing to read we were thrown back on our conversational resources to pass the time. Our existence in that small wattle hut was not unlike that of ten people who have to spend two years in a railway carriage, put on a siding and forgotten. In this respect I was lucky in the companions with whom I had been thrown together. It was only because our group included some highly intelligent people, much travelled, each an expert in a different form of human civilisation and with fundamentally good manners, that our life was bearable, though at times the strain was heavy.

Captain Holt, the most senior member of our group, was an Arabist with a lifetime spent at the very hub of the political problems and intrigues of the Middle East between the wars. His French colleague M Perruche, tall, dark, melancholic looking and the most warm-hearted of men, had served many years in various posts in China, was an excellent Chinese linguist and had travelled extensively in the interior of that vast country. Jean Meadmore had been born in Shanghai, spent a large part of his youth there and was also a fluent Chinese speaker. The other French Vice-Consul, M Martel, had lived all his life in Japan and Korea and spoke both languages well. His mother, who was in her seventies, was a formidable old lady. It must have been a great hardship for her and her daughter to live in such a confined space in the company of men, but she was German by birth and had all the thoroughness and determination of her race. She bore the privations of internment no worse than any of us. Although it was not always easy to like her, one could not but greatly respect her. M Chanteloup, the correspondent of *France Presse*, small, brisk, aggressively bearded and always ready with a caustic or witty remark, was a Japanese scholar who had lived many years in that country and was married to a Japanese wife. The most colourful figure of all was, undoubtedly, Philip Dean. Greek by origin, he was highly imaginative and extremely voluble, with a vast fund of stories and anecdotes. This had one drawback. He spoke English and French equally well and possessed a booming voice. Having spent a few hours talking to us in the English room, he would repair next door to the French room and, the partitioning wall being very thin, we had to listen to the same stories again, this time in French. Nevertheless, a kind and brave man, he did much to enliven the tedium of our captivity. Norman Owen, an easy-going young Englishman with an equable temper and warm friendliness was liked by all. During the war he had served in the RAF in an intelligence unit in Iraq. After the war he joined the Marconi Company, but, wishing to improve his conditions, had applied through a friend for a job with SIS and was accepted. Korea was his first appointment. He coped well with life in captivity, but suffered much from being separated from his young family.

In spite of such a large and varied fund of knowledge and experience as was found in our group, even the best of conversationalists among us eventually ran out of stories and reminiscences. After about three to four months, we began to repeat ourselves. This did not matter very much, however, as by that time we were quite ready to hear the stories again.

Though we were given enough to eat now, we were all obsessed by the thought of food. I remember that if anyone, even in passing, mentioned some dinner or lunch he had attended, we immediately stopped him and made him describe in great detail the dishes and beverages he had been served. We were also frequently plagued by frustrating food dreams. We would find ourselves in a pastry shop with all kinds of delicious cakes or a restaurant with tables piled high with food. All this disappeared just when we had with great difficulty made up our minds what we were going to have and were ready to start eating.

One day in the spring of 1951, quite unexpectedly, together with our monthly rice supply, a parcel of books arrived. It had been sent by the Soviet Embassy in Pyongyang. There was only one book in English, *Treasure Island*, which we read in turn several times over, having first cast lots for it. The others were in Russian and of political content. Two volumes of Marx's *Das Kapital* and Lenin's *The State and the Revolution*.

As Captain Holt and I were the only members of our group who knew Russian, we were the main beneficiaries of this consignment. It so happened, however, that Captain Holt, who suffered from failing eyesight, had lost his only pair of glasses in a scramble for shelter when two American fighters attacked our column with machine-gun fire. Without them he could not read and so he asked me to read to him aloud. In order not to disturb the others, we would retire during the fine summer and autumn days to a small group of low green mounds, a family graveyard, in the field behind our house. There I would read to him for hours on end, so that we finished the whole of *Das Kapital* and read certain parts twice before the winter set in. Naturally this reading gave rise to many interesting conversations in which we discussed Marx's and Lenin's theories and their effect on world history. Captain Holt had always been attracted by socialist ideas. He had at one time seriously considered retiring from the Foreign Service to stand for Parliament, but had never been able to make up his mind on behalf of which party. His personality, background and upbringing made him an obvious choice as a Conservative candidate, but his views and sympathies lay more with Labour. Thus he had never taken the decisive step.

He had witnessed, in the course of his career, the splendour and decline of the British Empire and had now reluctantly come to the conclusion that the next stage in the development of the human race was the advent of Communism. He would not enjoy living in a Communist society, he was too much of an individualist for that, but, as an expert on the Middle East, he could not but be favourably impressed with the achievements of the Soviet system in Central Asia. There the Russians had managed to raise the standard of living of the peoples of their former colonial territories to that of their own. Though by Western standards not high, this was much higher than that of the peoples, with the same traditions and culture, in the neighbouring countries of the Middle East. It was almost as if, in the short space of thirty years, the British had attempted and succeeded in raising the standard of living of the peoples of India to that of their own.

Having reluctantly come to accept the inevitability of Communism, his speculative mind was already engaged on imagining what form of society would take place. These views, which he shared fully with me in the course of our readings and conversations, were bound to have a strong effect on my mind. I looked upon him, in spite of his peculiarities, with affection and the respect due to a man of great knowledge and experience, much older than myself and my superior to boot.

Thus several factors worked together to bring about that fundamental change in my outlook which turned me from a man of conventional political views, and in the real meaning of the word a militant anti-communist, into a fervent supporter of the movement I had hitherto been fighting.

The creation of a Communist society, I felt increasingly sure, was both feasible and desirable. The universal aspect of Marx's teaching particularly attracted me. The aim of building a world union of free communities not separated by national frontiers and divided by mutual antagonism seemd to me the only certain way for mankind to get rid of the curse of war.

Another aspect of Communism which held a great appeal for me was the abolition of classes. The strongly marked class distinctions in Western Europe, particularly in Britain, had always strongly irritated me. I felt there was something fundamentally wrong, something decidedly un-Christian, in judging people by what class they belonged to, or, as an outward sign thereof, with what kind of accent they spoke rather than by their personal qualities or intellect. Class distinctions, to my mind, formed artificial barriers between people which prevented them from communicating freely with each other on an equal footing. I looked upon it as an evil which, if removed, could only benefit mankind and set it free from its own complexes. Another doctrine of which I very much approved was the gradual withering away of the state with its organs of repression, based on the ultimate use of force. Then there was something else in my character which made Communism very attractive to me. I have always hated competition between people. To indulge in it seems to me degrading and below human dignity. One should do something well not because one wants to outdo and outshine others, but for its own sake. I have always shunned competition and therefore shied away from it as soon as I saw it intruding in my life and withdrawn from the contest. That is probably why I have never enjoyed competitive games. I find the Olympic Games or football matches extremely boring, nor do I consider them a good thing. The Games have turned from pure sport into pure competition and given rise to intense national rivalry – as if the fact that a country has won a number of gold medals proves anything about the excellence of its social system or even its military power. I am not in the least astonished to see the rivalry between football teams turn into hooliganism and violence in the stadiums. These are its natural consequences. As for beauty contests, I think they are downright degrading, a modern form of the slave market. For the same reason I have never been attracted by business. I would hate to have to take part in the rat race where one either has to succeed or is thrown on the dust heap, where one is so taken up with making money that one has no time for anything else not even enjoying properly the fruits of that money, to acquire which one has had to distort one's life. I was not in the least sorry when my father's business went bust. I would have hated to have had to succeed him. I was glad it never came as far as my uncle in Cairo offering me to join his banking firm. I would have had to disappoint him. When on demobilisation from the Navy, I could choose between two offers of a career in business and a career in government service I opted without hesitation for the latter.

Many people look upon a competitive spirit and ambition as virtues and the lack of them as flaws in one's character. So be it. I fully recognise that these qualities are great incentives to action and a powerful motor to economic progress. But as for myself, I deplore that it should be so. If one compares oneself to others one becomes vain and bitter; for always there will be greater and lesser persons than oneself. I look forward to the day when man will have grown so in moral stature that this motor will no longer be needed and people will do things well, not because of what they stand to gain from it, but simply because they want to do them well. A society in which people do not have to compete and elbow each other out of the way, in which each gives of his best for the good of all, will always remain for me the ideal.

The formula, 'from each according to his ability, to each according to his need' defines, to my mind, the only right and just relationship between men, born free and equal into this world. To help build such a society, was this not to help build the Kingdom of God on earth? Was this not the ideal that Christianity for two thousand years had been striving for? Was this formula not taken almost word for word from the Acts of the Apostles (Acts 2–44, 45)? What the Church had failed to bring about by prayer and precept would not the Communist movement achieve by action?

If it was wrong, as I now had come to believe, to oppose Communism, to fight it by every means, fair or foul, as I certainly would be doing as an SIS officer, was it then not right to help to fight for it? Could one stand aside in a conflict where such great matters were at stake?

The question I now had to ponder was what action I should take. It seemed to me that there were three courses open to me in the particular situation in which I found myself. Firstly, I could ask to be allowed to remain in North Korea when the war ended and help in the reconstruction of that country. Secondly, I could return to England, resign from the service, join the Communist Party and sell the *Daily Worker* or do other propaganda work of that kind. Thirdly, I could make use of my position in SIS to pass to the Soviet Union such information as came my way on the operations directed by SIS and other Western intelligence services against that country and the countries of the socialist bloc and the world revolutionary movement, and by so doing frustrate them.

The first course I rejected almost at once. I possess no great skills and my contribution to the reconstruction of North Korea could only have been small. In practice, I would probably have been more of a burden and a worry than a help. For a long time I weighed up the relative merits of the two remaining courses. No doubt to leave the Service and openly join the Communist movement was by far the more honourable and at the same time the less dangerous course. The man who fights openly for what he believes to be right is a more attractive and respected figure than the one who acts in secret and wears a mask. If possible it is always better to take that course. But I could not hide from myself that the contribution I could make to the cause by adopting the third course would be incomparably greater. So after a long, inward struggle I resolved that this was what I should do. It was a grave decision, taken in grave and exceptional circumstances. Around me raged a cruel and bitter war. Violent times beget violent and extreme actions. Perhaps, if I had led a peaceful existence and been pondering these matters in a comfortable flat in London, my decision would have been different. Who can say?

There can be no doubt that the war I was living through acted as a strong catalyst. After what I had seen of the South Korean régime, I found it impossible to feel that keeping it in power was a worthwhile cause. From the very beginning, I saw the war as an internal conflict and although I was their prisoner, my sympathies lay with the North Koreans, just as earlier they had lain with the Communist partisans in the South. The destruction and the suffering of the civilian population and indeed of the young American POWs, with whom we had been thrown together, seemed utterly pointless to me. Nor could I feel that my own imprisonment and that of my fellow British inmates was for the good of our own country. Then it would have made sense and I would have borne it gladly. But I knew very well that this war was not in defence of any British interests, not even marginal ones. After all, the British government had not had the slightest intention of getting involved in Korea. I remembered how in Holland, during the war, when I heard at night the heavy drone of hundreds of RAF planes overhead on their way to bomb Germany, the sound had been like a song to me. Now, when I saw the enormous grey hulks of the American bombers sweeping low to drop their deadly load over the small, defenceless Korean villages huddled against the mountainside;

when I saw the villagers, mostly women and children and old people –
for the men were all at the front – being machine-gunned as they fled
to seek shelter in the fields, I felt nothing but shame and anger. What
right had they to come to this far-away country, which had done
them no harm and only wanted to settle its own affairs, to lay waste
its towns and villages, to kill and destroy indiscriminately? So I made
my choice, fully aware of its implications. I realised that I would be
betraying the trust which had been placed in me. I realised that I
would be betraying my friends and colleagues in the Service. I realised
that I would be betraying the country to which I owed allegiance. I
weighed all this up and, in the end, felt that I should take this guilt
upon me, however heavy. To be in a position to render assistance to so
great a cause and not to do so, would be an even greater wrong.

Why did I decide to approach the Soviet authorities with my offer
and not the Chinese or Koreans as would, probably, have been easier
in the circumstances? In the first place, because the Soviet Union was
the first country in the world to have embarked on the heroic and
arduous experiment of building a higher form of human society. It is
an experiment of the utmost importance to every other nation, to the
whole of mankind and it deserves to succeed. From the very beginning
this experiment has been beset by many difficulties – after all, nobody
had done it before – and has demanded enormous sacrifices from the
Soviet people. In the second place, it was the country against which
the main efforts of SIS and the CIA, the most insidious and extensive
of their subversive operations, were directed. It was by the same
token, the nation best placed to use the information I would be able to
supply. Finally, the Russians are a European people, I spoke their
language, had more in common with them than with the Chinese or
the Koreans and would find it easier, therefore, to work with them.

These then were the considerations that led to my decision. So,
when a suitable opportunity presented itself, I took the necessary
steps to put it into effect.

Late one evening in the autumn of 1951, when everyone was
asleep, I got up to relieve myself in the field behind the house, as
was our wont. On my way back, I opened the door of the guardroom
where the light was still burning. They were sitting on the floor
around a low table, listening to the major in charge, who, as he
frequently did in the evenings, was giving them a political lecture. I
put my finger to my lips as I handed him a folded note. He looked at
me somewhat surprised, but took it without saying anything. I closed
the door and went back to bed. I had written the note that afternoon

on the page of a copy book with which we were infrequently issued. The note was in Russian and addressed to the Soviet Embassy in Pyongyang. In it, I requested an interview with an official of the Embassy as I had something important to communicate which they might find of interest. I added that, for security reasons, not only I, but all the members of our group, should be interviewed separately, so as not to draw attention to myself.

For about six weeks nothing happened. Then, one morning, Captain Holt was summoned to accompany the major to Mampo, about three-quarters-of-an-hour's walk from our house. He returned late in the afternoon, obviously rather pleased with the outing. He had been seen by a pleasant, young Russian who spoke English. He had been asked for his views about the war, been given some propaganda material to read and asked if he was willing to sign a statement condemning the war in Korea. He had refused on the plea that he was a government official and could not sign documents of this kind without specific instructions from his government. The young man had not insisted. Captain Holt had taken the opportunity to ask for pen and paper and written a strongly worded protest against our internment which he had given to the young man for transmission to the Soviet Embassy in Pyongyang. Before leaving, he had been given a meal consisting of soup, a meat dish and a glass of real tea.

The next morning my turn came to be escorted to Mampo by the major. Mampo is situated on the Yalu river at a point where the railway line, the main artery between Korea and China, crosses that river. The railway bridge was, therefore, one of the most important targets of the American Air Force and was constantly under attack. Sometimes it got a direct hit and then it was out of action for several weeks and, on one occasion, several months. Frequently the bombs missed their target and fell on the town which, as a result, lay almost completely in ruins. Only a few buildings remained standing. The major took me to one of these. I was shown into a room on the first floor. It was quite bare, being furnished only with a bed, a table and two chairs. When I entered a European, whom I took to be a Russian, got up from the bed on which he had been sitting. He invited me in Russian to sit down and took the chair opposite me. He was obviously not the same man as Captain Holt had described to us. This was a big, burly man of about forty or forty-five with a pale complexion. What was most remarkable about him was that he was completely bald, so that he looked very like the film actor, Erich von Stroheim, and that, for reasons best known to himself, he wore no socks. He never told me his name, but many years later I learned that, at that time, he had been the head of the KGB in the Maritime Province. He showed me my note and asked me in a friendly enough tone what I wanted to tell him. I began by informing him that, apart from being a Vice-Consul, I was also a SIS officer and that I wanted to offer my services to the Soviet authorities. I then explained why I wanted to do so. I concluded by stating on what conditions I would be willing to co-operate. These were:

a) I would supply information on SIS operations directed against the Soviet Union, other socialist countries and the world Communist movement, but not on operations directed against any other country;

b) I would not accept any financial or material rewards for my services;

c) I should on no account be released earlier, receive any privileges or be treated in any way differently from my fellow prisoners on whose utterances and actions I was not prepared to give any information.

To clear up any misunderstanding, I would like to elaborate here on point b). During all the time that I worked for the KGB as an agent I never received a penny from them. When I finally arrived in Moscow, after my escape from Wormwood Scrubs, I was given a flat for which I pay rent and a modest sum of money to set myself up. Later I was given a pension which I still get. Any money I earn from my job is on top of that. But while I was in SIS, secretly working as an agent for the KGB, I was not paid anything by the KGB. I did what I did for ideological reasons, never for money.

The KGB chief, as I shall call him, listened attentively, occasionally interrupting to elucidate a point. He then asked me to write down in English all that I had just told him and left me alone in the room. When he returned he began to ply me with questions about my early life, the war and my work for SIS. While we were talking, a young, fair Russian, with pleasant, open features came in whom he introduced as the man who would interview my companions. We would probably have to meet several times to discuss all the questions and the whole process would take some time. There the interview ended. Back at the house, I told the others that I had been seen by the same young man as Captain Holt, that I had also been asked to sign a statement condemning the war and that I had also refused to do this.

In the course of the following days, all my companions were, in turn, summoned to Mampo, with the exception of the two ladies. On their return, they all told the same story which showed that all the interviews with the young Russian were conducted along the same lines. Philip Dean immediately thought up a name for him and called him Kuzma Kuzmich, a character out of a Russian novel, and from then on we referred to him by that name. Dean was also a good impersonator and took him off very well, especially the way he spoke, so that we had many laughs on that account.

In all, we were summoned three or four times so that the whole process took several months. I was always seen by the KGB chief, the others by Kuzma Kuzmich. On one occasion I was asked to write down everything I knew about the structure of SIS. After my return to England I realised that this had not been because they were interested in the information – they had that already in great detail from Philby and other agents – but because they wanted to check whether I was telling the truth. At one point, it was suggested that my offer was a provocation thought out by Captain Holt and that I had been put up to it. I strongly denied this and the matter was left at that. On the last occasion I was seen, the KGB chief told me that my offer had been accepted and that when the time came they would get in touch with me. When I was taken back to the house, he accompanied me part of the way, engaging in friendly conversation, and kissing me on both cheeks when he said goodbye.

I remember one other conversation I had with him. It was about Stalin. I told him that I couldn't understand the inordinate adulation of which he was the object. This seemed to me quite contrary to Communist doctrine which taught that it was the masses and not outstanding personalities who determined the course of history. Though Churchill had been greatly admired and respected for all he had done during the war, he had been removed soon after by a majority vote of the English people. Making a man into a semi-God was something we in the West simply could not understand. Moreover, there was absolutely no need for it. The KGB chief muttered something about different traditions, but took my remarks in good part and, indeed, I got the impression that somehow he agreed with me.

Thus, the first part of the operation was successfully completed. This was a matter of the utmost importance since any suspicion on the part of my companions would have flawed the whole plan from the start. Living in very cramped conditions and in close and constant contact with each other, I had of course to be on the alert all the time that there was no change in my behaviour and that my account of my interviews in Mampo coincided with theirs. That was not too difficult. They all had the same story to tell so I could pick up small details here and there and repeat them. They assumed that I, like they, was being seen by Kuzma Kuzmich, that we talked about the same things and that he asked me the same questions. They were never given any cause to think otherwise.

I now felt a great relief. My inward struggle was over. I had been accepted and was fully committed. There was no way back. I, too, could look upon myself as one of the many millions the world over who were actively engaged in building a new, more just society. My life would never be the same again, whatever happened. I had a purpose. Everything fell into its place.

I cannot say that I felt, then or afterwards, any pangs of conscience in respect of my companions. I had in no way prejudiced them, taken no advantage of them and, if anything, provided them with a not unwelcome break in an otherwise monotonous existence.

Looking back, I am often surprised myself how I could, then and later, keep up the deception so successfully. But with deception, particularly of this kind, it is like this. Once one has started with it, one has to go on with it, whether one likes it or not. I couldn't very well one day start saying to people, 'You know, I am really a Soviet agent.' If I had, the odds are that no one would have believed me, though they would certainly have thought I had a screw loose. Anyway, this is something one cannot seriously contemplate, the consequences would be too serious. It should also not be forgotten that, from my teens, I had been used to deception, albeit not of this magnitude. When I was acting as a courier for the Dutch underground and pretending to be a schoolboy who was carrying schoolbooks in his satchel instead of forbidden pamphlets or intelligence reports, I was already deceiving people, however justified this may appear. When, later, I was working for SIS and telling everybody, including my own mother and sisters, that I was a member of the Foreign Service, I was also practising deception. Once one adopts the profession of an intelligence officer, one must be ready to deceive and lie. If one has qualms on this score, one should take another job. Then there is another important psychological factor which comes into play. As an intelligence officer, any intelligence officer, one may be called upon, and almost certainly will be called upon in the course of one's career, to do things which if one did them as a private individual would bring

1985

Leaving Holland for Egypt, with my grandmother, mother and sisters seeing me off, 1935

Cairo, 1937

RNVR officer, 1945

Naval recruit, 1943

Off duty in Seoul, 1949

Mampo prison camp, Korea, 1951

My mother, 1960

With my children in Lebanon, 1961

With my family in England, 1960

My Russian wife,
Ida, 1968

In the Caucasus
with my son Misha, 1975

With Ida, 1983

In Moscow, 1990

1990

(Photograph by Kim Knightley)

one in conflict with the law. One may have to open other people's letters, listen in to their telephone conversations, seek to compromise, coerce or blackmail them and even, in exceptional circumstances, organise their assassination or plot terrorist actions. One will certainly have to subvert them and induce them by various means to break the law and be disloyal to their own country and government.

One would never dream of doing any of these things as a private individual in pursuit of one's own personal interests, but one is quite capable of doing them in one's official capacity when one is acting in what one believes to be the interest of one's country or one's cause. Perhaps I possess this ability to distinguish and separate the personal from the official to a high degree and it was this that enabled me to do my work as a Soviet agent. I was not acting in my own personal interest nor were my activities directed against my colleagues personally. Had they been I could not have done it. There is only one thing I should add: I do not consider there is anything clever in deceiving people who trust one and I never enjoyed doing it or exulted in it. I look upon spying as an unfortunate necessity. As long as there will be confrontation and rivalry, as long as armed forces continue to exist and the danger of war remains, it will be necessary to have spies. It is better, if possible, to be the captain on the bridge than the stoker in the hold. Both are needed to move the ship forward. Spies are like the stokers in the hold. Today stokers are no longer needed. I look forward to the day when spies too shall no longer be needed.

Our days in the farm house in Mampo, uneventful and dull, turned into months and the months into another year. We had now been in captivity for almost three years. We spent our days talking, sleeping and walking and occasionally, though fortunately rarely, quarrelling. From time to time, mostly at the instigation of the French and Philip Dean, who suffered the boredom less easily than we did, we staged an occasional hunger strike. These led to long palavers with the guards and a slight improvement in the food or permission to extend our walk another ten yards. Our gains never lasted long, however, and so there was always a good reason to start again.

To help pass the time, I began to teach my friend, Jean Meadmore, Russian using the Russian translation of Marx's *Das Kapital* as a text book. Being a gifted linguist, he learned fast. It was a great satisfaction to both of us when after about seven months of perseverance on his part, he was able to read the Russian text with ease.

During all this time we had been unable to communicate with our relatives, but one day, quite unexpectedly, we were allowed to send a Red Cross message. It had to be short. I don't think we could write more than twenty words. We all tried hard to cram as much reassurance about our health and hope for a speedy reunion as we could into this very limited space. Not so Captain Holt. Not even using up all the space available, he addressed his letter to the Foreign Office, asking it to arrange with his bank the transfer of £50 to his sister's account for theatre tickets.

When the Foreign Office got this letter, it was very puzzled and felt certain that it must contain a concealed message. A lot of time was spent trying to work out what it could mean – in vain, for it meant exactly what it said. As Captain Holt explained to us, he had been in the habit of giving his sister every year for her birthday a sum of money with which to buy theatre tickets. This letter was the only opportunity he had of getting the money to her. He felt this would be of more practical use to her than a message saying that he was well. She could anyway conclude that from the fact that he was sending her the money. This was typical of Captain Holt, always a most thoughtful and considerate man.

In the first days of March 1953, the news reached us that Stalin had died. The very next day his picture which, together with those of the other members of the Soviet politburo, adorned the walls of the guardroom, had disappeared. This must have been the first and most rapid de-Stalinisation measure in the whole of the socialist commonwealth.

A week later, while we were having our usual morning walk in the small farmyard, the British members of our group were called in and told to get their few belongings together. A quarter of an hour later, we were on our way to the capital on the back of an open lorry. We left our French friends behind with good hope that they would follow soon. They did so ten days later.

In Pyongyang we were put up in a mountain cave to protect us against American bomb attacks which occurred several times a day. Here we were joined by the three remaining British internees, Bishop Cooper, Commissioner Lord and Monsignor Quinlan, an Irish missionary. The latter I had always greatly admired. A big man with a red face and the gentlest of natures, he was always cheerful, however difficult the circumstances, always ready to help and give comfort to anybody who needed it. He was, to my mind, in every way a saintly man. I have in my life met only one other man who possessed these qualities. That was Donald Maclean, an English Communist and well-known diplomat.

Three days later, as night fell, we climbed on another lorry and, accompanied by two officers and four soldiers, left Pyongyang once more in the direction of the Chinese frontier. This was the first stage on the journey back to England and the beginning of a new life.

Chapter Seven

Slowly the Trans-Siberian express, Peking–Moscow, trundled through the no man's land, separating the People's Republic of China from the Soviet Union, past the mine fields, electrified wires, strips of raked sand, watchtowers and projectors, which marked the frontier between the two allied, socialist states. We watched these formidable obstacles from our compartment window with interest and, on my part, with mixed feelings. The brotherhood of men was evidently not for tomorrow. Half an hour earlier, we had said goodbye to the two extremely friendly and helpful officials of the Soviet Embassy in Peking who had met us at the Korean frontier and had accompanied us on our journey through Manchuria. Now we were on our own and designated henceforth as the 'British Delegation'. The train pulled up at the Soviet frontier station of Otpor. What struck me at once was the sudden transition from the Orient to Europe. When I had travelled to the Far East in 1948 by seaplane, it had been a gradual change from Southern Europe through the Middle East to India and Burma. Here it took the half hour or so for the train to pass through the no man's land to be suddenly back in Europe. Not, perhaps, the neat and prosperous Europe of Holland or England, but Europe all the same. Everything here bore witness to this, from the gabled, wooden houses with their lace-curtained windows and geraniums on the window sills to the tall, fair-haired frontier guards and the attractive, blonde girls with their well-shaped legs on the station platform.

An officer knocked on the door of our compartment and invited us to follow him. He led us into the customs house where he showed us into a large room with benches and told us to wait. After a while, he came back and asked Captain Holt to come with him. Fifteen minutes later he brought him back and invited Commissioner Lord to follow him. Captain Holt told us that he had had to show the travel document with which we had been issued and been asked to fill in a rather complicated form. When Commissioner Lord returned, it was my turn. The officer took me through a long corridor to a room where several customs officials and female clerks were working and then led me through an inner door to a small room at the back. Here the man, whom I was later to meet near Belsize Park Underground station, got up from behind a desk. He did not introduce himself, but simply said that in future we would be working together. Without losing any time he began to discuss plans for our first clandestine meeting. During the talks in Mampo, I had indicated that I wanted my first meetings to take place in Holland. My reason for this was that, somehow, I felt more on my own ground there and imagined that I would sense more quickly if anything was amiss. My opposite number said that this condition had been found acceptable and proposed a place in The Hague and a date in July with a number of alternative dates, in case either of us could not make it. As a sign that all was well, we would each carry a copy of the *Nieuwe Rotterdamse Courant* of the previous day. Having settled this question, he told me that he would be travelling back to Moscow on the same train and would occupy a compartment by himself in the third carriage from ours. If in the course of the journey I had an opportunity of slipping away, without raising the suspicions of my companions, to join him we would have an opportunity of getting to know each other better. I should not take any risks however. At that the interview ended and the officer took me back to the others. When everyone had finished filling in the forms, we were taken back to our compartments.

The journey to Moscow took a week. The train was quite comfortable, as we travelled 'soft' class, as opposed to 'hard'. People on the train were very friendly and several insisted on entertaining us in the restaurant car. In those days there was still plenty of caviar and vodka in Russia and this was pressed upon us in great quantities. At every station the passengers got out and walked up and down the platform till a bell rang to warn that the train was leaving again. On these occasions I frequently encountered my new partner, but of course we pretended not to know each other. In the end, I never visited him in his compartment. I thought it better not to risk it. Besides, as all the arrangements were clear to me, there was no real need for it.

On arrival at the Kazan station in Moscow, we were met on the platform by the British Ambassador and members of his staff. The man who was at that time Head of the SIS station in Moscow, Terence O'Brian Tear, with whom I had been good friends when we were both working in Head Office after the war, was not allowed to contact me for security reasons. He later told me that he had been watching our arrival in the forecourt of the Embassy from a garret window. We were at once instructed to avoid meeting the press and, on our arrival in England, to say as little as possible on the conditions in which we had been kept in North Korea in order not to affect the position of our fellow internees who had not yet been released.

We were put up for the night at the National Hotel and entertained to dinner at the Embassy. The splendour of the dining-room, the polite conversation of the guests, the refinement of the dishes and the deference with which they were served, formed a sharp contrast to what we had been used to all these years. Unfortunately, we had little time for sightseeing, but managed to visit the Metro, which we found very impressive. Life, however, was to provide plenty of opportunity to make up for this in years to come. Little could I then foresee that I would live in Moscow longer than in any other city.

Early the next day, an RAF ambulance plane which had been specially sent flew us to West Berlin. Though we were all in reasonably good health and not in need of any medical attention, it was a gesture we all appreciated. After a short stop-over in Berlin, we took off for the last stage of our journey.

The special RAF plane came to a halt in front of the main building on Abingdon Airfield. As it did so, a group of Salvation Army men and women burst into the hymn 'Now thank we all our God', which was soon taken up by the whole crowd of waiting relatives and friends. The door was thrown open and a moment later the six of us emerged into the soft light of a fine, English spring afternoon and stood huddled together, rather uncertainly, on the platform of the stairs and in the doorway of the plane.

We did not quite know what to do. To rush down the steps into the arms of our wives, mothers, sisters and brothers, whom each for himself was spotting eagerly in the sea of singing faces, or to wait respectfully till the solemn strains of the old hymn had died away. The singing, to us so totally unexpected, gave an even greater poignancy to this moment, to which we had looked forward with such intense longing.

We stood there waiting, for this was what we had decided was best, bare-headed, some of us bearded, dressed all alike in a strange combination of thick, grey overcoats, khaki trousers and light blue gymshoes.

We were the first prisoners to return from the Korean War.

Our return home, on this fine Sunday afternoon in early April 1953, was the first sign that the ice, which had kept the armistice negotiations at Pan Mun Yon bound for so long in a barren waste of frustration and procrastination, was beginning to break up and that the end of this cruel and particularly destructive war was, at last, in sight.

This was why our welcome not only bore a private character, but was something of a public event. Representatives of the Foreign Office, dignitaries of church organisations, as well as a large number of journalists, cameramen and television crews were there and formed, together with the many relatives and friends, quite a sizeable crowd.

The hymn had come to an end and our little group started to come down. I quickly walked towards the tear-stained, but happy face of my mother, who was standing in the first row and for the second time in our life we were reunited after war had separated us.

There was only one other person who had come to welcome me. An elegantly dressed, elderly man, whom I had never met before, and who introduced himself as the personal representative of the Chief of the Secret Service. After the official speeches by an Under-Secretary of State at the Foreign Office, two bishops – a Protestant and a Roman Catholic – and a General of the Salvation Army were over, he took me apart and welcomed me home on behalf of the Chief, gave me an envelope with some money, which he thought I might need in the next few days, and asked me to call at Room 070, the War Office, on the following Wednesday.

Then followed a confused half an hour, in which we were besieged by journalists, confronted by film and television cameras, asked to say something into microphones while, at the same time, trying to talk to our relatives and say goodbye to our companions, with whom we had shared such memorable and often bitter experiences. At last, happy, but dazed by all the turmoil and new impressions, I found myself bundled into a car with my mother, equally happy and dazed, and we were driven off to Reigate, where she was living at the time. That evening, we had a quiet supper together in her small but comfortable flat and went to bed early, tired from the many emotions of the day.

On Wednesday morning, I took the train to town and arrived at the War Office, in Horse Guards Avenue, at the civilised hour of eleven, as bidden, to report to Room 070. This room has acquired a certain amount of notoriety since then and is well known, for instance, to many British businessmen engaged in East–West trade, to scientists, students, musicians and others who are involved, one way or another, in cultural relations with Communist countries.

At the time I am speaking of, however, knowledge of its existence and purpose was much more restricted, and I myself, though I had heard of it, had never been there before. Situated on the ground floor of the main building of the War Office, it was set aside for the use of the Secret Service, commonly known as MI6. Officers of this Service interviewed people of British nationality there with whom they wished to establish contact without revealing, at that stage, which organisation they represented. Next to it, but separated from it by a small room occupied by secretaries, was Room 050 which was used for the same purpose by the Security Service, commonly known as MI5.

The reason why I had been summoned there and not to Head Office had been at once clear to me. Until I had been interrogated about my experiences in captivity in Communist hands and cleared from any suspicion that I might have been indoctrinated by them, I could not be allowed to enter the Holy of Holies.

I was conducted to the imposing, green door of Room 070 along a wide, dark corridor by a security guard in a frock coat with gold buttons. On entering I found myself in a room of spacious dimensions, furnished with some dignity – it even had a thick red carpet – and clearly designed to impress the visitor with the importance of its occupant.

Two men of about my own age were there waiting for me. They greeted me in an extremely friendly manner and at once ordered coffee from the adjoining room, it being shortly after eleven, the enchanted hour when everything stops and attractive secretaries bring round coffee to their masters who may relax then into some light banter or even, according to the relationship, indulge in a mild flirtation with them.

After some general conversation, appropriate to the circumstances, my two colleagues, for that is what they turned out to be, began to question me in detail on the circumstances of our arrest in Seoul in June 1950, our adventures in North Korea and the conditions in which we had been kept. One asked the questions in a friendly, sympathetic way while the other took notes, occasionally clarifying a point or seeking additional information. The questioning went on for about two hours, till lunch-time, and concentrated especially on the nature of the interrogations conducted by the North Korean authorities.

I was asked whether I had been subjected to any forms of torture or duress. Truthfully, I was able to say that neither I nor any of my companions had been deliberately ill-treated and that the hardships which we had suffered and which, at times, had been severe had been due to the conditions of war, the general poverty of the country, and the unprecedented scale of devastation caused by the massive American air attacks.

Well before our arrest, we had been able to destroy all SIS and other secret documents, including our codes, and nothing of any compromising nature had fallen into the hands of the North Korean authorities.

The interrogations, which I and my colleague Norman Owen had undergone, had been of a purely formal character and directed mainly towards establishing our identities and official functions. We had not been treated in any way differently from Captain Vyvyan Holt, HM Minister in Seoul, about whose genuine diplomatic status there could have been no doubt, or our colleagues from the French Consulate, who had been interned with us and from whom we had not been separated until the day of our release. The only brushes we had had with the authorities, apart from occasional hunger strikes for better conditions, had been on the subject of propaganda statements. From time to time attempts had been made, notably by a young Russian, to get us on various pretexts to sign statements condemning United Nations intervention in Korea. We had always firmly refused to do this on the plea that, as civil servants, we were not allowed to make any statements of a political nature.

At lunch-time we broke up and my colleagues asked me to come back the next morning to continue my account.

When we resumed the next day, my two investigators left the subject of security altogether and turned to pure intelligence matters. They were interested in such things as the Chinese lines of communication in North Korea and conditions on the Trans-Siberian Railway. One of them remarked what a pity it was that I had not brought a small sample of Siberian soil with me. From this they would have been able to deduce whether the Russians had carried out any atomic tests in the area and the strength of the explosion. I expressed regret that I had not known this, as it would have been easy to oblige. The best I could do now was to offer the shoes I had been wearing during the journey for a test. I had been wearing them since my return to England, but perhaps some traces of Siberian dust remained on them. This was thought unlikely and the offer was declined.

I must have satisfied my questioners in all respects for at the end of that day's interview, which lasted well into the afternoon, they informed me that I was to report to the Far Eastern Section at Head Office the following Monday morning. The Far Eastern Section was, of course, the section which controlled the Korean station and to which I was directly responsible.

When I arrived at Head Office on Monday morning, I found everybody extremely kind. Having been through a rather unusual experience for an SIS officer, few of whom have ever fallen into enemy hands, I found myself, for a short while, a bit of a celebrity. I must admit that this interest, especially on the part of the secretaries, who in SIS are chosen not only for their ability in shorthand and typing, but also for their good looks, was not altogether unwelcome.

One of the first people I was told to call upon, shortly after my arrival at HQ, was a man who at that time, officially, did not exist. Now, I believe, he does. To James Bond fans, however, he is well known as 'M', in Cabinet and high government circles he is referred to as 'C', in secret documents he appears as 'XYZ' and within the Secret Service itself people call him the 'Chief', while an expression of awe momentarily crosses their faces. So, straightening my tie, I made my way to the fourth floor where the Chief and the most senior officers of SIS had their offices.

The man who then occupied that post was Lieutenant-General Sinclair. During the war, he had been Director of Military Intelligence at the War Office and at the death, in 1945, of Sir Claude Dansey, a colourful figure in intelligence circles, had succeeded him as Vice-Chief of the Secret Service. Sir Claude had been in intelligence all his life and had served overseas in many guises. On being asked, once, how he had established his reputation as one of the shrewdest operators in the game, he is said to have replied, 'When people come to me with a proposal for a new operation, I always say that it cannot possibly work. If they, nevertheless, go ahead with it, in nine cases out of ten I prove to have been right. In the one case, when I turn out to have been wrong, I simply say, "Well, old boy, you have been bloody lucky."'

Before entering the Chief's office, one had to pass through an outer office, occupied by the formidable Miss Pettigrew, his Personal Assistant, supported by two younger secretaries. Grey-haired, with sharp, intelligent eyes behind a pair of rimless spectacles, and immensely competent, she had acquired vast experience in the many years that she had held her lonely post, raised high above the other women in the Service, and was looked upon by high and low with a respect not far removed from fear.

She smiled benevolently as I entered the office and said that the Chief would see me at once. She got up and opened the sound-proof communicating door for me and I now entered the room, familiar to all viewers of James Bond films. Though not altogether unlike its film version, it was in reality furnished more simply and in better taste.

I had met General Sinclair only once before, when as Vice-Chief he had had a talk with me before my departure for Seoul. He was a tall, lean Scot with the angular, austere features of a Presbyterian minister, blue eyes behind horn-rimmed spectacles and a soft voice gave him a kindly demeanour.

'Pleased to see you back with us, Blake,' he said to me as he got up from behind his desk to shake hands with me. 'I have read the report on your experiences, but I wanted to have a talk with you myself. How have things been?'

'Well, sir,' I replied. 'Only in the first year were conditions really bad.'

'A pity that you could not get out in time,' the Chief remarked rather sadly.

'But, Sir, we could have got out quite easily,' I answered with some surprise. 'But I had clear instructions to stay in the event of a war, instructions which you yourself repeated to me, before I left. Neither Captain Holt nor I had been given the slightest indication that the British government intended to intervene in a war in Korea. Otherwise, we certainly would have fled in time.'

He nodded sympathetically and said, 'Of course, of course. It was just one of those situations which nobody could foresee.' He then changed the subject and started to talk about Bishop Cooper, whom he knew personally.

At the end of the interview he suggested that I should take a few months' leave. They would be looking out, meanwhile, for a suitable new appointment for me. I had been away for a long time and it would probably be best, from every view of view, if I were given a job at home rather than abroad so that I could become familiar again with the working of Head Office.

He then got up and shook hands with me, wishing me a pleasant leave and success in my new job. As I walked out of his room, through the long, narrow, zigzagging corridor that led to the back of the building and down the small winding staircase to the second floor, where the Far Eastern section was located, I reflected on the conversation I had just had. I had thought, at the time, that I had done the right thing by staying. This had turned out to have been wrong. The Chief's words once more confirmed this. One may take a decision, which is generally accepted as morally right, and see it lead to results which are objectively undesirable or even bad. Conversely, one may make a morally wrong decision and bring about much good. Too many factors will always remain unknown for any man, however clever, wise and well-informed, to be able to foresee the outcome of his actions. That being so, the only certain guide in any circumstances is to act as one thinks right according to one's own light. As for the outcome, it is not in our hands.

The first thing I did with my accumulated salary was to buy a Ford Anglia. In this new car I took my mother and my youngest sister and her husband, whom she had married while I was away, on a three weeks holiday to Spain. On the way back, we dropped them off at Calais and my mother and I continued to Holland where we stayed for another month with several relatives. While we were at my aunt's in Rotterdam, the day came for my meeting with the man from Otpor.

On some pretext, which I have now forgotten, I absented myself for the morning and drove to The Hague, not a very great distance, only half an hour or so. I was to meet my contact in a square near the end of the Laan van Meerdervoort, the longest avenue in The Hague, which runs almost from the centre to the southern suburbs. I parked the car some distance away and with the *Nieuwe Rotterdamse Courant* in my right hand, as arranged, I walked slowly to the square. I was quite sure by now that I was not being followed. The square was built round a small garden with benches on one of which I recognised the man I had come to meet. He was holding the same newspaper and I sat down beside him. At that hour there were not many people in the garden. On a bench, not far away, but out of earshot, sat two young women with some small children who were playing. The weather was fine and the scene very peaceful. The first thing my Russian friend wanted to know was what had happened to me since my return to England and what welcome I had had. I told him about the interviews in the War Office and my meeting with the Chief of the Secret Service. I was quite sure now that none of my companions had had an inkling of the real purpose of the Mampo interviews and that no one had alerted the authorities. I was almost certain that I was not under any suspicion and I had been cleared for further work in SIS. In the beginning of September, I was to take up a new appointment in Head Office.

We then discussed plans for our next meeting. My friend thought it would be much better if we met in London. He pointed out that in actual fact this represented no greater danger than meeting in Holland, which required that I should absent myself for at least two days every time we met. It would also be easier from their point of view. I realised that there was much truth in what he said and, having acquired more confidence already, I went along with the suggestion. The next meeting was fixed accordingly for the beginning of October near Belsize Park Underground station. Before parting, I could not refrain from drawing his attention to the headlines in the newspaper we were both carrying. These announced in big letters that Beria, the head of the Soviet Security and Intelligence services, had been arrested as a British agent. My Soviet contact looked somewhat embarrassed and had obviously hoped that I would not refer to this painful event. He hastily began to explain that I should not take this literally, that it was only by way of speaking. He could assure me that I had nothing to fear. I quickly put his mind at rest. Of course, I had not taken it literally as, otherwise, I would certainly not have come to the meeting. We then parted company the best of friends, the whole encounter not having lasted more than twenty minutes.

I walked back to my car by a round about way and, instead of the motorway, I took the old road back to Rotterdam, which runs through the town of Delft and along which I had often cycled as a boy. As I drove along and looked across the canal to the green meadows beyond stretching to the horizon in the haze of the warm, summer morning, I felt a great relief that this first meeting had passed safely. I was quite sure that I was not being followed. That this might have been very easily otherwise, I discovered nearly seven years later. After a break of several years in Berlin, I was at that time again working in Head Office and my contact in London was again the man from Otpor. We knew each other well by then and had full confidence in each other. On one occasion, when we were making arrangements for emergency meetings, he told me that his name was Korovin and he gave me his home telephone number in case I wanted to get hold of him in a hurry. I happened to be working against various Soviet targets in Britain, among which was the Soviet Embassy in London and my duties entitled me to request the MI5 file on any member of the Embassy I was interested in. Naturally, I at once asked for Korovin's file. When I got it, I read it with mounting interest. I learned that he held the rank of General in the KGB, that he was the official KGB resident in London and that, previously, he had been for several years the resident in Washington. The file contained an extensive correspondence between the FBI and MI5 in which both services spoke highly of him as a particularly clever intelligence operator and a formidable opponent. What attracted my special attention, however, was an exchange of letters, in the summer of 1953, between MI5 and the Dutch Security Service. In July of that year, Korovin had made a mysterious journey to Holland. He had been followed by an MI5 surveillance team and then been passed on to the Dutch who had taken up the trail. They had kept track of him until, at a certain point, he had succeeded in eluding them. They had not picked him up again until he boarded the ferry back to England. There was much speculation on what the purpose of the trip to Holland could have been. I could have told them the answer. Far from causing me concern, the fact that the followers had lost Korovin heartened me. If this Russian was so good that he could shake off professional surveillance teams then my confidence in him was justified. If I were to be exposed, then it was not going to be his fault.

I cannot say that Korovin was the kind of man who naturally evoked very warm feelings in me. There was too much of the iron fist in the velvet glove about him for that, but I had great admiration for his skill, even before I had seen his file. I photographed its contents and at our next meeting presented it to him. I hope he enjoyed reading it and, even more, that it impressed his superiors in Moscow. I cannot say that passing on information ever gave me any pleasure, but, on this occasion, I actually felt satisfaction at being able to show my Soviet contact his own file and in what laudatory terms his opponents referred to him.

It is generally held that once an intelligence officer is 'blown', i.e. known as such, to the other side, his usefulness, at least in that particular country, has come to an end. The Korovin case shows that this is not always so. Was it not remarkable that, though he was known to MI5 to be the KGB resident in Great Britain and constantly followed by a highly experienced surveillance team, equipped with fast cars and modern radio communications, he always managed to get rid of his tail and meet me, punctually, at the appointed time and appointed place?

He once told me how it was done. In order to meet me at seven o'clock in the evening, he left his house at eight o'clock in the morning and was on the move all day. The operation involved several people and cars and a few safe houses. It was difficult and time-consuming, but it worked every time. If, eventually my activities came to light, it was not the result of surveillance, but of betrayal.

Later that summer, I took my eldest sister for a holiday to France. We stayed at the hospitable home of Jean Meadmore and his mother in Paris and visited M Perruche, who had a house in a village on the Loire, where he was spending his leave, happily reunited to his wife and children he had missed so much. All in all, it was a most enjoyable holiday, enhanced by many good dinners and lunches in small inns and restaurants.

Back in England, I continued to see my English companions from Mampo, until life separated us. Our families met and we frequently had lunch together. Captain Holt was knighted and appointed Ambassador in El Salvador. Two years later, he retired from the Foreign Service and went to live in Clacton-on-Sea. There he died, quite suddenly from a heart attack some six months later. Philip Dean left England for a new assignment in the United States and I never saw him again. About a year after his return, Norman Owen fell seriously ill. He suffered from a mysterious disease which nobody could diagnose. He slowly wasted away and after a long illness died in hospital, having had little time to enjoy the family life which he had looked forward to with so much longing.

In September 1953, I started work in section 'Y' and soon became absorbed in my new duties and my new life. An important part of that life were the regular meetings with my Soviet contact and the photographing of the documents, which I passed on to him.

In the beginning, I felt rather nervous when photographing, but one gets used to most things and my apprehensions gradually left me. Of course, there always was a danger that I might be caught in the act, but this was a danger, I felt, I could control. I usually chose a time when the secretaries in the room next door were away for lunch or waited till after office hours when everyone had gone and I was ostensibly working late. As an additional precaution, I left the door open between my room and the outer office, through which every one had to pass to enter my room, so that I would hear at once if anyone came in and have time to put the camera away. What feelings did I experience when I was photographing these top-secret documents? The answer is none. It was as if I had ceased to exist. Concentrating on getting the lighting and the distance right, I was reduced, as it were, to nothing, having become only the eye which looked through the viewfinder and the hand which pressed the button.

At that time there was much talk of treason. The year before, the two British diplomats, Burgess and Maclean, had fled to Russia, having obviously been Soviet agents. A man called Philby who, I thought, also worked in the Foreign Office, was suspected of being the person who had tipped them off. All this I heard for the first time after my return from Korea. Later I realised that Philby had, in fact, been an SIS officer,though I had never met him and not even heard of him. This is not so strange if one bears in mind that I had been away for five years and that we had worked in quite different fields; he in counter-espionage and I in espionage.

The Burgess and Maclean affair, not unnaturally, formed a frequent subject of conversation in SIS and Foreign Office circles and, frankly speaking, it was a subject I did not enjoy. It was too near the bone and made me feel very uncomfortable. I tried to avoid it as much as possible.

In the spring of 1954, my work in 'Y' was interrupted by a short assignment abroad. In the beginning of May of that year, the Foreign Ministers of the USA, the USSR, Britain, France and China gathered in Geneva to seek a settlement to the wars in Korea and Indo-China. The head of Berne station immediately suggested that the telephones of the Soviet and Chinese delegations in Geneva should be tapped in the hope that useful information might be obtained, which would affect the course of the negotiations.

It is, of course, not possible for an SIS representative, operating in an independent country, to carry out an operation of that type and on such a scale without the connivance, if not the actual assistance, of the security services of that country. This presented no particular problem in this case as there existed an excellent liaison, at all levels, between SIS and the Swiss Sûreté.

The project looked promising and was swiftly approved. Since it was confidently expected that information of the highest urgency might come our way, it was thought essential to have a small team of transcribers on the spot. Two excellent Russian speakers were selected for this purpose, while I was sent out to study the material and extract what was of value.

Our small party, consisting of a matronly Armenian lady, a young, rather attractive woman of Rumanian origin and myself, was accommodated in a small flat in one of the suburbs of Geneva, not far from the shores of the lake. It had been equipped with two recording machines to play back the reels and a few desks. This was all we needed. The two ladies worked and slept in the flat, while I lived in a nearby *pension*. We had, of course, no contact with the official British delegation and did not share in the social life of the conference. Such leisure time as we had was spent in exploring the beautiful surroundings of the city.

After the first week or so, it became clear from a study of the material that if anybody had hoped to rush to the Foreign Secretary with a vital piece of information, which would dramatically alter the negotiating position of the Western powers, disappointment awaited him. The staff of the Communist delegations observed strict telephone security. They never discussed anything with even a remote bearing on their position and tactics at the negotiation table, or gave an inkling as to what concessions they might be prepared to make. They discussed only routine questions such as meetings between the heads of delegations, dinner and cocktail parties, official receptions and supply, travel and transport arrangements.

This did not mean, however, that the operation was entirely valueless. A study in depth of the material, which I was able to make later that summer at the end of the conference, gave us some interesting background information on the relationship between the various Communist delegations, as well as on certain of the personalities. It showed, for instance, that the Soviet and Chinese delegations dealt with each other on a footing of complete equality. The staff of both delegations were most deferential, in this sort of way: 'Would it be convenient for Comrade Molotov to call on Comrade Chou this afternoon?' asks the Russian private secretary. 'Certainly,' answers the Chinese, 'But if it suits better, Comrade Chou could call on Comrade Molotov instead.' 'No, certainly not, Comrade Molotov will be at the villa at four o'clock.'

There was a great deal of traffic between Geneva and Moscow. This was concerned mostly with administrative arrangements, but there were also a number of private conversations with wives and relatives. These threw up a most unfashionable and unexpected picture of the unbending Molotov. It showed him to be very much a family man, who had frequent and long conversations with his wife. He discussed with her the difficulties which their married daughter had in feeding her new baby, in which matter he sometimes tendered practical advice. He also had long talks with his six-year-old grandson, listening patiently to his detailed accounts of what he had been doing.

This was the first time I came across the 'telephone call' system, the Soviet equivalent of the British 'old boy network' and equally widespread. One evening, Mrs Molotov told her husband that the son of a friend of hers had difficulty in getting into Moscow University. Could he ring the rector and arrange it? Rather grudgingly, Molotov consented.

Shortly after we recorded this conversation, the conference ended and we returned to London.

I have already mentioned that not very long after I started working in section 'Y', I began to take the youngest secretary, Gillian Allan, out to the occasional dinner or play. I liked her a great deal and as the feeling was mutual, our friendship, gradually and insensibly, developed into a steady relationship. We saw a great deal of each other, both in and out of the office. She lived with her parents in Weybridge and I became a frequent visitor at her house. Her father, Colonel Allan, also worked in SIS, was also connected with Soviet affairs and spoke Russian, which he had learned while serving with the British Expeditionary Force in Russia, during the years of the intervention. This gave us something in common and, both he and his wife, obviously approved of my friendship with their youngest daughter. After my absence in Geneva, it became clear that we were both in love and that the natural thing for us to do was to get married. This was the sort of marriage that SIS welcomed – it kept everything nicely in the family and avoided the strains that can occur when an officer marries 'outside'. (I was intrigued to learn later that the KGB has the same approving attitude to 'office' marriages.) Gillian was ten years younger than I, tall, dark and attractive and would, in every respect, make an ideal wife. Nothing seemed to stand in the way of a marriage, except one thing. I fully realised that, in my position, to marry anyone would be the height of irresponsibility and, of course, I should never have allowed things to develop to this point in the first place. How to get out of it now? I was faced with a terrible dilemma and my conscience was greatly troubled. She was a girl of conventional English upbringing, whose political views, in so far as she had any, were decidedly conservative. If I told her that I was a Soviet agent, she would be absolutely horrified. What is more, I would confront her with a choice with which nobody should be confronted, let alone a young and inexperienced girl. She would either have to betray me, the person she loved, or betray her country, to which she was deeply attached. On the other hand, if I broke off the relationship, without giving a very convincing reason, she would never understand and be terribly hurt.

I made some feeble attempts to put her off by telling her that I was half-Jewish and that her father, who was the kind of Englishman who had little time for Jews, blacks and dagos, would not like this. This had no effect and so, faced by these two evils, I decided that the best course would be to go ahead with the plans for a wedding. I tried to quieten my conscience by arguing that I was really in no different position from a soldier during the war who got married before he was sent to the front, and consoled myself with the hope that it would all work out in the end and nothing terrible would happen to me.

In October 1954, we were married in St Peter's Church, North Audley Street, by the Reverend John Stott a well-known preacher in those days. We spent our honeymoon in the South of France and on our return moved into my mother's flat in Baron's Court.

Many years later, when I was already in prison and she knew everything, my wife told me that my decision had been the right one. My sons, whom I met again after more than twenty years and to whom I told the whole story, thought the same. This is some consolation, but it does not take away the guilt which I feel towards my wife and my whole family for the pain and grief I have caused them.

Realising that I had obtained all the operational intelligence which section 'Y' could provide, I began to make it known that I would be interested in a posting abroad. Since the reorganisation of 'Y' in connection with the Berlin-tunnel operation meant that my place as number two would, anyway, have to be taken by an American official, this seemed to suit everybody. At the beginning of 1955, I was posted to Berlin.

Chapter Eight

Berlin station was the largest station SIS had in the world. The reasons for this were not far to seek. The Western Sector of Berlin was a small island, an outpost of the Western world in Communist territory. It lay in the heart of the German Democratic Republic, in the immediate vicinity of large Soviet land and air forces. What made its position even more unusual, at least up to 1961, when the Berlin Wall was built, was that there was no physical frontier worth speaking of separating this outpost from its surrounding territory. Although the sector boundary was in fact a frontier separating not just two countries, but two worlds, with radically different ideologies and economic systems, it was as easy to travel from West to East Berlin and back as from Hammersmith to Piccadilly. Although there were check-points on the main streets, people could cross freely in both directions. On the Underground there was no check at all. All this made Berlin an ideal centre for intelligence activities, and the opportunities it offered in this respect were exploited to the full.

Not only did the British, the French and especially the Americans have large intelligence agencies operating there, but the West Germans, though newcomers, were also strongly represented in the field.

All these organisations, some with great professionalism, others with tragic amateurishness, were sending large numbers of agents into

East Germany against all sorts of targets and with a variety of tasks. To those must be added, of course, the Eastern intelligence services, in the first place the Soviet and East German, which, naturally, were no less active. All this turned Berlin into one vast espionage web, with wires crossing in all directions. One had the impression that at least every second adult Berliner was working for some intelligence organisation or other and many for several at the same time.

Apart from the operational facilities created by the special conditions obtaining in Berlin, the status of Great Britain, as one of the four occupying powers, offered financial and administrative advantages to SIS which did not exist elsewhere. In Berlin SIS was operating not under diplomatic cover, but under that of the Army or the Control Commission. Both organisations were large enough to provide an umbrella for any number of personnel the Berlin station might require without attracting attention. Financial considerations were equally unimportant. The whole SIS establishment was paid for out of occupation costs, which were borne in their entirety by the German taxpayer. All this was fully exploited.

Not long after my arrival, in the summer and autumn of 1955 a series of conferences and meetings were held to discuss the reorganisation of the SIS establishment in Germany and the reallocation of responsibilities between the various stations. The principle subject discussed was how to tackle the main task of SIS – the penetration of the Soviet Union and the other socialist states in the changing conditions of the post-Stalin era. It had become increasingly clear as the years went by that an armed conflict was unlikely to break out and that preparations had to be made for the long haul of the Cold War which might well last several decades.

Berlin occupied an important place in these deliberations. It was there, it was thought, that the most favourable conditions existed for establishing contacts with Soviet citizens and with personnel of the armed forces. It was from there that the main drive should be launched. Other places which were thought suitable for operations of this kind were Finland, India, Austria and, possibly, Bonn. In these places there was a wider intercourse than elsewhere between Soviet diplomatic personnel and the local politicians and public and it would be easier therefore for our agents to establish contact with them.

In the course of the Berlin conferences George Young laid down the two main directions in which, from now on, the British Intelligence effort should be deployed. These were to obtain 1) political information, so as to be able to gauge Soviet intentions and

2) scientific intelligence on research so as to assess advances in the field of Soviet armaments.

At about this time George Young, who must have been one of the most energetic and active Vice-Chiefs SIS has ever had, issued a circular in which he gave his view on the role of the spy in the modern world, a view which though to my mind paints a too flattering image of the spy nevertheless contains an element of truth in it.

In the press, in Parliament, in the United Nations, from the pulpit, there is a ceaseless talk about the rule of law, civilised relations between nations, the spread of democratic processes, self-determination and national sovereignty, respect for the rights of man and human dignity.

The reality, we all know perfectly well, is quite the opposite and consists of an ever-increasing spread of lawlessness, disregard of international contract, cruelty and corruption. The nuclear stalemate is matched by a moral stalemate.

It is the spy who has been called upon to remedy the situation created by the deficiencies of ministers, diplomats, generals and priests.

Men's minds are shaped, of course, by their environment and we spies, although we have our professional mystique, do perhaps live closer to the realities and hard facts of international relations than other practitioners of government. We are relatively free of the problems of status, of precedence, departmental attitudes and evasions of personal responsibility, which create the official cast of mind. We do not have to develop, like the Parliamentarians conditioned by a lifetime, the ability to produce the ready phrase, the smart reply and the flashing smile. And so it is not surprising these days that the spy finds himself the main guardian of intellectual integrity.

Berlin station had a complement of about a hundred officers, secretaries and ancillaries. Each officer had his own car. Every day these fanned out in all directions from the Olympic Stadium, where the British Headquarters were situated, to take their occupants to clandestine meetings on street corners, near Underground stations, in cafés, night-clubs or safe flats in the Western sectors of the city.

The station was divided into several sub-stations, each with its own particular sphere of activity. There was a section responsible for the collecting of political intelligence and the penetration of the Soviet

Headquarters in Karlshorst (a suburb of East Berlin). Another had the task of collecting information on the Soviet and East German armed forces. A third was exclusively concerned with the collection of scientific intelligence. Finally there was the section concerned with the planning and execution of technical operations of various kinds.

I found myself attached to the section which was responsible for collecting political intelligence on the Soviet Union and penetrating the Soviet Headquarters. In this framework, I had the special task of trying to establish contact with Russian personnel in East Berlin, and, in particular, with members of the Soviet Intelligence Services with a view to their ultimate recruitment as SIS agents.

This was something much easier said than done. The Russians seldom came to West Berlin and then mostly on official duty. Many, no doubt, would have liked to come. Russians are human, and West Berlin has a lot to offer to the frailties of human nature. It boasts a throbbing nightlife, many good restaurants, bars, cafés and beautiful shops which display a glittering array of goods.

The Russian authorities were well aware of the dangers lurking behind the bright lights of West Berlin. They therefore discouraged their citizens from crossing the sector boundary in every possible way, though they could not physically prevent them from doing so. Apart from the knowledge, however, that they were incurring the grave displeasure of their own authorities, there was one other very real obstacle to Russians wishing to come to West Berlin for a night on the town. This was the question of money. The value of the East-mark was many times less than that of the West-mark. This made everything in West Berlin prohibitively expensive for Russians and East Germans. The British, in their turn, were also discouraged by their authorities from visiting East Berlin except on conducted tours. As for members of SIS, being in possession of state secrets, they were categorically forbidden to go there at all.

If we could not go to them and they could not come to us, how then could we meet? We spent a lot of time and effort trying to solve this problem. We used several approaches, which in the end all boiled down to exploiting common human weaknesses.

We knew that they were interested in such things as silk stockings and underwear, jewellery, watches and cameras. Since they had difficulty in getting them SIS decided to make it a little easier. A plan was conceived to open a shop, not far from the sector boundary, which would sell such goods. It would not look like a shop from the outside, but be located in a luxury flat and the customers would be brought to it by touts, some of whom were female. These would be especially recruited for the purpose by a German head-agent, who was to act as the owner of the shop and would pose as a blackmarketeer. The touts would not know that in fact they were working for the British Secret Service.

The head-agent selected for the job was a man called Trautmann, who had extensive contacts in Berlin black-market and criminal circles. His mistress was to act as his assistant and take charge of the shop when Trautmann was away on other business.

The idea was that when a Russian came to the shop, everything possible should be done to interest him in placing an order for goods. He was to be promised that these would be obtained especially for him. On purpose the shop would carry hardly any stock, since the whole idea was to get the Russian to come again and, if possible, bring friends and acquaintances. To this end, advantageous conditions were to be offered to him in respect of payment and currency exchange. At some suitable moment, either during the first visit, if it proved possible to keep the customer long enough on the premises, or on a subsequent occasion, Trautmann was to introduce a friend. This would, in fact, be an officer from the Berlin station, summoned in haste by telephone. He would appear on the scene as a Russian-speaking acquaintance of Trautmann who had come to facilitate the negotiations. It was the officer's job to take the case from there and interest the Russian in such a way that this casual contact would grow into a permanent relationship. This, it was hoped, would lead to recruitment and the acquisition by SIS of an agent in the Soviet Headquarters in Karlshorst or some other Soviet establishment in East Germany and, who knows, maybe even in Moscow itself.

To bring this about much depended on the skill of the officer in finding out and exploiting the weaknesses or interests of their victims. It might be black-market deals to start with, or women, or perhaps some other vice. But it need not be this sort of thing at all. If a common interest in art or some form of sport would bring about the desired result, so much the better. This was the general theory behind the shop scheme.

It never produced the desired results. We met no Russians that way, but nearly became the victims of a hoax.

One Saturday evening, not long after I had arrived at my new post, the telephone rang in my flat. It was Trautmann. A Russian woman officer was in the shop. This was her second visit already. She was interested in buying a fur coat. Could I come along and meet her? I jumped in the car and drove, as fast as I could, to the shop which was located in a truncated house, standing in a desolation of rubble, not far from the Friedrichstrasse check-point.

Through thick velvet curtains, I entered the discreetly lit room where Trautmann's mistress was talking to a fair-haired, slightly built girl. I was introduced to her as Herr Stephan, a name I sometimes used on such occasions. She smiled brightly and said, 'Nina.' Though not good-looking, she had a trim little figure and was not unattractive. She was dressed in a cheap, blue coat and skirt and there was nothing to indicate that she was not Russian. At first, we talked in German, which she spoke well, but with a strong Slavonic accent. Then we switched to Russian. This she spoke fluently, but with grammatical mistakes, and it seemed to me there was something foreign about it. Trautmann appeared and the conversation, which was at first about fur coats, took a more general turn. He brought out a bottle of brandy, I played the role assigned to me and Nina's attitude can only be described as forthcoming.

When the bottle was finished, Trautmann suggested that we should all move on to a night-club. Nina accepted the idea with alacrity.

The rest of the evening I spent dancing with her on the tiny floor. She told me that she had the rank of a lieutenant and was working as a supervisor in the Karlshorst telephone exchange. She lived in a hostel and in her free time she could do what she wanted. This was only her second visit to West Berlin. As the evening wore on my suspicion that she was not a Russian lieutenant grew stronger. The only way I could find out for certain was to try and meet her again alone.

I could not help noticing that Nina was not indifferent to my person and, during one of the dances, I asked her if she would go out alone with me one evening. She at once agreed and we arranged to meet the following Wednesday near one of the U-Bahn stations.

When I reported the meeting in the office, I at once voiced my strong doubts that Nina was a genuine Soviet officer. I suggested that we should arrange for her to be followed, after our meeting, to see where she was going. If she was seen to enter the Soviet compound at Karlshorst it could be assumed with some certainty that she was whom she claimed to be. If not, we would have to think again.

The following Wednesday evening, she turned up as agreed, this time much more smartly dressed than on the previous occasion. As we walked to the restaurant where I proposed to have dinner, I noticed the tall figure of the head of the German private detective agency, which we always employed for this purpose, not far behind us. The evening went off extremely well. When, towards eleven o'clock, we left the restaurant, I don't think Nina would have said 'no', if I had suggested that she should accompany me home. But I pretended that I was anxious for her safety and that she should return to East Berlin in time. We would meet again the following week. As I waved goodbye, I noticed our sleuth taking a seat at the other end of the carriage.

The next day we received his report. Nina had got out at the next station, well before the train reached the sector boundary. She had then taken a bus in the direction of the Grunewald, in the American sector. She had got off the bus not far from the American Headquarters and had walked to one of the streets nearby, entirely reserved for American personnel. There she had let herself into one of the houses with a latchkey. A few subsequent enquiries established that it was the house of a CIA officer, well-known to us and with whom we frequently liaised. Nina was his housemaid and a refugee from one of the Baltic republics. This accounted for her knowing Russian and speaking German with an accent. We suspected that she must have been one of Trautmann's innumerable acquaintances and that it was he, himself, who had arranged for her to pose as a prospective Russian customer in order to keep our interest in the shop scheme alive. We confronted him with the facts, but he denied knowing anything about it and said that Nina had been brought to the shop by one of his touts.

Not very long afterwards the shop scheme, the image of which had already badly suffered from the Nina incident, received a blow from which it could not recover.

One morning it was found that Trautmann and his mistress had disappeared from the flat. Not a word of warning, not a message, no signs of violence. They had left in good order, taking their belongings and the small stock kept on the premises with them. With its manager, its saleswoman and its stock gone, the shop had to be closed. The Berlin police were approached and asked to start discreet investigations into the whereabouts of the couple.

A few days later, the Berlin newspapers announced in big headlines that Trautmann had defected to East Germany in the interests of which country he appeared to have worked for some time. There he had given an interview to Communist newspaper correspondents and told the full story of his activities on behalf of SIS. It included lurid details of the shop, its address and its real purpose.

In Berlin I resumed my regular contact with a representative of the

Soviet Intelligence Service. For the first meeting, which had been arranged before I left London, the man, whom I later got to know as Korovin, came over to introduce me personally to the new officer who was to run me. Conditions for meeting my Soviet contact in Berlin were much less dangerous than in London, and much more convenient. The only rule I was breaking was that, as an SIS officer, I was not supposed to visit East Berlin. Otherwise, this was just one more clandestine meeting among several in a day and the danger that I would be caught out was not very great. I had a false German identity card, provided by the British authorities in connection with my SIS duties, and if I had been stopped and asked for my papers, I could produce that document. I boarded the U-Bahn some two or three stations from the sector boundary and got out at the second or third station inside East Berlin, usually at the Spitalmarkt. By seven o'clock the centre of East Berlin, which in those years still lay in ruins, was almost deserted. As I walked slowly along the pavement, past the empty shells of the houses that were still standing, a large black car, with drawn curtains, would pull up beside me and the door be thrown open. I quickly jumped in and was driven at high speed to a safe flat in the neighbourhood of Karlshorst. There the table was laid for a light supper and, while we had a drink and something to eat, we discussed the business in hand. The first thing I did was to hand over the films and receive enough new ones to last me till the next meeting. Then there were always questions to be answered and explanations to be given in connection with previous material. After an hour or so of leisurely conversation in complete security, I was taken back to the centre of the town and dropped off in the vicinity of a U-Bahn station. Ten minutes later I was back in West Berlin.

My new contact used the name Dick. Why he took that English name I do not know for we always spoke Russian. He was a thick-set man of about fifty with a pale complexion and a friendly twinkle in his eyes behind thick, horn-rimmed spectacles. His manner was quiet and fatherly. He always listened attentively and his opinions when he gave them were well-considered. In the course of five years of regular monthly meetings, I got to like him a great deal and felt truly sad when, at the end of my term, I had to say goodbye to him. I never saw him again. Shortly after I arrived in Moscow, I enquired about him and was told that he had died of cancer a few years earlier.

What struck me in my relations both with him and the other KGB officers, with whom I had dealings in the field, was how little they interfered. The running of the operation was left almost entirely to my own judgment. They never gave me any instructions what to do and trusted me entirely to keep them informed of everything important that came my way. This seemed to me to be quite at variance with what I had heard was the common Soviet practice of never taking a decision without express sanction by higher authority. My experience of more than twenty years of life in the Soviet Union has confirmed that this is, indeed, a marked feature of the system and one of its weaknesses. Even decisions on what would seem trifling matters are not taken without them being referred first to what is called 'the leadership', often at the highest levels. I can only explain the departure from this principle in my case by the fact that I was a professional intelligence officer and they felt that I was quite capable of judging what was the best course to take in any given situation.

If conditions for meeting my Soviet contact in Berlin were easier than in London, those for photography were less so. This was because, whereas in section 'Y' I had an office of my own, here I had to share one with a colleague. Because of operational requirements, attendance at the office was very irregular and I could never be quite sure when my colleague, if he was out, might return. If he had come back and found the door locked, this would certainly have caused eyebrows to be raised. Nevertheless, as I was always on the look out for an opportunity to photograph, I usually found one, though sometimes, in cases of great urgency, I had to take a deliberate risk and just hope for the best. Once every six weeks, however, a very favourable opportunity for taking photographs presented itself. This was when my turn came to be duty officer. I was then alone in the building for the whole night and had the keys and combinations of safes to which, at other times, I had no access. I could work quietly without fear of being caught. Nobody could enter the premises without previous warning and only I could let them in.

If the shop venture turned out a failure, the Boris case became, at least for a time, a real success story.

I met Boris through a man nicknamed Mickey. The reason for the nickname was obvious the moment one saw him; he bore a strong resemblance to Mickey Mouse. He was small, agile, with bandy legs and large ears. If the expression on his face had been less cheerful, it might have been called ratlike.

Mickey had worked for SIS for some time before I took him over from my predecessor. He originated from East Germany, where he still had a large number of contacts. These visited him in Berlin, from time to time, and brought him snippets of political and economic information which he hotted up and presented to us as reports from his agents. It was mostly of little value. Nevertheless, he drew regularly a small salary and was given a certain amount of money to pay his agents.

He had a young and attractive wife, who had been an intelligence agent in her own right. While still a teenager in East Germany, she had been part of an American network. It had been rolled up by the Soviets and she had been arrested and sentenced to twenty-five years hard labour in Siberia. After five years, she had been amnestied and returned to East Germany. She settled in West Berlin where, shortly afterwards, she met Mickey and married him. I write about Mickey and his wife in some detail as, later, they played a role in the events which led up to my arrest.

I had been running him for about a year when one day my Soviet contact warned me that Mickey and his wife had been recruited by the GRU, the Soviet Military Intelligence organisation, and that, therefore, they were double agents. I should bear this in mind in my dealings with him. They, of course, had no idea that I too was working for the Soviets. I thought the recruitment of Mickey by them pretty pointless, but, as a sister organisation was involved, it was apparently difficult to do anything about it. On the other hand, it did not seem to matter very much and so it was left at that.

The working-class district of Wedding lies just on the Western side of the sector boundary. Heavy bombing and shelling had turned large parts of it into a wasteland. On this, in the years immediately after the war, a shantytown of little shops, selling all kinds of oddments from ready-made clothes to old furniture, interspersed with cheap cafés, dancehalls and amusement galleries, had sprung up. This jumble of shacks, crowded and sordid, had become a hotbed of prostitution and black-market activities. It was here that Mickey spent a lot of his time. Among his acquaintances was the Jewish owner of a ready-made clothes store frequented by people from East Berlin and, occasionally, by Russians. On my prompting, Mickey got himself a job as a part-time assistant in this shop, with a view to looking for possible useful leads among the customers.

For some time my Soviet contact and I had been discussing the possibility of planting a genuine Soviet official on me whom I would eventually recruit as a full-blown, conscious agent. This would be a feather in my cap and at the same time provide an extra link with the KGB which could be used in case of an emergency. We now decided to use Mickey and his shop as the means of establishing initial contact between me and the Soviet official. The latter would not know anything about me, but be instructed to show himself co-operative.

One day, Mickey asked me to meet him. He told me that a Russian had come to the shop, where he worked, and wanted to buy a fur-lined windjacket. The shop did not have these in stock, but Mickey had promised to try and get one and asked the Russian to come again the following week. I instructed Mickey to buy a good quality jacket in one of the more expensive men's outfitters on the Kurfürstendamm and sell it to the Russian at half the price.

About a week later, the Russian called again, appeared delighted with the windjacket and bought it at once. He then told Mickey that he wanted to buy a Swiss watch for his wife, but could not afford a too-expensive one. Mickey promised that he would try to get one and asked him to come back three days later. This time, we decided to ask a price somewhat higher than the Russian had suggested. Mickey would tell him that if he had difficulty in finding the money, that could be arranged. Mickey had a friend who was interested in buying caviar. If the Russian could bring a dozen pots, he could pay for the watch that way.

This arrangement suited the Russian and he promised to bring the caviar the next time he came. We decided that a suitable occasion had now been created for me to meet him. Mickey should suggest that they go to his flat for a drink. If he agreed, I would drop in during the evening to collect the caviar.

Again, everything went according to plan. When I got there, the wine and brandy were already on the table and a convivial atmosphere had been established. The Russian, who spoke excellent German, told us his name was Boris, that he was an economist and worked for a Soviet economic agency in East Berlin. I mentioned, in passing, that I spoke a certain amount of Russian and we at once switched to this language. In the course of the evening, I told him that I was a Dutch journalist, correspondent of a newspaper in Berlin, and that my name was de Vries.

At about ten o'clock we both took our leave from the Mickeys and I accompanied Boris to the nearest U-Bahn station. On the way, passing the discreetly lit entrance of a night-club, I asked him if he had ever been to one of those places. He said he hadn't, so I suggested that the next time he came to West Berlin, we should go to one so that he could see what they were like. He agreed at once and we arranged to meet the following week.

This was the beginning of a relationship which lasted for several years and only ended with my arrest. From now on, I met Boris on my own and Mickey dropped out of the case. He was recommended for his good work and given a bonus of 500 marks.

In the course of subsequent meetings with Boris, who came to West Berlin about every three weeks, I began to cultivate him as a journalist who was more interested in information than black-market deals. In the initial stage, I used to take him to a quiet, but good restaurant or one of the smaller, intimate night-clubs, where one could spend a whole evening over a bottle of Mosel wine. Neither Boris nor I were heavy drinkers. Later, I rented a small furnished flat where we met over drinks. He began to speak freely about his work and told me that he was employed as a senior interpreter with Comecon (the economic organisation which links the socialist countries) and that it was part of his duties to interpret at high-level negotiations between the Soviet Union and the DDR and accompany important Soviet delegations. Though, ostensibly, the luxury articles which I obtained for him as gifts for his wife were in exchange for the caviar he continued to bring me, it was well understood between us that what I was really interested in was the information he was in a position to supply. He apparently accepted my explanation that I needed it as background material and my assurance that nothing he told me would ever be published by my newspaper. The intelligence which I obtained from him in this way was mainly of an economic, but, occasionally, also of a political nature and received an enthusiastic reception from our London customer departments. Head Office was delighted and thought that Boris represented a source of great promise and should be carefully cultivated. Though he was not 'our man' in the Kremlin yet, there was a good prospect that he might become one. There was no doubt that he was a high-level interpreter who sat in on important negotiations. From time to time, London would send me special questions on some matter of current importance and nearly always Boris came back with the required information.

Our relationship continued in this way for nearly two years. Then, one evening, he told me that he was going back to Russia at the end of that month. He had been transferred to Comecon Headquarters in Moscow. It meant promotion and his new job would involve travel to foreign countries, accompanying high-level Soviet delegations.

On his last visit, I offered him a farewell dinner and presented him with an expensive fountain-pen. I gave him an address in Holland, to which he could write and told him that if, on any of his visits to the

West, he needed money for personal expenses or had difficulties with currency, I could always help him out.

I met him again more than a year later. By that time I had left Berlin myself and was working in the Russian section at Head Office in London. I received a letter from him posted in Austria, saying that he would be in Dusseldorf on a certain date, as a member of a Soviet industrial delegation and be staying in a certain hotel. The safest way of making contact with Boris, I thought, was to instal myself in the lounge of his hotel in a place where I could easily be seen and then leave the initiative to him on the appointed day. I had been sitting there for about twenty minutes when he came in, together with some other Russians. He could hardly fail to notice me where I was sitting, for the lounge was small. Though he made no sign that he had recognised me, I felt sure he had. He went up with the others and about half an hour later came down alone and joined me. We had a brief conversation and arranged to meet outside.

We spent that evening in the customary way. Dinner first, followed by a night-club. He passed a considerable amount of information to me, some of which turned out to be quite valuable to SIS. (The KGB was obviously trying to establish Boris's bona fides as my agent.) I on my part 'lent' him a hundred pounds to buy presents to take home with him. We parted in the early hours of the morning and never met again. Before another meeting could be arranged, I had been arrested and had ceased to operate.

In the summer of 1985, I was spending my summer holidays in the DDR with my family and staying a few days in Berlin. While I was there, I was asked if I would like to meet an old acquaintance. I said certainly and wondered who it could be. The next afternoon, to my great surprise, Boris turned up at the house where I was living. Time had done its work on both of us, but we recognised each other at once. He had risen to a high position in the Soviet diplomatic service and was on an official visit in Berlin. We passed the afternoon reminiscing about the old days. He told me that he had never suspected that I was connected with the Soviet Intelligence Service and had only discovered this when he read about my trial in the newspapers. Since then we have met several times in Moscow.

My memories of the years I served in West Berlin are pleasant. I lived with my wife in a large flat on the top floor of a house reserved for British officials. It was situated about ten minutes' walk from the British Headquarters in the Olympic Stadium, in a smart, residential area, with lots of trees, and which had suffered comparatively little from war damage.

The SIS staff in Berlin was sufficiently large, together with wives and secretaries, to form a separate group within the large British community there. Cocktail and dinner parties given by members of the staff and to which very few outsiders were invited formed a regular feature of our life. It sometimes even happened that there would be two or three such parties on one evening. One would start at one house and after three quarters of an hour or so move on to another, where one would meet the same people, continue the same conversation, drink the same drinks, eat the same snacks, and then go somewhere for dinner. This could be very trying, but one was more or less expected to take part in this round.

Once or twice a year we were invited, in turn, to the house of the commanding general for what Captain Holt would have called our 'hot meal' and to such official functions as the Queen's birthday party, but otherwise we mixed little with official Berlin. Some of us knew a few Americans or French, if it so happened that it was part of our job to liaise with them, but, in general, there was little visiting between the foreign communities. As for contacts with the Germans, these were mostly restricted to professional relations. There seemed, on their part, little desire to have any social contact with the British. This was in striking contrast with my experience in Germany immediately after the war. Then one could have as many German friends as one wanted and it was often difficult to get rid of them. Now it was a different matter. They had everything we had and, in many cases, more and better. So, on the whole, they no longer wanted to know us. Not that we minded very much. Maybe thirty years of common membership of Europe has changed all that.

Our annual leave we always spent with our families in England, but for our local leave we usually went somewhere on the continent. In that respect, Berlin was ideally situated. With the car one was in one day in Holland or in Austria and in a day and a half on the Italian lakes. I remember one happy week with my wife in an old hotel, situated on a promontory in Lake Garda. It was there that an important change in my life took place. The hotel provided facilities for water-skiing, which we both enjoyed very much. In this way we got to know two French couples, who were also staying at the hotel. They were very health conscious and constantly doing exercises and watching their diet. Though my obsession with food had gradually subsided, I had put on a great deal of weight and my wife was constantly urging me to do something about it. Their example infected me and I, too, started to do exercises and eat a great deal less. Not very long afterwards, I happened to come upon a book, written by a Dominican monk, in which he described a series of Yoga exercises which he had found very helpful in his meditation. The exercises and the philosophy behind them appealed to me and I decided to switch from ordinary to Yoga exercises. Since then I have practised Yoga daily for about an hour, and I am convinced that it is to these exercises that I owe the good health that I have enjoyed all these years and the relative equanimity with which I have been able to meet the vicissitudes of life.

In the summer of 1956, my wife told me that she was expecting a child. Again I was faced with the inner struggle which I had faced when I got married. On the one hand, I was delighted with the thought of becoming a father, on the other, I was deeply aware of the fact that, in my position, I should not have any children. But how could I explain this to my wife without telling her the truth? She was young and healthy and, naturally, wanted to have children. As before, I persuaded myself that all would be well and that I would pass unscathed through all the dangers, even though an inner voice told me that the chances of this being so were slight. So, in the spring of 1957 my first son was born to the delight of both of us and our respective families. My mother came over to help out during the first months and soon we settled down to this new, more complete form of family life.

During the night of the 22nd of April, 1956, Soviet signals troops, carrying out urgent repairs on a cable which had shown signs of sagging, 'stumbled' on a telephone tap. They discovered a tunnel leading in the direction of an American army store, just on the other side of the sector boundary. They penetrated into the tunnel but were unable to advance beyond the point where it intersected the boundary. A barrier of sand-bags prevented any further progress and they made no attempt to break it down.

As soon as the tap was discovered, alarm bells began to ring in the listening station in the American compound. The Americans, not knowing at that stage the intentions of the Soviet soldiers, rushed reinforcements to the compound to stop any Soviet military personnel from entering it either through the tunnel or across the boundary. The military commanders in Berlin were alerted and for nearly a whole day the situation on the border remained tense.

It soon became clear, however, that the Soviets were not

contemplating any strong-arm action to destroy the installations which had been eavesdropping on their military telephone traffic. They limited themselves to calling a press conference the next day, at which they accused the Americans of being responsible for this particularly flagrant incursion into their territory, in proof of which they took the assembled journalists for a conducted tour of the tunnel. This unmistakably led in the direction of the American army compound.

In the Western press the tunnel operation was generally hailed as one of the most outstanding successes of the CIA in the Cold War. Although it was noted that most of the equipment found was of British manufacture, there was no suggestion by anybody that the British had in anyway participated in or had known about the project. This was too much for Peter Lunn. As soon as the news broke in the press, he assembled the whole staff of the Berlin station, from the highest to the lowest, and told the whole story from its inception to its untimely end. He made it quite clear that this had been essentially an SIS idea and his own to boot. American participation had been limited to providing most of the money and facilities. They were, of course, also sharing in the product.

Up to then hardly anyone in the station had known about the existence of the tunnel. Apart from himself and his deputy, I had been the only officer who had been in the 'know' and that only by virtue of my previous job in 'Y'. My former colleagues in that department, who were in Berlin working on the tunnel operation, lived completely isolated from the Berlin station and I had had no further contact with them. My information on developments affecting the project had come henceforth only from the Soviet side.

I, for my part, had naturally been watching these developments, which I knew were about to occur, with some anxiety, on the alert for any signs of suspicion on the part of SIS or the CIA that the Soviets might have been forewarned. So skilfully had the 'discovery' of the tunnel been stage-managed, however, that a subsequent SIS/CIA enquiry into the circumstances surrounding the collapse of the operation produced the verdict that the cause had been purely technical and that there was no question of a leak. What the KGB had done was to wait until a real fault had developed on a cable so that it had to be inspected, thus giving the signals troops an apparently genuine reason to discover the telephone tap. Since the Americans were monitoring the cable, they too knew about the fault so they considered the Soviet action perfectly logical. Still, I must confess that I passed some anxious weeks until the results of the inquiry became known and I could heave a sigh of relief.

Only in 1961 did SIS discover, as a result of my arrest, that the full details of the tunnel operation had been known to the Soviet authorities before even the first spade had been put in the ground.

After the discovery of the tunnel, Peter Lunn began to lose interest in the Berlin station and made it known that he would like a transfer. So, in the summer of 1956, he was appointed Head of the Bonn station, a post with important liaison duties. He was replaced by Robert Dawson, the Head of one of the Berlin sub-stations. This solid, fatherly figure, with the air of a countryman, assisted by his sensible and able wife, had the gift of making the members of the staff feel part of a large family. Just as in the Navy there are happy ships and unhappy ships, so in SIS there are happy stations and unhappy stations. Berlin became a happy station.

Robert Dawson left Berlin in the beginning of 1959 to become Head of the Directorate of Production 4 (DP 4). He was anxious that I should join him there and that summer, having been in Berlin nearly five years, I returned to London to take up an appointment in the Russian section of the Directorate.

Chapter Nine

Shortly after our return to England, my second son was born. For some time we lived with my wife's parents in Chester Row, within walking distance of my office, and then moved to a furnished flat in a large old house in Bickley. Our daily existence now centred very much on the family, not only because there was one more small child to look after, but because our social life in London was very different from that in Berlin. There we had been part of a closed community, the members of which all lived at a short distance from each other. Here I was just one of a rather amorphous mass of civil servants who lived dispersed over the enormous area of greater London and rarely met outside the office. We were now thrown back on our own friends, of whom my wife had many and whom we saw occasionally, and our families whom we saw regularly.

The atmosphere in the Directorate, in Head Office, to which I was now attached was very reminiscent of that in the Berlin station, especially after Robert Dawson had become its head.

In the late 1950s, as a result of Khrushchev's co-existence policy, contacts with the Socialist Bloc countries became easier. A thin, but constant flow of visitors began to move in both directions between Great Britain and the Soviet Union. These ranged from official trade delegations, businessmen and scientists to artists, exchange students and an increasing number of tourists. British firms began to carry out large Soviet orders which required, in some cases, the attachment for lengthy periods of Soviet technicians to their plant and, in others, the sending of British technicians to the Soviet Union to advise on the installation of equipment.

It had always been a strict rule that SIS should not carry out intelligence operations in Great Britain, which was the exclusive preserve of MI5. It was now decided to abandon this rule in order to be able to exploit the rich field of opportunities provided by the thaw in relations between East and West.

SIS always had a section specialising in useful contacts at home. It was a sort of support section. If anybody needed expert advice on some technical or commercial aspect of an operation, or a particular kind of cover or facility for an agent, which could best be provided by a British firm or organisation, it was the job of CPR (Controller of Production Research, as it was called) to try and arrange it. In this way, it had built up over the years a vast reservoir of contacts in all walks of life, but chiefly in the City and in Fleet Street. It was now decided to make direct use of these contacts and transform CPR into an agent-running organisation, doing a similar job to that of SIS stations abroad. It was made into a new Directorate, in Head Office, and reorganised into a number of separate sections, each with its particular sphere of activity.

As before, the section in which I now worked concentrated on intelligence operations directed against the Soviet Union and, as before, it was my job to explore every opportunity to establish contact with Soviet citizens with a view to developing them into regular sources of information. Its Head and my immediate boss was a man called Dicky Franks. He had left Cambridge with a good degree and, from the start, had been one of the promising young men of the Service. His subsequent career has justified the high hopes of him and he ended up as Chief of the Secret Service. Now, in his late thirties, he was very much a with-it man, and had more of a public relations officer or a high-powered advertising executive in him than a conventional civil servant. His trim figure had something boyish and, with his glistening, rimless glasses, slightly too large head and snap reactions, he reminded me irresistibly of the brightest boy in the class. When we were at a meeting together, I always expected him to raise an arm before starting to speak. He was very energetic and hard-working and knew how to delegate responsibility so that, all in all, he made a very good station commander.

His particular responsibility was the relations with the chairmen and managing directors of large companies and newspapers, whose assistance and co-operation we required. It was a strict rule that no employees of British firms were to be recruited as agents, or used in any way, without the prior consent of the chairman, or managing director of their company. Large concerns like Shell or ICI we were frequently reminded, were as much identified abroad with the British government as any Embassy. If one of their employees was caught spying, the political and economic consequences could be both expensive and embarrassing. We should think hard before using them.

One way of establishing contact with Soviet officials visiting Britain was through the interpreters attached to them for the duration of their visit. I spent a great deal of time and effort to try and bring as many of these on our books as possible. In addition, we set up our own interpreter agency. It had its offices in a couple of rooms in an old house off Leicester Square. Two White Russians, with a long connection with SIS, were its joint directors. The aim behind the agency was to provide commercial cover for their intelligence activities and to attract as many free-lance interpreters, as were suitable, by offering them full or part-time employment.

As the two partners were extremely competent interpreters and provided excellent service to their customers, they soon began to build up a reputation and were more and more frequently approached by British and even Soviet firms and organisations which needed interpreters. In this way, SIS was able, in time, to have its agents attached, in the guise of interpreters, to almost every Soviet visitor of interest and to send them to the Soviet Union with British delegations of various kinds.

All these interpreters were given a standard brief. Apart from obtaining information directly connected with the field their customer was engaged in, they were instructed to establish, whenever possible, good personal relations with the Soviet people they came in contact with. In the course of this, they were to collect as much information as they could on their work, character, weaknesses and their attitude to the political system in the Soviet Union. They should try to arrange things in such a way that they could start a correspondence with them, and at some later date, resume the relationship.

Apart from the interpreters, it was my task to recruit businessmen, university dons, students, people in the world of art and scientists who, one way or another, were in direct contact with Soviet citizens. The initial approach was always based on an appeal to patriotic sentiments and there was no question of any financial rewards. As many of the people concerned were businessmen, it was usual to invite them to lunch in order to establish the right atmosphere. I got to know a great number of London restaurants this way, but found it exhausting work. From the beginning I made it a firm rule not to drink more than half a bottle of wine a day. I was, as always, concerned that my health should not be affected.

Most of the people I approached agreed to co-operate, but always made one proviso: that they should not be asked to do anything that might harm their commercial interests or the particular project they were working on. I found, in practice, that this proviso enabled them to keep up the pretence of co-operating with us, while, in fact, doing very little. Others, from the very start, refused to have anything to do with intelligence work on the grounds that they considered it unethical and that their conscience did not permit it. I had always much respect for these people and, of course, did not pester them any further.

My work in the Directorate confronted me with a small handicap from which I did not suffer when I worked abroad. I speak English very well and don't think I am boasting when I say that to all intents and purposes I am bilingual. I have retained, however, a slight Dutch accent. This never worried me at all with people who knew my background, but it did become a source of unease whenever I had to meet new people – English people I mean – as I had to do in my job in the Directorate. Had I been able to do so, I would have said, the moment I met somebody new: Look, this is who I am and this is why I speak like this. This I obviously couldn't do and so, until I could bring the subject up in a natural way at some later stage, I was all the time imagining to myself what the other man was thinking: Who is this Foreign Office official – a cover we nearly always used – who is obviously not English, although he has an English name? I found this distracting and not conducive to establishing an easy relationship from the start.

My accent had however one advantage. It not only baffled people, but it also precluded them from immediately determining to what social stratum I belonged. The English and, especially, the English middle classes are great classifiers and have a, to my mind, exaggerated sense of the importance of class. One of the first questions a middle-class Englishman asks you is what school you have been to and whether you are not related to the Blakes of somewhere or other. As I had not been to any school in England and was not related to any Blakes from anywhere, it was difficult to classify me, and people had no alternative but to take me at my own worth. In Holland I had also been accustomed to class differences, but there they were softened by the fact that that nation, apart from being divided horizontally in classes, is also sharply divided vertically in religious denominations. As a result Dutch society does not so much consist of layers as of squares, within each of which there is a certain amount of solidarity, transcending class differences.

I always have been and still am a great admirer of the many sterling qualities of the English people, but about two marked characteristics I am less enthusiastic. One is the exaggerated class consciousness, to which I have alluded, and which often degenerates into sheer snobbishness. The other is a general tendency to over-value themselves in relation to other nations. I am told that both these characteristics are much less evident in the younger generations and if this is so, it is all to the good.

In London I resumed my regular contact with the Soviet representative who, as before the Berlin period, was again Korovin. Occasionally, he was away and his place taken by a younger man, called Vassili, who differed from Korovin in that he had a much more cheerful disposition and looked typically English so that if he didn't open his mouth nobody would have dreamt of taking him for a foreigner. I always enjoyed my evening strolls with him through the quiet streets of a London suburb.

By now, I had come to acquire such confidence in the skill of my Soviet friends in evading MI5 surveillance that I looked upon these meetings as the least of the dangers that threatened me. The photographing of documents had now also become a routine process which I was able to carry out at times and in conditions when the danger of being caught was virtually nil. There were only two dangers against which I could not guard and upon which, in consequence, I looked as acts of God. One was, if I had a road accident while I was carrying on my person the Minox camera with compromising films. The other was if an official in the Soviet Intelligence Service or in that of one of the socialist countries, who knew my identity or possessed information that could lead to it, decided to defect to or work for the British or American intelligence services, in fact, would do for the West what I was doing for the East.

Although my motto in life has always been to hope for the best and to reckon that everything will come out all right in the end, I was well aware of the fact that the chances that I could go on operating indefinitely without being caught were slight and would become less with every year that passed.

One fine summer evening, as we were walking in a quiet road in the Croydon area, I decided to talk to Korovin about this subject. I had never done so before and I was interested to know what attitude the Soviet authorities wanted me to adopt if I were caught and had to face trial. Did they want me to stage a political show trial, for instance, and denounce the subversive operations of the Western intelligence services directed against the Soviet Union and its allies? Did they want me to deny, out of hand, that I had been spying for them or, on the contrary, confess? It may be argued that all this was rather naïve and that a man in my position ought to know, and the sheer instinct of self preservation dictate, what course to take if this happened. I felt, however, that I should adopt in such an event any attitude which the Soviet authorities thought in the higher interests of the cause that I was supporting.

If I thought I was going to get a clear answer to my question, I had disappointment coming to me. Korovin squarely refused to discuss the subject at all. He was a man of the old Stalinist school and, evidently, held that there was nothing beyond human control. He argued that if I did everything right and made no mistakes and if they did everything right and made no mistakes, nothing could go wrong. The very fact of discussing this subject was already an admission of defeat and one might as well give up there and then. So that was the end of that conversation.

It may well be that according to the textbook Korovin was right and that it was inadvisable, in general, to discuss the possibility with an agent that he might be caught. But to my mind, each individual case was different and one had to take very much into account the character of the person concerned. I, for instance, have always been deeply conscious of the forces which determine our destiny, over which we have no control and to which we have no choice but to submit. So his answer did not convince me in the least and had he given me, then or on another occasion, clear instructions as to how to behave if I were caught, I would have followed these instructions when the time came.

After all, the KGB must have had plenty of precedents to go by, if only the Philby case, to name but one, and the latter's attitude when he was interrogated. Unfortunately, the accumulated experience of intelligence services – of all intelligence services – is often lost in old registry files and seldom brought to light, studied and crystallised into practical guidance in individual cases. I, for instance, knew nothing about the Philby case at that time, and, I think, that if I had, it would have made a difference. Whether in the end that would have been better is another matter altogether. As the lawyers like to say, 'in all the circumstances' things could hardly have worked out better for me than they did.

One day, that same summer I was asked to call at the Personnel Department, where I was seen by Ian Crichley, its deputy head. He wanted to know if I would be interested in being sent to Lebanon for a year to study Arabic at the Middle East Centre for Arabic Studies (MECAS), with a view to being posted, afterwards, to one of the Middle East stations. I asked for a short period of reflection in order to consult my wife. This I did, but I also consulted Korovin. Both were in favour so I accepted with much pleasure.

It was the fulfilment of an old wish. The years I had spent with my father's family in Egypt had left me with an interest in the area and I had always hoped that I would go back there one day. This desire had received a strong fillip from the stories of life in Iraq and dealings with the Arabs which Captain Holt had told us to while away the time spent in captivity. The Service had been recruiting quite a few young Orientalists straight from university. What it now needed was a small number of experienced officers with a good knowledge of Arabic and Middle Eastern problems to fill the more senior posts in the area. I felt, therefore, that this course should affect my career favourably, which was another reason why I was keen on it. The Middle East might well become the crucial battleground in the conflicts which divided the world and would offer many opportunities for interesting and important work.

Besides, a posting abroad carried with it all kinds of allowances and perks and offered a good opportunity for replenishing one's bank account, always seriously depleted after a spell at Head Office where one had to make do with one's bare salary. Finally, the prospect of a year's break from the constant pressure and dangers of operational work to devote myself to the study of a difficult language and live with my young family in the beautiful surroundings of a Mediterranean mountain retreat was most pleasing.

And so it turned out, at least for a while. In September 1960 I travelled out alone in my car, crammed with suitcases, prams and children's toys. My wife and two small boys were to follow by air.

Shemlan is a village of low, white terraced houses, strung out along a winding road high on the coastal mountain range of the Lebanon. MECAS itself, was housed in a modern, white stone and glass building, surrounded by spacious balconies and terraces. It had been set up and was financed by the Foreign Office to train its own Arabic experts and those of the Colonial and Armed Services. Originally located in Jerusalem, it had been moved at the end of the Mandate to the Lebanon. The bulk of its students were members of the Foreign Service and the Services, including always one or two from SIS, but a few were sent there by British oil companies, banks and other commercial concerns with interests in the Middle East. There even were two Dutchmen from Shell, with their families.

The Director of the Centre was always a senior FO official while the director of studies was usually an Orientalist, seconded on a sabbatical year from one of the British universities. The remainder of the teaching staff were Palestinian Arabs, all Christians and former Mandate officials.

Shortly after my arrival, I rented a small house, within a few minutes' walking distance from the school. It had a spacious veranda from which there was a splendid view over the sprawling white city below and the blue sea beyond. Two weeks later my wife and children joined me there.

Then followed six very happy months. The course was an intense one of eighteen months, divided into two parts of nine months each. The first part provided us with a sound working knowledge of spoken and written Arabic and the second prepared us for the Civil Service Higher Interpretership Examination. Frequent tests and stiff exams at the end of each term kept up our spirit of competition and saw to it that we had little time to relax. One day a week I did absolutely no work, however, and allowed my mind a complete rest. On that day, often in the company of other families on the course, we would go for picnics in the mountains or seek out a lonely cove along the rocky coast. In the evenings we would usually have dinner in a small restaurant and might end up in one of the hundreds of Beirut's night-clubs. Apart from that, we would seldom go down to the city. Occasionally, we were invited to a dinner or cocktail party given by friends in the Embassy. But, on the whole, we took little part in the intense social life of Beirut. I did not even meet Kim Philby, one of the best known Englishmen in town at that time. In fact it was not until I was in Wormwood Scrubs in 1963 and read about his escape to the Soviet Union that I learnt that he had been an officer in SIS and, like me, a Soviet agent. I really had thought that he was a Foreign Office official.

Shortly after my arrival in Beirut, I established contact with the representative there of the Soviet Intelligence Service. Being fully engaged now in the study of Arabic, there was little information of operational importance which I could pass, so we decided that a meeting once every two months would be sufficient to keep in touch. He gave me a telephone number where I could contact him in case of emergency.

We were approaching the end of the Easter term. I had passed the exam at the end of the first term well and hoped for even higher marks in the second exam. I found the study entirely absorbing and got a deep satisfaction from the beautifully logical, almost mathematical construction of the Arabic language. We had now reached the stage when we would soon have to put the knowledge we had acquired to the test. After the short Easter break, we were due for dispersal to various parts of the Arab world to live for a month with Arab families and acquire practice in speaking. Some of the students took this opportunity to visit exotic lands and went as far afield as the Yemen and the Hadramaut. But as my wife was due to have her third child during this period, I had arranged to stay with a Lebanese family in the next village of Souk El Garb in order to be at hand. My mother was to come out to look after the children while my wife was in hospital.

About two weeks before Easter, my small son got pneumonia. During a walk on the mountainside we had been caught in a sudden, drenching downpour. He had to be taken to hospital in Beirut, where my wife stayed with him, sleeping in the same room. I was doing some last minute swotting for the end of term exam while an Arab nurse looked after our second son.

One afternoon, when I was in the hospital visiting them, one of my wife's friends came to see our little boy. She was an SIS secretary who, at one time, had worked in the same section as my wife and was now PA to Nicholas Elliott, the Head of Beirut station. She told us in the course of conversation that she was going that evening to a play, 'Charley's Aunt', produced by the local British drama group. The play was supposed to be very amusing. She had a spare ticket and wondered if I would like to come. I was not very keen, but my wife insisted that a break from the books would do me good and I allowed myself to be persuaded. The play was indeed funny and I was enjoying myself. In the interval we went to the bar. There we ran into Nicholas Elliott and his wife who asked us to join them for a drink. In the course of conversation, he drew me aside and said he was glad I happened to be there as this saved him a trip up the mountain to see me. He had received that morning a letter from Head Office with instructions for me to return to London for a few days' consultation in connection with a new appointment. It suggested that I should travel on Easter Monday so as to be available in London early on Tuesday morning.

After the play, I dropped the girl at her flat and then drove back up the dark mountain road to Shemlan. It was well that I knew every turn and precipice on the way for my mind was not on my driving. It was entirely taken up with the news I had been given that evening. I could not make it out. There was something wrong somewhere. Why recall me now? Head Office knew that this was an intensive course and that every day counted, especially with the final exams in sight. In July there would be a few weeks' holiday when I would go home anyway. Surely any consultations could take place then? Why this highly inconvenient, sudden interruption? True, the civil war in the Congo had just broken out and it was possible that this had set in motion a series of emergency appointments requiring my services urgently for operational work. But this explanation did not really satisfy me. The more I thought about the whole thing, the less I liked it. By the time I was home, there was no longer any doubt in my mind. There was only one thing to do. I had a valid visa for Syria, just a few hours' drive from Beirut. As soon as my son was out of hospital in a few days' time, I would take my wife and children to Damascus. There I would explain the situation to her exactly as it was, however painful this might be, and leave her to decide whether to accompany me to the Soviet Union or take the car and the children back to Beirut and return to England.

I slept little that night, all the time turning things over in my mind. By the morning the sun and the warmth brought other thoughts.

It had happened before that I had been recalled rather suddenly to London. Every time I had gone with a certain apprehension but every time it had been all right – a conference, a course, a consultation. Why should it not be the same now? If I fled on no more evidence than a hunch, would I not be haunted for the rest of my life by the uncertainty that I had abandoned my post for perhaps no good reason at all? And my wife? What would I say to her and how would she take it? Was I not about to cut myself off from all that was most dear to me for a mere shadow? Was this not a case of the coward fleeth when no one pursueth?

The first thing to do was to arrange an emergency meeting with my Soviet contact and ask him to get in touch with Moscow without delay. Perhaps they had some information which might indicate that all was not well and advise me accordingly. I met my friend the same evening on a deserted beach near Beirut and explained the situation to him. He promised to get in touch with his headquarters at once and hoped to have a reply by the following evening.

When I met him again, he told me that Moscow had no reason to suspect that anything was wrong and that, in their opinion, I could safely go. This was exactly the news I wanted to hear. The moment of truth had been put off. I did not have to confess to my wife that I was a Soviet agent. I felt such a relief that I deliberately pushed any doubts that still lingered right out of my mind and the next day began to make arrangements for my journey to England. The last days passed in a whirl. The end-of-term exams, which lasted two days, had started. I was now only worried whether I had used the right case with this or that pronoun or the correct plural form. After each paper we crowded into the coffee room, anxiously comparing notes, exultant one moment on discovering that we had made the right choice in translating a tricky passage, kicking ourselves the next for having put down the wrong answer when we had known the right one. The following day we waited tensely for the final results. Then the satisfaction of seeing my name among the first four, and the feeling of complete relaxation looking forward to the few days' Easter vacation. That evening there was a stag party, a black-tie affair, in one of Beirut's more expensive restaurants followed by some mild gambling in the Casino. I won; then lost all my gains in a single throw. I had let it be known that I had been recalled to London for a few days. There was general speculation as to the reason, but the consensus of opinion was that I had been earmarked for an important appointment. The last days before my departure passed in a pleasant whirl. My son came home from hospital and was quite spritely again. My wife made shopping lists of things which it had suddenly become essential to bring back from England. I sent a telegram to my mother that I was coming. In the excitement, generated by my unexpected trip, my last doubts vanished. I called at the Embassy in Beirut to collect the money for my air fare. Nicholas Elliott showed me the letter from Head Office. It read innocuously enough. He could add nothing to it and wished me a pleasant journey with a bland smile. (Of course, I now realise that Elliott must have known why they wanted me back in London. Head Office would have had to consider the possibility that I might run, or at least make contact with my Soviet control. Elliott would have had to be in the know so as to be ready for anything.) In parting, he asked me if I wanted him to make arrangements for me to stay at St Ermins hotel, just opposite Head Office, while I was in

London. I declined, saying that I would be staying at my mother's. Was I sure? Would it not be easier? No, indeed not. For a moment the shadow of a doubt again crossed my mind. Strange, this insistence on staying at the St Ermins. But it passed away again.

The last day remains a pleasant memory. We left early by car for an excursion to Byblos. Easter Sunday, the church bells ringing, the crowds in their Sunday best outside the Maronite churches in the villages. The majestic Greek temples against the intense blue sky. The picnic on the edge of the desert in the shade of a fig tree. The return drive back through the festive villages. A good friend and fellow student, Allan Rodney of the Foreign Service, and his wife asking us to dinner. The happy conversation afterwards on the terrace with the myriad lights of Beirut glittering below us. My friend insisting on opening a bottle of champagne to drink to my new appointment.

The next morning early, the drive to the airport. A last wave to my wife as I pass through the customs. My eyes remain riveted to the white cluster of houses against the mountain side which I know to be Shemlan. Then suddenly the land drops away behind me and we fly over the glistening blue sea.

Something wrong with our aircraft in Rome. A long, uncertain wait broken by a bad lunch. Then the relief as we are driven to board another aircraft bound for London. At Heathrow a grey drizzle, calling for my raincoat. I walk briskly through the controls – into the trap.

That night I stayed with my mother in her small flat in Radlett. We sat talking till well after midnight. I had a lot to tell her about our life in Shemlan and to discuss her forthcoming visit and my wife's shopping list. My mother, being a very practical person, made suggestions on who should buy what and where. Everything had to be ready by the Friday as I counted on being able to return to Beirut that day to be in time for my eldest son's birthday party on the Saturday.

The next morning, it being the Tuesday after Easter, I reported to the Personnel Department in Petty France, shortly after ten, as instructed. I was shown into the room of Ian Crichley, the Deputy Head of the Department. There an old acquaintance of mine, Harry Shergold, one of the SIS experts on Soviet affairs, was already waiting for me. They both welcomed me in a friendly manner and Shergold suggested that I should come with him as he wanted to discuss certain questions which had arisen in connection with my work in Berlin. Instead of taking me to Head Office in Broadway, a stone's throw away, he led me across St James's Park to the house in Carlton

Gardens, so familiar to me from the days when I worked there in Section 'Y'. We were shown into the rather splendid reception room on the ground floor. At a large table two of my colleagues were seated. I knew them both since they also worked in the Soviet field, but their names, I must admit, I have now forgotten. They got up to greet me and then we all sat down round the table. After some general conversation, they got down to business. Shergold did most of the talking. He began to tell me about an event which had happened in Berlin, some time after I left.

As I have already mentioned, the agent Mickey – his real name was Horst Eitner – was married to an attractive, young woman who had spent five years in a prison camp in Siberia, having been sentenced by the Soviet authorities in East Germany to twenty-five years imprison-ment for espionage on behalf of the Americans and subsequently been amnestied. I have also mentioned how Mickey and his wife were recruited by the Soviet Military Intelligence service so that both were, in fact, double agents.

Mickey and his wife were in the habit of celebrating every year her release from Soviet imprisonment with a dinner in one of Berlin's many restaurants in the company of one of her girlfriends who had been an inmate in the same camp as she and had been released on the same day. It was, as always, a very convivial party and all concerned had more to drink than was good for them. In the course of the evening, Mickey started making passes at his wife's girlfriend which, of course, Mrs Mickey did not like. She showed her irritation and asked him to stop. He ignored her entreaties and went on with his flirtatious behaviour. At last, driven to exasperation, Mrs Mickey threatened to go to the police and tell them that her husband was a Soviet agent. Mickey didn't take this threat seriously and told her to do what she liked. Without another word, she got up and went straight to the nearest police station. They thought at first that she had had too much to drink and did not want to believe her story. To prove that she was telling the truth, she asked them to accompany her to her flat. There she showed them two hidden microphones, installed by the Soviets. Mickey was arrested the same evening and Mrs Mickey herself the next day.

What had happened was this. While I was in Berlin and Mickey's case officer, there had been no need for the Soviets to listen in to what passed between us. But when I left and handed him over to Johnny Spears, another expert on Soviet affairs, they became interested in my successor. They therefore asked Mickey if he would allow them to put microphones in his flat so that they could monitor the conversations between him and his case officer. Mickey agreed to this and two microphones were installed.

Having told me this story in some detail, Shergold began by asking me why I thought the Soviets had wanted to install microphones only after I had left and another officer had taken over. To this I could only answer that I did not have the faintest idea.

It was now also clear – Shergold continued – that, since Mickey had been a Soviet agent, Boris, the Soviet Comecon official, must have been a plant. How could I explain that? I agreed that the evidence pointed to Boris having been planted on us, but as to why, well, all I could say was that Mickey had obviously been a convenient link for this purpose.

Thus the discussion went on till lunchtime. When we broke up, nobody suggested, as would normally have been the case, that we should have lunch together. I thought this was a bad sign. I walked alone to Soho and had lunch in a small Italian restaurant I sometimes used to go to. I can't say that I had much appetite. My thoughts were on other things.

By itself, of course, the fact that the Soviets had placed microphones in Mickey's flat only after my departure could quite easily be explained as pure coincidence. That Boris was, in all probability, a plant followed from the fact that Mickey, as was now known, had been a Soviet agent. But in all this there was nothing criminal. These things could happen and did happen in the career of any intelligence officer, especially in a place like Berlin where many agents were double or even triple agents. If they had no more than this circumstantial evidence, I had not much to worry about. On the other hand, would I have been called back from Beirut, at a particularly crucial point in my studies, just to discuss a matter which was now only of academic interest. Why did we have to discuss this in Carlton Gardens and not in Shergold's room in Head Office, which would have been more normal, and why was it necessary to have three people there?

When I returned to Carlton Gardens, my three colleagues resumed their questioning. The subject now shifted from Berlin to Poland. They said that they had evidence that certain important SIS documents, bearing on Poland and with a very restricted distribution list which included me, had found their way into the hands of the Polish Intelligence Service. How could I account for this? I said I couldn't and that their guess was as good as mine.

In the course of further questioning, it became clear to me that they must have a source in the Polish Intelligence Service at a pretty high level. Many years later, I found confirmation of this in Peter Wright's book *Spycatcher*, in which he relates how one Michael Goleniewski (codename Sniper), allegedly a deputy head of the Polish Intelligence Service, who defected in 1959 to the Americans, had reported to the CIA that the Russians had two very important spies in Britain, one in the British Intelligence Service and one somewhere in the Navy. This report eventually led to the arrest, first, of Gordon Lonsdale and his group and then, a few months later, of myself. I also discovered in this book that I had been given the codename 'Lambda 1' and Lonsdale that of 'Lambda 2'. The questioning went on all through that afternoon, in ever decreasing circles, till, towards the end of the day, my interrogators – for that is what they were more and more becoming – openly accused me of working for the Soviet Intelligence Service. This I flatly denied. At six o'clock we broke up and they asked me to come back the following morning at ten. On the way back to Radlett, I kept on turning over in my mind all that had been said that day. Of one thing I was no longer in any doubt – SIS knew that I was working for the Soviets. Otherwise such a grave accusation would never have been levelled against me.

Thinking back now, that evening and the two following evenings were, without doubt, the most difficult hours in my life. Knowing that I was in serious danger, that, whatever happened, life would never be the same again for any of us, I had to pretend to my mother that all was well and continue to discuss with her the plans for her forthcoming trip and all the purchases we had to complete before the end of the week. I remember in particular how one item, high on my wife's shopping list, was mosquito nets. My mother had found out that these could only be bought at Gamages and she instructed me to make sure to go there the next day and order them so that they could be delivered in time.

To cut a long story short, all the next day my interrogators continued to accuse me of being a Soviet agent, revealing little bits of additional evidence in the process, and all the next day I stubbornly continued to deny this. At lunch time, though my mind was on quite different matters, I managed to go to Gamages and order the mosquito nets and some other items. That evening, I went home again to my mother and her cosy flat seemed to me cosier and safer than ever. It became increasingly difficult however to pretend that I did not have a worry in the world and I pleaded a busy day ahead to go to bed early and be alone with my thoughts.

The next morning found us again, all four, sitting round the table in the sumptuous ground-floor room in Carlton Gardens. One of the reasons this venue had been chosen, I now realised, was that recording apparatus was installed in the next room so that everything that was said could be taken down. Round and round we went over the same ground, without getting any further. I must stress, however, that, throughout, the tone remained courteous and no threats of any kind were made.

When we resumed after lunch, my interrogators changed tack. Looking back now, I don't think this was only a ploy on their part. It seemed to me that they themselves genuinely believed that it had all happened the way they suggested and it was this that lent special weight to their words. Be that as it may, the fact remains that, whether by luck or by planning, they hit upon the right psychological approach. What they said was this: 'We know that you worked for the Soviets, but we understand why. While you were their prisoner in Korea, you were tortured and made to confess that you were a British intelligence officer. From then on, you were blackmailed and had no choice but to collaborate with them.'

When they put the case in this light, something happened which to most people would seem to go against all the dictates of elementary common sense and the instinct of self-preservation. All I can say is that it was a gut reaction. Suddenly I felt an upsurge of indignation and I wanted my interrogators and everyone else to know that I had acted out of conviction, out of a belief in Communism, and not under duress or for financial gain. This feeling was so strong that without thinking what I was doing I burst out, 'No, nobody tortured me! No, nobody blackmailed me! I myself approached the Soviets and offered my services to them of my own accord!'

A gut reaction this outburst may have been, but it amounted well and truly to a confession. Having now admitted to my interrogators – as unexpectedly to them, I am sure, as to myself – that I was a Soviet agent, I now went on to explain exactly the reasons that impelled me to become one. They listened to me in amazed silence, but their courteous attitude to me did not change nor did they question, either then or afterwards, that I had acted for other than ideological motives. At no time, then or later, did they offer me an immunity from prosecution in return for what I might have been able to tell them. My reaction in the end was no different from that of my friends Michael Randle and Pat Pottle when it became known, in 1989, that they were the people who had helped me to escape and had been named in the press. They wrote a book *The Blake Escape* in which they admitted their role in the escape. What was important to them was that everyone should know exactly why they had done it. They chose to face the danger of prosecution and a prison sentence rather than have the wrong motives ascribed to them.

By the time I had finished it was nearly six o'clock and time to go home. It was arranged that a chauffeur-driven car should take me to Radlett where I could spend the night at my mother's. I was not to say anything to her, however, only that my return to Beirut had been postponed as I had to attend an urgent conference which would take me away from London for a few days.

The next morning, another chauffeur-driven car came to collect me and I said goodbye to my mother as if I really was going away for a few days. As I waved to her from the car window, I wondered if and when I would see her again. At Carlton Gardens, Harry Shergold, one of the other interrogators whose name I have forgotten and John Quine, an old friend of mine were waiting for me. I had known the latter well in the Far East, where he had been Head of Tokyo station at the time that I was in Korea. He had on two or three occasions visited me there and I had stayed at his and his charming wife's hospitable house in the Embassy compound whenever I had been in Tokyo for consultation or to deliver the diplomatic bag. Now he was there, partly because he was head of R5, the counter-espionage department in SIS which worked closely with MI5, and partly, I think, because he was a friend of mine.

With a police car ahead and another following the party then drove in two cars to a small village in Hampshire – I have forgotten its name – where Harry Shergold had a cottage. There we were met by his wife and his mother-in-law, a charming old lady with snow-white hair, who reminded me of my grandmother. It was now Friday, the day I had hoped to return to Shemlan.

The next three days had something surreal about them with everyone pretending that this was just an ordinary weekend party among friends. The only difference was that the house was surrounded by Special Branch officers and, every time we went out for a walk, a police car drove slowly behind us. It was a bizarre situation which struck me as very English – I should say endearingly English. I particularly remember one afternoon which I spent in the kitchen making pancakes with the old grandmother. I am something of a specialist in this and when it was suggested that we should eat pancakes, I offered to make them. At night John Quine shared a bedroom with me, and when we were alone he spoke a lot about my family and wanted me to tell him again what had been my motives for doing what I did. I had a feeling he was trying hard to understand. During the day, there were frequent telephone conversations with London, conducted in another room so that I could not hear what was being said. In the course of the weekend it became clear to me that we were all waiting for something, though for what I had no idea.

Somehow, I felt no longer worried about my own fate, but all my thoughts were with my wife and children, my mother and my sisters. How would they be told, how would it affect them and what would now become of them?

Watching the Special Branch men and police cars around the house, a strange thought struck me. Up to now, it had been I who had been on guard against the authorities, watching out for any signs of suspicion on their part, afraid that I might be caught. Now that I had been caught, a subtle transference had taken place. It was no longer I who had to be on guard, but the authorities who had to worry and keep a constant watch on me to make sure that I would not slip through their fingers.

On the Sunday afternoon, we all drove back to London, where we spent the night in a large house in one of the western suburbs. That evening there was a telephone call which, I noticed, did not please my colleagues. Some decision had evidently been taken and it was not the one they had hoped for.

The next morning, as we were finishing breakfast, two officers of the Special Branch, led by an inspector whose name, if I remember rightly, was Smith, came to arrest me. I said goodbye to my colleagues who at that moment, I somehow sensed, felt some sympathy or perhaps pity for me. Anyway, they shook hands with me and wished me strength.

A police car drove us to Scotland Yard, where I was officially charged by a superintendent under article 1(1)(c) of the Official Secrets Act. My fingerprints were taken and I was searched, but they forgot my watch which I carried in a small pocket in the belt of my trousers. From Scotland Yard we drove straight to Bow Street Magistrates Court, where I was remanded in custody for two weeks. The proceedings did not take more than ten minutes. From there I was taken by the inspector and his two assistants to Brixton prison.

After the usual reception procedures, I was put in a large room in the hospital wing, furnished with a bed, a table and chair and a small radio. The date was the 12th of April 1961. That evening a short report appeared in the newspapers to the effect that one George Blake, civil servant of no fixed address, had been charged under the Official Secrets Act and had been remanded in custody.

The next day, I heard the news over the radio that Yuri Gagarin, the Soviet cosmonaut, was the first man to travel in space. This news, at that time and in those circumstances, was a great boost to my morale. I experienced it as a confirmation that I had not laboured in vain, that I had helped those who were in the vanguard of progress, who were opening up new horizons and leading mankind to a happier future. I felt then that it showed that Soviet society was ahead. Now I realise that it was ahead only in one small area. Up to the 1970s one could keep up the illusion that we were moving forward all the time, moving towards Communism. As a result of *glasnost* we now know that we were actually moving backwards.

I spent nearly a month in Brixton on remand. For me that period was mostly remarkable for the great number of books – I was allowed as many as I liked – which I devoured and by the visits, from time to time, of the solicitor and Counsel assigned to me through Legal Aid. I felt that both of them were well-disposed towards me. I liked them from the start and trusted them to do what they could on my behalf. I did not envy them their task, however, which seemed to me pretty thankless after the confession I had made.

I was also seen, occasionally, by the prison doctor who chatted with me and was invariably kind. Looking back on that period, the impression remains in my mind that people who came in contact with me treated me more as a curiosity, as a person with whom there was evidently something wrong, than as a dangerous criminal.

On the 2nd of May, I was visited by my wife. She was accompanied by John Quine and we met in a small room in the hospital wing. The day I had been arrested, John Quine had flown out to Beirut to break the news to her. He had done this as carefully and sympathetically as he could to soften the shock. He had then taken her and the children back to England, assisted by one of the Embassy wives, who happened to be an old schoolfriend of my wife. In order to shield them from the press, she and the children and my mother were temporarily living with one of my former colleagues from Berlin, who had a large house in the country. Both my wife and my mother are women of strong character, who, fortunately, get on well together. This enabled them to be a support and comfort to each other in those dark days. My arrest and the disclosure that all these years I had been a Soviet spy, that I had deceived them and led a double life came as a terrible shock to them and caused them much grief. For a long time I could hardly bear to think about the suffering I had caused them. It was too painful. If I have any regrets for what I have done, it is for the pain they have suffered and the way I have deceived my colleagues and friends, though this was in no way directed against them personally.

It was a sad reunion for us, but my wife never uttered one word of reproach. She told me how John Quine had broken the news to her and what a shock it had been. She was not angry and there was no sign of rejection in her demeanour. She continued to visit me for the next five years. (It was, of course, all a great blow to her father. He took it very badly. But his wife, my mother-in-law, coped very well and visited me twice in prison – I suspect without telling him.) Though I knew that Gillian could not possibly approve of, or even begin to understand, what I had done, I felt her full loyalty and support in my hour of need. In the course of conversation, I learned from her that the trial would take place the very next day. Nobody had told me anything about this and it all seemed very sudden to me. In a way, I was quite unprepared. On the other hand, I reflected, what was there to be prepared about? Whether I would be found guilty or not guilty? That had already been settled by my confession. That left only the sentence. I knew that the Official Secrets Act provided for a maximum sentence of fourteen years and, contemplating that period, it seemed to me a very long time. I hoped against hope that perhaps my Counsel could persuade the judge to give me less, but, on sober reflection, that seemed unlikely. On the other hand, I couldn't exclude the possibility that the British judiciary would rake up some old law, dating from the Middle Ages, which everyone had forgotten about, but had never been abrogated, under which I could be sentenced to death. Thus, between hope and despondency, I spent the last night before my trial. I realised later the weakness in my position – I had not seriously studied the law relating to these matters. If I had understood the law better I might have been able to throw all sorts of spanners into the works.

The old judge looked kindly enough, as he sat there opposite me – he and I, the two principal participants in this show, raised high above the others – he busily taking notes hardly ever looking up, I wondering what there was to write. For him it was now so simple. I had pleaded guilty and he knew the facts. I had already written them all down for him. All he had to do was to determine the sentence. His small wig, pushed forward, almost rested on the golden rim of his spectacles and made him look slightly old-maidish.

The fear for the future, the uncertainty of how I would stand up to years of imprisonment, the nagging regret that, if only I had followed my hunch, I would not have come back to England, these thoughts, which in endless new mutations had passed through my mind during the weeks of waiting in Brixton prison, had gone for the moment, pushed right down somewhere in the depths of my mind, leaving it empty and detached.

My eyes wandered around No. 1 Court at the Old Bailey. It looked grand and dignified after the sordid shabbiness of prison, to which I had not yet had time to get accustomed. The judge was not sitting in the highest chair in the middle, under the coat of arms, but in one nearly at the end. It spoiled the symmetry of the room. This worried me, but only for a passing moment.

So the Chief himself had come. His white head and tall, distinguished figure stood out in the well of the Court among some of my former colleagues, who were there because they had been working on my case. I say 'former' as I imagined that, as prisoner in the dock, charged with five – why five I could not quite make out – offences under the Official Secrets Act, I was no longer their colleague, though I had not received any notification that my employment with the Secret Service had been terminated.

The Attorney-General, Sir Reginald Manningham-Buller, appearing for the Crown, was finishing his address. As I sat watching him, not really listening to what he was saying, I thought what an unprepossessing figure he cut, with his wobbling crimson cheeks and the apoplectic, bulging eyes of the over-indulgent, beside the thin, intellectual-featured Jeremy Hutchinson QC, who appeared on my behalf and rose immediately afterwards to address the Court.

Hutchinson spoke very well and movingly. I felt sure that his words would make an impact on the judge and all who heard him. Before the case started, he had come to see me in the little waiting room below the Court where I was kept. He had asked me if in his address to the judge he could say that I was deeply sorry for all I had done. That might help a lot. I replied that I could not agree to this. In the first place, it was untrue, for I felt that what I had done was right and, in consequence, I could not feel sorry for it. In the second place, it seemed to me undignified that somebody, who in the course of nearly ten years, had photographed almost daily every important and interesting document which had passed through his hands in order to transmit it to the Soviet authorities, should suddenly feel sorry for having done this, simply because he had been found out and arrested. If my activities had not been uncovered, I would still be continuing them. He saw the point and did not insist, though obviously it made his task of moving the Court to leniency much more difficult.

When Counsel had finished, the judge suggested a short adjournment. He got up and it struck me that he was quite tall. During the ten minutes that he was away I was wondering how much I would get or would I perhaps be sentenced to death? On the other hand, if I was lucky, after that very able and eloquent speech by Jeremy Hutchinson, in which he had so lucidly and with such understanding, explained my motives and which, I felt, must have moved the judge, it might even be less than fourteen years. These thoughts were cut short by the judge's return. There was a commotion as the public was now admitted to the gallery. The judge was going to pronounce sentence and this part of the proceedings was no longer in camera.

He made a short preliminary speech in which he said that by my activities I had undone most of the work of British Intelligence since the end of the War. He recognised that I had acted out of ideological motives and not for the purpose of gain. Nevertheless, he felt that an exemplary sentence should be imposed which would punish and deter. He then sentenced me on each of the five charges to fourteen years' imprisonment, three of these to run consecutively and two concurrently. He added in clarification, lest I or anyone else should not have grasped it, that this meant that I would go to prison for a period of forty-two years.

There was an audible gasp in the Court as he spoke these words. To me they sounded utterly unreal, so much so, in fact, that I could hardly suppress a smile. Somehow, if he had said fourteen years, that would have made a far more fearful impression on me. It was a period the length of which my mind had wrestled with and shrunk back from. Forty-two years was beyond the limits of the conceivable and therefore had no more real meaning than if he had said two thousand years. Besides, who could foresee what might not happen over such a long period and what great changes might not take place?

When the judge had left the Court room, I was taken down to one of the cells below. It was small and dark, designed only to wait in, with just a wooden stool and a small table as furniture. Dirty and damp, its walls were covered with inscriptions, some merely obscene, but most witnessing to the moods of despair, bitterness, defiance or hope of those who had waited there. While I sat there the medical officer of Brixton prison came to me. I had not yet lost the habits of the diplomatic world in which I had moved. Since he had evidently come to enquire how I felt, I took this to be a sort of courtesy visit and was touched by his kindness. Only later did it occur to me that this had been purely a duty call, to see how I had taken the blow and if any sedatives were needed. Later in the afternoon I was handcuffed to two prison officers and taken in a small van to Wormwood Scrubs prison. On the way, I saw the newspaper vendors carrying placards with my photograph, taken eight years earlier on my return from Korea, announcing the news of the sentence in the early evening editions. For a short moment I had become headline news.

Presently the two huge prison gates swung open to let through the van and closed behind it again almost immediately. I had reached another turning point in my life. Another stage was beginning and it looked as if it would be a long one.

Chapter Ten

In Wormwood Scrubs I was handed in to Reception. I was duly entered in the books of the prison and my earliest date of release recorded as 1989 and the latest as 2003. All my clothes and personal belongings were removed and, after a bath, I was given prison clothes and taken to the hospital. There I had to undress once more and was issued with a pair of pyjamas, much too large for me and with all the buttons and the trouser cord missing. I was locked in a cell, the only furniture of which was a rubber mattress on the floor. This was not because I was in a state of shock or unduly depressed as has been rumoured in the press, though I might well have been, but normal prison routine. All new arrivals, sentenced to life or other long sentences of imprisonment, are first taken to the prison hospital, where for a week or so they are kept under observation to see how they take it. The next day turned out to be a busy one for I received a whole string of callers, the chief medical officer, the Governor, the Deputy Governor, the chaplain and others whom I could not place. They all kindly enquired how I felt, looking rather curiously at me. I had a vague impression that when they received the reply 'Quite well, thank you,' they were slightly disappointed.

I also received a visit from my kind and very able solicitor, Mr Cox, for which purpose I was given back my prison clothes and taken to the visitors' block. He had come to urge me to appeal against my sentence and I agreed to this, more in order to please him, for he was so insistent, than that I had any hopes myself that it would make the slightest difference. I felt sure that this sentence had not been the result, in the first place, of the sentiments or mood of the judge. It represented a deliberate act of government policy.

This was clear to begin with from the number of charges that had been brought. In the magistrates' court and at the committal hearings there had only been one charge. At the trial this was suddenly increased to five. Why? The maximum punishment under the Official Secrets Act, laid down by Parliament, is fourteen years. But this was clearly not enough. It had not deterred in the past nor, above all, would it satisfy the Americans, who were raising hell and crying for blood. So a way had to be found to make it more.

A conspiracy charge, which had served well in the Portland spy trial a few months earlier, and had made it possible to send Lonsdale and the Krogers to prison for periods of twenty-five and twenty years, would not do in this case for there was only one accused. So somebody in the Director of Public Prosecutions Department remembered the Tichborne case, the dispute about a title in the last century, in which the judge had imposed a separate sentence on each of a number of charges relating to the same offence. The years during which I had passed information to the Soviet Intelligence Service were therefore divided into five periods, corresponding to the different appointments I had held in that time, and a separate charge was made for each period. That this was an arbitrary division is clear from the fact that one charge covered a period of five years, another one of two weeks, while the other three referred to periods varying from one to two years. On each charge I was given the maximum of fourteen years, three to run consecutively and two concurrently. That made forty-two years. A few months after my trial, allegations were made in the press to the effect that I had been responsible for the death of some forty agents, working for the British and other Western intelligence services, and that the prison sentence of forty-two years imposed on me represented one year's imprisonment for each agent.

In the first place, it is on record that at my trial it was no part of the prosecution case that I was responsible for the death of any agents. No such allegations were or could be made. I do not deny that I did reveal the identity of a large number of agents to the Soviet intelligence service, not forty as alleged, but nearer four hundred. I challenge anybody, however, to name one who has been executed. Many of them are today taking an active part in the democratic movements of their respective countries in Eastern Europe. I revealed their identities on the express understanding that they would not come to any harm. I felt particularly strongly about this. It was my aim that prophylactic measures should be taken against them, that they would be prevented from having access to information of any importance and thus could not harm the interests of the countries of the socialist bloc. This was done.

Secondly, there is another point I should like to make in this connection. The agents whose identities I revealed were not innocent persons. Rather they were persons who deliberately set out, more often than not for financial gain, to harm the interests of their own country and government, knowing the risks attached to this. In other words, they were in the same position as I was myself and exposed to the same risks. They were betrayed in the same way that I was betrayed.

They are often referred to as British agents. This is correct in the sense that they worked for the British Intelligence Service, but not in the sense that they were British nationals, as the term is often understood. They were all citizens of socialist bloc countries and there was not one British national among them. I point this out to put the record straight, not because I think it makes any difference. To me, it makes no difference, especially in this context, whether a person is British or Hottentot. We are all human beings and life is equally precious to all of us.

Apart from the identities of agents, I also, together with the structure and organisation of SIS, passed on the names of many SIS officials (who were all British) and the posts they occupied at the time. This did not put their lives and liberty in danger. At most, if they were posted to a socialist bloc country, they would not be given an 'agreement', i.e. permission to serve in a diplomatic capacity at the British Embassy in that country, or, if they did get permission, and were subsequently caught spying, all that would happen to them was that they would be asked to leave the country at three days notice.

In his book *Blake Superspy*, the late H. Montgomery Hyde, a writer on intelligence matters, specifically accused me of being responsible for the death of two agents. The first was an important East German defector, Lieutenant-General Robert Bialek, Head of the DDR Security Service, who, according to Mr Hyde, was kidnapped in West Berlin in 1956 and taken to his old Headquarters and after prolonged interrogation executed. I can truthfully state that I was in no way involved in this case and that this was the first I had heard about it.

In this connection I should like to point out two things. The first is that Mr Hyde alleged that Lt-Gen. Bialek lived in the same block of flats as I did at 26 Platanenallee in West Berlin. This cannot have been true. The block of flats in question was occupied entirely by members of the British Control Commission and officers of the Armed Forces and their families and no Germans lived there at all. Secondly and more importantly, if the man kidnapped was who Mr Hyde said he was – i.e. Head of the DDR State Security Service – I am quite sure, knowing defector procedure, that the British authorities would never have installed him in a flat in West Berlin, about three miles from the sector boundary, which at that time could be crossed without any let or hindrance. What is more, is it likely that Lt-Gen. Bialek himself would have agreed to live in such an extremely exposed position? In reality, a defector of this status and importance would have been flown out of Berlin to West Germany or England the very day after his arrival and, after debriefing, be settled in either of these countries or another safe country. Whatever the truth about this kidnapping, I can only repeat that I had nothing to do with it.

The other case which Mr Hyde cited is that of Lt-Col. Peter Popov of the GRU, the Soviet military intelligence service, who, to quote:

. . . was originally stationed in Vienna, where he volunteered his services to the Americans, by the simple expedient of dropping a note on the front seat of an American diplomat's car. His services were accepted and he was assigned a CIA case officer, one George Kisvalter, who had been brought up in St Petersburg before the Revolution and spoke Russian fluently. During the next two years Popov supplied Kisvalter with the names or codenames of upwards of four hundred Soviet agents in the West. In 1955 he returned to Moscow on leave and was then posted to East Berlin since the GRU had no suspicion of his duplicity. However, this transfer meant that the CIA had no means of communicating with him. Popov also realised this with the result that he wrote a letter to Kisvalter explaining his difficulty and he handed this letter to a member of a British military mission touring East Germany. This officer passed the message to the MI6 office in the Olympic Stadium in West Berlin where it landed on George Blake's desk with instructions to forward it to the CIA in Vienna. This Blake did but not before he had read the contents and informed the Russians who took some time to react.

Popov continued his meetings with Kisvalter, but it was not until Popov disclosed that he was sending a young girl, a secret agent, named Tairova, to New York on an American passport which belonged to a Polish-born hairdresser living in Chicago and had been 'lost' during a visit to her native Poland, that Popov definitely came under suspicion. The girl, to whose mission the FBI had been somewhat reluctantly alerted by the CIA, was subjected to such a degree of surveillance by the Bureau that she felt she had been 'blown' and returned to Moscow of her own accord. The GRU now recalled Popov to Moscow where he blamed Tairova for what had happened. His explanation was accepted and for the time being he continued to work as usual at the GRU headquarters. At the same time he was assigned a CIA member of the US Embassy, named Russell Langrelle, as his American contact.

The KGB who were keeping an eye on Popov took action on 16 October 1959 when they arrested him on a Moscow bus in the act of passing a message to Langrelle. The CIA man was arrested at the same time, but successfully pleaded diplomatic immunity and was released. But Popov met the fate which similar defectors had suffered in the past, having admitted (according to *Izvestia*) that he deserved the 'supreme penalty'. It took a grim form. He was thrown alive into a blazing furnace in the presence of an audience of his GRU colleagues.

I have quoted this passage in full as, in my opinion, it contains the true explanation as to why Popov was caught. First of all I must state that I had never heard of Popov until I read about his case in Mr Hyde's book. It was not I who alerted the Soviet Intelligence Service to the fact that he was a CIA agent. The message he handed to a member of the British military mission in East Germany could not have landed on my desk. I was not the officer in the Berlin station responsible for liaison with that mission, nor was I responsible for liaison with the CIA. The letter would have been passed on via quite a different channel. Secondly, it is clear that the Soviet authorities did not know as early as 1955 that Popov was an American agent, as they would have if they had been tipped off by me as Mr Hyde alleged. Had they known, they would not have a) allowed Popov to send the girl Tairova to the US on a secret mission; b) accepted his explanation that it was Tairova herself who was to blame for the failure of the mission and c) allowed him to continue working as usual in the GRU headquarters for several years.

The Soviet authorities discovered that Popov was a CIA agent simply as a result of shadowing Langrelle who, as an official of the US Embassy in Moscow and a suspected CIA officer, was under constant surveillance. They waited till Popov was in the act of passing material to Langrelle to arrest them both. As to the manner of Popov's execution, one wonders how Mr Hyde came to hear about it. If it really happened in the way he described – which I very much doubt – such a fact would have been kept a close secret in any country, let alone in a country as secretive as the Soviet Union.

Whether the sentence imposed on me was just or unjust, is a matter of opinion. What, it seems to me, is not a matter of opinion is that it was manifestly unjust when compared to the way two other Soviet spies, Blunt and Philby, were treated. Blunt was given a free pardon, and allowed to remain in his high position at Court and retain his title, until he was finally publicly exposed in 1979. In the case of Philby, who I am sure did not do less than I to frustrate the operations of the British and other Western intelligence services, a high SIS official (Nicholas Elliott, the same man who had handed me in Beirut the instructions to return to England) was especially sent out to Beirut to warn him not to return to England. He would have done so in the course of that summer for his annual leave – he told me this himself many years later – and could have been arrested then and tried. Why were they let off while I had to stand trial and was given such a heavy sentence? The only answer I can give is that further scandals had to be avoided at all cost. They, moreover, were both English and, what is more, members of the establishment – though that, it would seem, should have made what they did more and not less reprehensible in British eyes. I, on the other hand, did not belong to the establishment, was of foreign origin and could, therefore, safely be made an example of.

However, I do not complain for it is to this long sentence that I owe my freedom. It secured me the sympathy not only of many of my fellow inmates, but also of the prison staff. It made me determined to attempt to break out of prison, as I truly could say that I had nothing to lose but my chains. These factors enabled me, in time, to effect a successful escape. Had I been given fourteen years, not only would it have made a much deeper impression on me than the rather surreal forty-two years, but it would have excited much less interest and sympathy in others and, very likely, I would have served my sentence to the end.

The week in hospital, fortunately, passed fairly quickly for I was anxious to start as soon as possible on normal prison routine, and get used to the new conditions and the communal life with my fellow inmates, which might at first not be easy. I spent most of my time reading, thanks to the hospital librarian, another prisoner, who, against the regulations, provided me with an unlimited number of books. This helped me get through the first days. In between books, I would try vainly to make sense of the news which came drifting into my window from a distant radio. Occasionally, I could make out a few words and my name, but never enough to make sense. It was a tantalising experience.

A week after my arrival in the prison, I was taken from the hospital back to Reception. I was told to take off the blue prison uniform I was wearing and instead was given another with large white patches sown on the jacket and trousers. The prison officer who gave me these much worn articles told me that from now on, by order of the Governor, I was on 'Special Watch'. He did not explain what this meant and as he did not appear in a communicative mood, I did not ask. But I soon found out. It is a special régime for prisoners who have escaped and been recaptured, or of whom evidence has been found that they are planning an escape. Normally, it is imposed by the governor who also has the right to take prisoners off Special Watch.

In a large prison like Wormwood Scrubs, which also serves as an allocation centre, there are usually from five to ten prisoners on Special Watch. They are only let out of their cells for work and exercise and move about the prison in a group under close escort. They have to change cell every day so that nobody can know beforehand their exact location or they can't have the opportunity to saw through bars or manufacture false keys. They are frequently searched and at seven o'clock every evening all their clothes are removed except for a shirt to sleep in. A light is kept burning in their cell all night and there are frequent checks to see that they are still present.

The first six months of my imprisonment I spent in C Hall, one of the five long structures in pseudo-Gothic style, built parallel but unconnected to each other, which make up the prison. C Hall housed prisoners who had recently been sentenced and were awaiting transfer to other prisons, as well as those who were serving sentences of less than three years. The high, hollow shell of this caravanserai, with its steel staircases and four landings, on each of which the doors of a hundred cells open up, resounds all day to the tramp of marching feet, the shouting of orders, the ringing of bells, the banging of cell doors, the clatter of steel foodplates and a Babel of voices.

When I arrived at Wormwood Scrubs, it already housed another Soviet spy. Lonsdale, a so-called 'illegal resident' of the Soviet Intelligence Service and the principal figure in the Portland spy trial, had been sentenced a few months earlier to twenty-five years imprisonment. On the day I was removed from hospital, Lonsdale, who until then had been kept in normal conditions, was also put on Special Watch.

I met him on my first day in C Hall when I was taken down to the yard for the half-hour daily exercise after lunch. As we were both on Special Watch, we walked together with some six others 'on patches' in a small inner circle which moved in the opposite direction to the large, slowly shuffling circle of some seven hundred prisoners around it. He must have known who I was for he came at once towards me and shook hands with me as he introduced himself. Lonsdale was a stockily built man of medium height with a broad, cheerful face and very intelligent eyes. He spoke with a marked 'overseas' accent and his speech was larded with transatlantic expressions. When I got to know him better, it struck me with what skill he had been cast for his role. Nobody who met him would for a moment have taken him for anything else but the hail-fellow-well-met, hard-living, hard-working, pushing Canadian businessman he was supposed to be.

He bore his fate with remarkable fortitude and was invariably in good spirits. He was an excellent story-teller and I found his company in those first weeks of my imprisonment a great morale-booster. During our daily walks in the grey prison yard we naturally often discussed our chances of getting out. Lonsdale was a Soviet citizen and there always was a chance that if the Soviets caught a British spy an exchange might be arranged. I realised from the very beginning that for me this hope did not exist. I was a British subject, a former government official, and the authorities, who anyway did not like these kind of deals, would never agree to let me go. Amnesties are no part of British penal practice, so for me that left only escape.

I remember in this connection one conversation we had only a few days before he was suddenly transferred to another prison. 'Well,' he said in his customary optimistic way, 'I don't know what is going to happen, but of one thing I am certain. You and I are going to be on Red Square for the big parade on the 50th Anniversary of the October Revolution,' (in 1967). It sounded fantastic at the time when we were both at the beginning of very long sentences. Life, it so happens, can be fantastic. He turned out to be dead right. We both attended the parade and there was champagne afterwards as well.

One day he did not come down to the yard for exercise. In the middle of the night, without any previous warning, he had been moved to a prison in the north of England. I was sorry he had gone. I missed a good friend and cheerful companion.

There has been a lot of speculation on how it was allowed to happen that we met. After all, one of the first security rules is to prevent communication between two spies in custody. It has been suggested that Lonsdale and I were put on Special Watch in order to force us into each other's company – for that was in fact what this measure amounted to – in order that the Security Service could overhear our conversation. Lonsdale had persistently refused to reveal his true identity and maintained that he was a Canadian and it might have been hoped that in conversation with me he might reveal who he really was.

As former number two of section 'Y', I venture to say that this is of course an unrealistic assumption. Even with the most up-to-date listening devices available at that time our conversations in the prison yard, and that was the only place we met, could not possibly be overheard. We were walking in a large, open yard beside each other, in the centre of a vast, slow-moving circle of some seven hundred chattering, shouting and shuffling prisoners. No microphone could have picked up our conversations.

The explanation is much simpler. MI5 got worried when it realised that two important Soviet spies were held in the same prison. Special watch should be kept on them to make sure they could not establish contact with each other. The order was passed on to the Prison Department and from there to the Governor, who at once implemented it. That was where things went wrong, for the term 'Special Watch' in the language of the prison administration has a very definite meaning, which differed from the one MI5 attached to it. This order, therefore, had exactly the opposite effect of the one MI5 intended it to have. Instead of preventing Lonsdale and me from communicating, it ensured, on the contrary, that we did and in the most favourable conditions at that. Just another typical bureaucratic mix-up.

That this explanation is very likely the right one is, I think, borne out by the Home Secretary's reaction, when questioned about this matter in Parliament in 1964. Mr Brooke, the Home Secretary of the day, firmly denied that any meetings between us had taken place and affirmed that care had been taken to keep us separated while we were in the same prison. When challenged again, he repeated this denial on several occasions. Later, when an ex-prisoner swore an affidavit to the effect that he had seen us together a number of times, the Home Secretary told the House that the prisoner concerned was of doubtful mental health and had been sent to Wormwood Scrubs for psychiatric investigation. All this, in spite of the fact that not only this prisoner but the whole staff of the prison and at least a thousand other prisoners could witness to the fact that what he told the House was not true.

I had been in the prison about six months when, one morning, I was called over to Reception and given an ordinary prison uniform. I had been taken off the Special Watch list. The same day I was transferred to D Hall. Already earlier, I had been put to work in the canvas shop, where somebody with a sense of humour gave me the job of sewing diplomatic mail bags.

D Hall is a so-called Central prison, reserved for those sentenced to more than three years' imprisonment. Paradoxically, it has a lighter régime than C Hall where short sentences are served. The Prison Department suffers from an acute shortage of staff. It has therefore worked-out a system which reduces the strain on long-term prisoners to the minimum and makes it easier to manage them with the staff available. Much trouble is avoided this way, with which it would find it hard to cope. So behind the double grilled gates and bars of the hall there is a certain amount of freedom. Prisoners are unlocked at seven o'clock in the morning and not locked in their cells again until eight o'clock in the evening. They have their meals at tables in the body of the hall and out of working hours are free to associate, watch television, play cards or go to their cells to read. Those who have been there some time are allowed to have their own radio. There is a large urn with constantly boiling water for tea or coffee, which can be purchased from earnings in the canteen. Once a week there is a film show.

This régime is an admirable example of English compromise. It keeps the prisoners reasonably contented and enables the authorities to guard them with the minimum of staff. There are about 370 prisoners in D Hall of whom some seventy are murderers doing a life sentence and at least another hundred are in for various other crimes of violence. But during the hours of association there are only two officers on duty. Yet there is seldom any trouble, at least not during the period I was there.

Although I was now no longer on Special Watch and was allowed to mix normally with my fellow-inmates, I remained carefully guarded. An intermediary régime was worked out for my benefit, something of a cross between Special Watch and the ordinary prison régime.

Prisoners were moved about the prison in groups, conducted by trusted prisoners, called 'leaders' or 'blue-bands' because of the blue band they wore round their arm. I, on the other hand, was taken everywhere by a prison officer and a special book was kept to record my whereabouts at any time of the day. For me, personally, this had the advantage that I never had to queue and was always helped out of turn. The canvas shop was the most secure workshop and that was why I was assigned to it. I stayed there five years. It is considered the lowest form of labour in the prison and is used as a form of punishment. Most longterm prisoners don't stay there longer than a few weeks before they are given more congenial work or taught a trade. The vast majority of people who work there are epileptics, mental defectives, people on punishment and those on transfer to other prisons. Finally, I had to have my monthly visit in a small room in the presence of a prison officer. This was the most painful of the restrictions imposed on me. The other inmates had their visits in a large canteen at separate little tables under general supervision of a prison officer, who sat out of earshot.

It is only fair to put on record, however, that the prison authorities tried to lighten this restriction by assigning, as much as the duty roster allowed, the same prison officer to sit in on my visits. He was a kind man, of cheerful disposition, an ex-Army sergeant, who, in time, became almost a member of the family. We, in turn, never took advantage of his kindness and did not use the visits to pass messages or in some other way break the prison rules. My wife came regularly every month and shared her visits with my mother or some other member of my family. They always brought sandwiches or home-made cakes which for me were a real treat. Otherwise, food parcels were not allowed. Most of our conversation concerned family matters and, sometimes, I told them little incidents of prison life. A month after my trial, my wife gave birth to another son, our third. From the beginning, we agreed that it would be better if she did not bring the children to visit me and to this we stuck throughout. These visits, though I would not have wanted to do without them, were a considerable psychological strain on all of us and always left a feeling of great sadness at the thought of the happiness that had been destroyed. Fortunately, both my wife and my mother, apart from sustaining each other, met with much kindness and support from all their friends and relatives and this, to some extent, helped to lighten their burden. Most people showed themselves from their best side.

It was clear to me from the very beginning that if I wanted to escape, I had first of all to create the firm impression all round that I had no intention of doing so. This was no easy task. Every one, from the Governor down, seemed to assume that anybody with such a heavy sentence could not possibly resign himself to it and was bound to make at least an attempt to escape. One prison officer even fell into the habit, whenever he saw me, of asking me whether the escape would be soon now. As time went on and nothing happened, he seemed to be genuinely disappointed that I had not yet gone. Still, I think I can fairly claim that when I eventually did go, it came as a great surprise to almost every one. The authorities and inmates alike had come to believe that I had settled down, resigned myself to my sentence and decided to make the best of prison life. This was to a large extent true, but it did not necessarily exclude plans for an escape.

The most important thing I felt was to try and keep mentally and physically fit. I saw no point in wasting my energy in attempting to beat the prison system, which anyway couldn't be done. Instead, I resolved, right from the beginning, to go along with it and preserve my strength and faculties, so that when an opportunity came to escape, I would be in a position to seize it.

This attitude, incidentally, earned me the goodwill of the staff. I was little trouble to them and no trouble means less work, something most people appreciate. A lot of prisoners take their bitterness out on the prison officer and reserve all their pent-up hatred and resentment for him. This is as unreasonable as taking your resentment out on the prison wall. The officer is only its human counterpart and as little responsible. I found them, on the whole, reasonable men and fair, doing a difficult job with restraint and tact. Some of them were even kind and genuinely tried to help a prisoner if he had run into trouble or had domestic difficulties. Only a few were clearly sadists and, had the regulations allowed, would gladly have ill-treated us. But they were exceptions. In my relations with the staff, I was always distant but polite. We got along with the least friction – an important factor if you have to serve a long sentence.

With most of the prisoners I got on well. I had expected that, at first, I might encounter a certain amount of bad feeling. Professional criminals tend to hold extreme conservative views which is, perhaps, not surprising if one bears in mind the large stake they have in free enterprise and private property. I didn't think these people would be particularly well disposed towards me. To my surprise, the contrary proved to be the case. There exists in prison a strict hierarchy with big-time criminals, such as bank robbers, fraudulent businessmen and confidence tricksters somewhere at the top. I now found myself because of the length of my sentence and the nature of my crime belonging to this prison aristocracy. Most people looked upon me as a political prisoner in spite of the British government's position that no such category exists in Britain.

Because of, perhaps, the importance of dissent in their history and the long struggle for civil and religious liberties, English people are inclined to show respect for the convictions of others, if they feel these are sincerely held. They may not share them, indeed disapprove of them and severely punish the actions which may spring from them, but they still respect the person who holds them. This is, I think, a very admirable quality which, as experience has shown me, is not a myth but a fact, reflected in the attitude of my fellow inmates, the prison staff and various people I came in contact with after my trial.

In a small way, I was able on my part to help several of my fellow prisoners. I listened to their stories, the accounts of their crimes, their encounters with the 'law' and their family troubles. Many of them were not very good at expressing their thoughts on paper, so I was able to help them by drafting their Home Office petitions if they wanted their case reviewed, became eligible for parole or to be transferred to another prison for family reasons. Many inmates, I found, wrote petitions only to vent their grievances against the authorities and insisted that invective and disparaging remarks be included. I refused to do this and asked them what precisely they wanted: to get if off their chest or to run a reasonable chance of having their petition granted.

Another way I could help was to keep tobacco for people. In prison tobacco is the accepted currency to pay for all sorts of services, from having one's cell cleaned out by another inmate, one's uniform pressed by a man working in the laundry, or real steak and chips provided by somebody working in the kitchen. One young American hippy, who was in for drug offences, earned tobacco by writing pornographic stories, tailor-made to the tastes of his customers. As a result, a great deal of tobacco smuggling was going on especially during visits. The prison authorities tried to counter this by frequent searches both of persons and cells. As it was known that I didn't smoke and didn't purchase any tobacco in the canteen, I was often asked by people to keep their surplus tobacco for them in my cell. Later, when after five years in the canvas shop, I was made the manager of the prison canteen and had control of the stock of tobacco which was sold there, I was able to keep larger surplus quantities. I did this by simply adding these to the stock in the shop which was never searched. Thus I became the prison's banker. I think my uncle in Cairo would have enjoyed the irony of this.

As is only to be expected in prison, I came up against some pretty nasty characters, but I also met a number of people with sterling qualities; courage, mental toughness and selflessness. The people I enjoyed talking to most were the conmen and fraudulent businessmen who were mostly highly intelligent and exceedingly amusing people with rich funds of stories. In the course of time I made some very good friends whom I shall always remember with affection.

Five years of close association with criminals of all kinds has brought me to the conviction that they are no more to blame for being in prison than are patients for being in a hospital ward. In a way, it was an experience which confirmed my belief in the absence of free will and in the truth of St Paul's words in Chapter 7 of the Epistle to the Romans, v. 19–21: 'For the good that I would I do not; but the evil which I would not, that I do. Now if I do that I would not, it is no more I that do it, but sin that dwelleth in me. I find then a law, that, when I would do good, evil is present with me.'

It seems to me, therefore, that the first reason why the present system meets with so little success in doing what it is meant to do, i.e. to punish, to deter (I consider these two notions to be, in practice, the same) and to reform, is based on a wrong concept of the human mind. The second reason is that it is designed to deal with large groups of prisoners and not with individuals.

Conditions 'inside' are such that prisons are a recruiting ground for further crime. Many inmates, because of their bitterness and the lessons they have learned in prison, are a greater danger to society when they leave prison than when they come in. This is not surprising when one comes to think of it. Imagine a hospital in which all the patients, irrespective of their disease or injury, whether it be cancer, cholera, pneumonia, appendicitis or a broken leg, are all put in the same ward and given the same treatment, say, a strong dose of purgatives. Nobody would expect many of the patients so treated to leave the hospital cured. The mast majority of them will carry their disease back into society and may well have been infected with new ones. Yet that is how the prison system works.

What then is the answer? Humanity over the last two hundred years and, especially, over the last fifty years, has made momentous discoveries about the Universe in which we live, discoveries which have had a far reaching effect on our way of life and our attitude towards it. Until recently, in contrast, comparatively little research was undertaken of that other Universe – no less mysterious – that lies within each of us.

I believe that, as our knowledge about this inner universe grows, a point will be reached when yet another breakthrough will enable the old penal system to be discarded and a new one adopted. The most outstanding feature of such a system will be, I should imagine, its prophylactic rather than its remedial aspect. Much time will be needed, much more knowledge acquired before this point is reached and society will be willing to assign the necessary funds to carry out the research, train the staff and build the institutions which will make it possible to treat offenders individually in the same way as mental patients are increasingly being treated today.

Meanwhile, until that time comes, there is no alternative but to carry on with the present system. The wrong answer must remain better than no answer for no answer is tantamount to society giving up the very function for which it was instituted. Whatever its faults, prison acts undoubtedly as a deterrent and as such is a real factor influencing many, though not all, people's behaviour.

I am sadly aware as I write this that my escape has been the immediate cause of a serious worsening of the conditions in which inmates, and especially those among them who have been sentenced to very long terms, are kept and that the picture painted here is no longer true. I am deeply sorry about this.

The authorities panicked and had recourse to the measures which defeat the declared purpose of the prison system, the reform of the criminal. Though it is true that fewer inmates now manage to escape, their existence in many gaols, to quote *The Times*, 'has become an affront to human dignity'.

To keep my mind in working condition, I resumed my Arabic studies, which my arrest had abruptly interrupted. I asked if I could avail myself of the possibility, open to prisoners with the necessary qualifications, to study for an Honours degree at London University.

This request was granted by the prison authorities. I think they were rather glad of this initiative. They were faced with the problem of keeping me in a reasonably normal state of mind while I was in their care. It was a long term project and when they saw, as the years went by, that I was taking my studies seriously and passing each year the required examinations, this became an important factor in bringing them round to the view that I had no intention of escaping.

The system of Yoga exercises, which I had already been practising a number of years, helped enormously to keep me physically fit. I did them every evening before going to bed and they ensured that I had a good night's sleep. One evening I was standing on my head when the night watchman peeped through the spy-hole to see if all was well before turning off the light. He must have been rather taken aback to see me in this unusual position for he asked me with some alarm in his voice if I was all right. When I assured him I was, he shuffled away muttering, 'Well, I suppose that's what you can expect from a man who is doing forty-two years.'

Prison food is very starchy. The bulk of it is porridge, bread, potatoes and dough. Combined with the lack of exercise it can easily lead to overweight, especially at my age. So I watched it carefully and accustomed myself to eat very little. I found this régime suited me. Apart from a short period when I suffered badly from boils, I was never ill all the time I was in prison. I even stopped having the bad colds which outside had always plagued me in spring and autumn.

So I cannot say that I suffered any mental or physical damage as a result of my sojourn in Wormwood Scrubs. I can even claim that the experience of prison life, by giving me a new insight into human nature, broadened my horizons and rounded out my personality.

When I now think back on my life in the Scrubs, it seems to me as if all that time I was wrapped in a dense fog which, like cotton wool, deadened all the sensations and isolated me from the joys and satisfactions of ordinary life, but also from its jolts and stresses and reduced everything to one long, grey monotony. Every day was the exact replica of the previous day and formed the exact pattern for the next one. The experience of five years could be compressed in one day and that of one day extended over five years. Though Wormwood Scrubs is located in West London, life inside is so different, so disconnected from the life that goes on all around its high walls that it might just as well be situated on another planet. In my mind, I did not leave England in December 1966, as was actually the case, but in May 1961 when I first entered Wormwood Scrubs, that other Universe.

Chapter Eleven

I had then adapted myself well to prison life and worked out for myself an existence which I found bearable and which, I felt, I could keep up for a long time. In many ways I looked upon myself as a monk in a contemplative order, a calling I, at certain moments in my life, had thought of following. Yet not for a moment had I given up my intention of attempting to escape. The sentence was such that it became almost a question of honour to challenge it. Moreover, I looked upon myself as a political prisoner and as such, like a POW, had a duty to escape.

I had no illusions about the KGB being able to help in this. I fully realised that they could not run the risk of a major international scandal if something went wrong and it was discovered that they had been involved. Besides, it would have been very difficult for them to establish contact with me. I had therefore no choice but to rely on my own resources.

All the time, I was on the look out for people, both inside and outside the prison, who would be prepared and able to help me. I well realised that without such help, it could not be done. Even if I managed to get over the wall by myself, where would I go to and what would I do? I needed friends who could hide me while the hunt was on and later smuggle me out of the country. The smuggling out presented possibly the most difficult part of the operation. England is an island and far from easy to get out of. Without dedicated friends with resources at their disposal it could hardly succeed. Before I got out of the prison I had to be absolutely sure that I had somewhere to go and a good chance of getting away to a country where I was certain to find sanctuary. I could not afford to be recaptured. I would not get a second chance.

Sometime in May 1962, I think it was, I met two members of the Committee of 100, Michael Randle and Pat Pottle, who were both serving an eighteen months sentence for organising peace demonstrations at a USAF base in Wethersfield. It so happened that both of them attended the same Musical Appreciation class and English Literature course as I. These were organised by the Tutor, Mr Sloan, a kind, energetic, but slightly fussy, Irishman, who was in charge of the prison education system. This system included classes in a whole range of subjects from woodwork, bookbinding and drawing to classes for people who could not read or write. They were held after working hours and attended by inmates from both C and D Halls. I enjoyed these classes very much as they enabled me to listen to good music and interesting lectures on literature and meet people with the same tastes of whom one finds relatively few in prison. From the very beginning there was a good rapport between us. We all three considered ourselves political prisoners, had all three been sentenced under the Official Secrets Act, been prosecuted by the same Attorney-General and defended by the same QC, Jeremy Hutchinson. This gave us a great deal in common. It is true, that they in no way approved of what I had done— they condemned spying in general—and made no secret of this. But they thought the sentence I had been given vicious and inhuman, to use their words, and had a great deal of sympathy for me. We continued to meet regularly and soon a friendship sprang up between us. On one occasion when no one else was in earshot they offered to help me in any way they could if I ever thought of escaping. I was much moved by this generous and unexpected offer and said that if I could work out a sound plan and needed their help I would certainly get in touch. Shortly afterwards they were released so we had no time to make any definite arrangements. The years passed, but they did not forget me and every year sent me a Christmas card. I, in turn did not forget them and their offer. They seemed to me the ideal people to help me, not only because they had offered to do so and I could trust them, but they were activists with experience of organising anti-government demonstrations and actions and with a large number of contacts in left-wing circles. To begin with, however, I needed someone who could establish contact with them and act as go-between and make the necessary arrangements.

The man I was looking for to do this had to have initiative, courage and single-mindedness to see the job through. He had to be willing to do it and to end his sentence in the not too distant future, otherwise there would be obviously no point in it. Above all, he had to be a man I could trust not to go to the authorities and give the game away, irrespective of whether he agreed to help or not.

During the years I was in the Scrubs, I looked at various people from this angle. Though some possessed a few, only one combined all these qualities, Sean Bourke. He possessed one other great advantage. He had attended the same literature course as Michael Randle, Pat Pottle and I and knew them both well. They would trust him.

Sean Bourke and I started our life in prison at roughly the same time and I got to know him quite early on. We used to walk together during exercise and I liked listening to his stories. He had typical Irish charm and he talked well. In colourful details, he would describe his boyhood in a small Irish town and his years at a boys reformatory, run by monks, who looked upon the stick as the most important principle of education.

Sean was a good-looking, rather heavily built man, who gave the impression of being placid and easy-going. When one got to know him well, one discovered that this rather stolid exterior hid an intelligent and highly imaginative personality, with a strong sense of the dramatic, an ability to dissemble, an obsessive pride and a deep-rooted hatred of anyone in authority. He was in prison for sending a bomb to a police-man who in the course of his duties had wrongfully voiced a suspicion that Sean had an illicit relationship with a boy. Most people would have shrugged this off or looked for some other form of redress. Not Sean. He manufactured a bomb, wrapped it in a parcel and sent it off by post. When the policeman opened it, the bomb exploded and only by a miracle did not kill him. The operation was carefully planned and skilfully carried out. But for a small, though vital, oversight it could never have been proven against him, though of course he came immedi-ately under suspicion.

Sean was coming to the end of his eight year sentence and would soon appear before the hostel board. He had been a highly successful editor of the prison magazine, a job for which he had shown a natural ability. He had become a trusted prisoner, a blue-band, and stood a very good chance of being accepted for the hostel. This meant that for the last nine months of his sentence he would work in a normal civilian job outside, and only sleep in the hostel, attached to the prison. I decided that the time had come to approach him.

On one of our regular walks, I put my proposal to him. He at once agreed to help. I suggested that he might wish to think it over for a few days first. But he said at once that he had already made up his mind and was determined to see it through; it was a wonderful chance I offered him. He hated authority, still had an important account to settle with the police, and this was a hoped for opportunity to get his own back on them. He liked me and had always considered the sentence I had been given monstrous. Nothing would give him greater satisfaction than to help me get away.

We immediately started planning. The first requirement was good communication. The hostel was located in the prison and was in process of enlargement. The work was carried out by prisoners from D Hall and it was not difficult to find among them someone willing to carry messages. For greater safety, we decided to ask a friend, whom we both liked and trusted, to act as cut-out.

A few weeks later Sean appeared before the hostel board and passed with flying colours. One afternoon in the beginning of November 1965, we said goodbye to each other and he was on his way. The first part of the operation had started.

As soon as he was in the hostel and free to move about London till 10 o'clock in the evening, Sean contacted Michael and Pat. They both agreed at once to help, first by raising a small sum of money, essential for buying a get-away car, renting a flat to hide and other sundry expenses. The final cost of the operation, from start to finish, amounted, I heard later, to some £800.

Sean kept me informed of developments by sending messages through the cut-out. This was dangerous. Sean enjoyed writing—his ambition was to become a writer—and he had little sense of security. Indeed, as we discovered later, he had a foolhardy streak in him. His letters, though colourful and entertaining, would have hopelessly compromised the escape, had they fallen into the wrong hands.

This nearly happened when another prisoner received in error a missive intended for me. The other fellow, however, proved to be a true friend. Although he most certainly could have benefited by giving me away to the authorities, he passed the letter to me and kept quiet, for which I was most grateful.

Sean hit upon a brilliant idea. He had now some money to work with and from this he bought two walkie-talkie sets. The one for me he managed to smuggle in by handing it to our cut-out during a concert party in which he took part. At that time he was still living in the prison hostel.

By then, I had already been in charge of the prison canteen several months, which was located in a cell converted into a shop. As I had to work there for stock-taking, book-keeping and the ordering and taking delivery of new supplies, I had the keys of this cell. It was, therefore, an ideal place to hide the walkie-talkie set, all the more so as it was hardly every searched. I am sure I would have found a good hiding place, anyway, even if I had not been manager of the shop. Only this simplified matters considerably. It has been suggested that my appointment as manager of the prison canteen represented a relaxation of the security conditions under which I was held. This is a misconception. On the contrary, it enforced those conditions since, as a result, I never left D Hall and was in the constant view of the officers on duty at the central desk to which both my own cell and the one which served as the shop were quite close.

The night after the walkie-talkie set had been smuggled in, we used it for the first time. I was lying in bed with my back to the door and had the set concealed under the blankets while talking into it. Had the night watchman suddenly switched on the light and looked in through the spy-hole he would have noticed nothing unusual.

At eleven o'clock, as agreed, I went on the air with the call sign. A few moments later Sean came through, loud and clear. I had to turn the set down to its lowest volume. Reception was perfect and that first time we talked well into the night. Apart from its immense usefulness, it was a wonderful experience to communicate once again completely freely with someone in the outside world, to which Sean, though only some fifty yards away in the hostel, to all intents and purposes now belonged.

After that first long talk, we communicated regularly once a week, usually on Saturday nights when most hostellers were away. One Sunday lunchtime, after we had talked at length the previous night, a young man came into my cell and closed the door carefully behind him. He looked worried and excited. In a hoarse voice he whispered to me, 'George, for God's sake be careful. I heard everything.'

'What do you mean?' I asked.

'I heard you and Sean talking on my radio last night. I heard every word you were saying. It was as clear as a bell.'

'But that is not possible,' I said.

'I can assure you it is. You want to be careful with that thing. I had been listening to the messages of the squad cars and was just going to switch off. I was still twiddling the knob when I suddenly came upon this conversation. At first I thought it was a play, but then I recognised your voices. I could hardly believe it.'

'Well, I am glad it was you and not somebody else who heard it,' I said, still very worried.

'I bet you are. A lot of people here listen to the police messages and might quite easily stumble on your wavelength. I lay awake all night worrying that somebody else might have heard you too, who might give you away. Of course, I won't say a word to anyone, I promise you, but do be careful.'

I thanked him for having warned me and said I would let Sean know. He left wishing us the best of luck.

We had been extraordinarily lucky that it had been this man who overheard us. He worked on the hotplate, serving food and cleaning plates and was therefore like me, the shop manager, all day in D Hall while most of the other inmates were in the various workshops. We naturally often chatted together and I got to know him quite well. He was a young man from the East End who was doing 'life' for having killed a man in a brawl. As a 'lifer' the length of his sentence depended, in practice, entirely on the decision of the Home Office. Denouncing an escape of this kind would have undoubtedly earned him the gratitude of the authorities. He knew this, yet his honour forbade him to take advantage of the knowledge he had so inadvertently gained. He never breathed a word to anyone.

Sean had assured me that the set had quite a different wavelength from those of an ordinary radio. This was so, but it turned out to be fairly close to the wavelength used by the police. What to do now— revert to letters? Anyway, that had its own risks. The best thing was to reduce the number of contacts to the absolute essential, remain on the air as short a time as possible, and trust that our luck would hold out. This is what we did.

Soon afterwards Sean was discharged from the hostel. He took a room not far from the prison, but it proved to be out of range of the walkie-talkie, so late at night he went out on Wormwood Scrubs Common and called me from there. We could hear each other only very faintly; he had to crawl so close that he was almost lying under the prison wall before reception was good enough to carry on a conversation.

Then three policemen were shot in Braybrook Street, just next to the prison. For nearly three weeks there was so much police activity in the area that Sean could not come out on the Common to make contact.

Meanwhile preparations for the escape were coming to an end. Sean had bought a second-hand car and after much searching had acquired a small flat about five minutes walk from the prison where I would hide to start with. From thin, nylon rope he had manufactured a ladder and ingeniously reinforced the struts with knitting needles, so that they would remain taut as I climbed. In the middle of September he gave up his room and his job at the factory, and returned to Ireland, ostensibly for good.

Three weeks later, he came back under a different name and took up residence in the new flat. He was posing as a free-lance journalist. Everything was set now and we fixed the date of the escape for Saturday the 22nd of October. Zero hour was to be 6.15 P.M. At that time it was almost dark and most of the prisoners would be out of the Hall, watching the weekly film show.

On the advice of our friend, the cut-out, an expert at breaking and entering, we had chosen for my exit one of the tall windows which take up nearly the whole wall at each end of the hall. They look like church windows, matching the pseudo-Gothic style of the building, and like church windows are divided into a number of thick glass panels set in cast-iron frames. Each second panel swivels open to act as an air vent. The panels are too narrow for a man to pass through but if one removes the iron bar between the fixed panel and the one that swivels, the space becomes large enough for the passage of a man of my size. A further advantage was that if one stepped out of the panel on the second landing there was only a short drop of about three feet on to the roof of a covered passageway from which, by hanging down from the gutter, it was again a short drop to the ground. From there, I had only to run some fifteen yards to reach the wall. One of the small turrets at each corner of the hall conveniently marked the exact spot where Sean should throw the ladder.

On the Thursday before the operation we had a final conversation. We had chosen for this the same hour as the one fixed for the getaway. Sean was sitting, as he would be on the night, in his car parked opposite the side gate of Hammersmith Hospital, in Artillery Row, the narrow road which separates it from the prison. He had his set concealed in a bunch of flowers to create the impression that he was waiting to visit someone in the hospital. I had gone for the purpose to the cell of my cut-out on one of the landings, from where I called Sean.

We both confirmed that all was well at our respective ends and that the operation could go ahead as planned. As an extra precaution we decided to make contact once more at lunch time on Saturday to make sure that there were no last minute hitches. Before breaking off contact, Sean sang to me in his melodious voice 'I'll walk beside you'.

It was high time. There had been a spectacular escape from the Hall earlier in the summer when six prisoners had got out together. Several of them had a record of violence. There had been an outcry in the press as a result of which the authorities had started taking extra security measures. The tall windows at each end of the hall were being reinforced with thick steel netting. Those on A and B Hall had already been fitted and they were now working on C Hall. Another week or so and it would be the turn of D Hall. A good thing that, as good bureaucrats, they did the job in alphabetical order.

Prison officers were now permanently stationed in booths at each end of the wall. From that vantage point they could observe the whole length of two walls. We had worked out, however, that if they spotted me and gave the alarm there was sufficient time for us to get away before the patrols could reach the wall.

We had planned the whole escape in such a way that there was no need to use any violence and I and Pat and Michael had expressly stipulated that Sean should carry no arms or resort to force in any circumstances.

At one o'clock on Saturday afternoon we had a final talk. There had been no last minute hitches, the film show was on that day and we could go ahead as planned. The glass in the fixed panel in the corner near the landing floor had been removed the day before. It had been easy for it was already cracked and nobody had noticed it. All that remained to be done at the last minute was to remove the cast-iron bar.

Many inmates used the free Saturday afternoon to clean out their cells and usually hung their blankets over the steel railings on the landings to give them an airing. There was nothing extraordinary, therefore, that a couple of blankets were hanging over the railings just in front of the panels through which I had to pass, effectively shielding them from the view of the two prison officers who were on duty at the centre desk in the hall.

Tea, the last meal in the Scrubs, is at half past three on Saturdays. At half past four the greater part of the prisoners filed out to the cinema, attendance at which was voluntary. The Hall became quiet and almost deserted. At the opposite end a group of prisoners were sitting round the television. Here and there at the tables in the body of the hall men were playing cards. One of the two officers on duty was watching television, the other sat reading at the centre desk. This was the most peaceful hour of the week.

Time seemed to pass very slowly. I wandered down to the television. All-in wrestling, I watched it for a while and started back to my cell. In passing I exchanged a few words about the match with the prison officer who stood watching at the back. I decided to have a bath. It would have a soothing effect and I would be clean, whatever happened. In the showers, I took my time and chatted to a few fellows there. On my way back to my cell, I made a mug of tea. The officer at the desk had gone into the pantry now to play chess. Another half-hour to go. I looked out of my cell window and to my joy noticed that the dull afternoon had turned into a fine drizzle. It would soon be dusk and visibility bad. This was more than we had hoped for.

Slowly I drank my tea and read the paper. Time to get ready, I put on a pair of gym shoes and took the walkie-talkie set out of its hiding place, tucked it into my sweater, keeping it in place under my arm. A last look round my cell, taking leave of the objects I had grown fond of, and I stepped out. The hall presented the same peaceful scene. One officer was still watching television, the other still in the pantry. It was 6.15. From my friend's cell, I called up Sean. After a short while he answered. He was in position at the other side of the wall.

'All set?' I asked.

'Yes, fine,' came the answer.

'Can we go ahead with knocking out the bar?'

'Yes, you can proceed.'

My friend, who had been anxiously waiting beside me, immediately went down. In exactly three minutes he was back again. I thought he must have come up against an unexpected snag and hadn't been able to remove the bar.

'Something went wrong?' I asked. 'You are back so quickly.'

'No, everything is fine, you can go ahead. That bar was so rusty that one kick was enough for it to give way.'

I called Sean again who answered at once.

'The bar is out. Are you ready for me?'

'What already? Yes, you can come now, I am ready for you,' came Sean's voice.

I tucked the set into my jumper, shook hands with my friend, who wished me luck, and walked quickly to the second landing without encountering anyone. It was only just in time. The first cinema-goers were just beginning to pour in through the centre gate, filling the hall with their clamour. They were unexpectedly early, the film must have been a short one. Soon they would be stamping and shouting down the landings on their way to their cells. I slid through the opening in the window and felt with my feet for the roof of the passage way. It was the work of a moment. I carefully let myself down the tiles, slippery from the rain which, now no longer a drizzle, was pouring down. It was almost completely dark. I got hold of the edge of the gutter, hung on to it and dropped easily to the ground. I found myself now in a small recess formed by the passage way and the jutting turret at the corner of the hall. Pressed against the wall it was unlikely that any passing patrol could see me, even if the weather was not driving them to shelter in a porch. As soon as I was down, I got out my set and called up Sean. He answered almost immediately.

'I am out now and ready for the ladder,' I reported.

'Hang on just a sec, I am up against an unexpected snag,' he replied in an agitated voice and went off the air.

I stood in the dark recess and waited. The rain was coming down heavily and in a moment I was drenched. Time passed and nothing happened. No ladder. The walkie-talkie remained silent. I called repeatedly, but got no reply. Had he got into trouble and made a rapid getaway? Or had he got cold feet at the last moment? It was unlike him, but one never knew.

Inside I heard the bell ordering everybody to their cells to be locked up and counted. The noise of shouting and running men rose to a crescendo. It must have been ten to seven. There was little time left now before they would discover I was missing. The walkie-talkie remained silent. Sean must have gone. I began to get visions of Parkhurst. There was no point in trying to get back into the hall. I decided to wait.

Then suddenly loud and clear in came Sean's voice again. I gave a deep sigh of relief. I had almost given up hope of ever hearing it again. 'Sorry, there was a hitch, I will throw it soon now.'

'Please, hurry,' I shouted with desperation in my voice, 'Time is very short.'

'Just one more sec,' he replied and there was another long silence. I stood in tense expectation, ready to rush to the wall as soon as the ladder came over. But nothing happened. Only the noise of the rain and the banging of doors inside as cells were being locked. It must have been about five minutes, though it seemed to me an eternity, before Sean's voice came through once more, firm and certain this time.

'It is coming now!' The next moment in the light of the arc lamps I saw the ladder flash over the wall, writhe for a moment and hang still. It looked incredibly thin and fragile, but the instant I saw it I knew that nothing now would stop me. I pushed the walkie-talkie set into my soaking wet sweater and, bending low, rushed to the wall. I grabbed the ladder and started up. It seemed amazingly easy. In a moment, unseen by the officers in the observation booths at the end of the wall, but watched, I am sure, by several pairs of eyes bursting with excitement from the cell windows, I reached the top of the wall. As I climbed astride it I looked down and saw a car and, beside it, looking up at me with anxious expectation, Sean.

'Let yourself drop,' he shouted, his voice high with tension. 'Hurry.' I moved along the wall to avoid falling against the car and lowered myself till I was hanging from both hands. As I let go, I saw Sean move right underneath me to try and break my fall. It flashed through my mind that if I dropped on top of him, I might injure him and then where would we be? At the same time, I made a move in mid-air to avoid him. He stepped aside, but as I fell I glanced off against him and landed badly. Through the impact my head swung forward and hit the gravel. At the same time, I felt a sharp pain in my arm. For a moment I was dazed, but Sean pulled me up and pushed me into the back of the car. He jumped into the front seat and started the engine. The blood was streaming down my face and blinding me. I got out my handkerchief and wiped my face. Just as we pulled out, a car with its headlights full on swung into the narrow road. We had to wait till it turned into the gate of the hospital, before we could drive off. If it had been a moment earlier, its occupants would have seen me drop from the wall.

We reached the end of the road and turned into the main stream of traffic. I could feel Sean's tenseness. He had put on a pair of glasses as a disguise. These had got wet and now, in the car, were beginning to steam up. He started to curse and bumped into the car ahead. We were moving fairly slowly in the traffic and the bumpers, fortunately, did not lock. But the driver turned into the kerb to look at the damage and must have been indignant that we did not do the same. We got to the traffic light which just jumped to red. It looked as if Sean was going to drive through. 'Take it easy, Sean,' I said. 'Just take it easy and we will be all right. Everything is going fine.' Sean had taken his glasses off and was calming down now. Soon we turned into a quiet, suburban avenue. A few more turns and the car pulled up. Meanwhile I had got into a raincoat and put on a hat which were lying on the back seat. We got out, crossed the road and walked up a street of three-storeyed houses. At one of them we stopped. Sean got out a key and let us in. We had not passed a soul in the street, shiny with rain. We walked down a long, dark corridor and with another key Sean opened a door at the end of it. We entered a brightly lit room. The curtains were drawn and a gas fire was burning. In a corner stood a large television set. The room seemed homely and secure to me after the drabness of the prison and the adventures of the last hour. We looked at each other and shook hands.

'We have done it! We have done it!' we exclaimed almost simultaneously, moved by the same emotion of immense relief and triumph.

So far so good. But a lot remained to be done. Sean said he was going off again, straight away, to get rid of the car. He would be back in about an hour and a half. Before he left, he showed me a set of civilian clothes which he had bought for me to change into. He left and I locked the door behind him. I took off my wet prison clothes and washed my face. It looked a terrible mess. But after I had carefully cleaned the wound, it appeared that the damage, though extensive, was only superficial. Anyway, it made a good disguise.

I looked at my left wrist which was hurting. My hand was bent at a strange angle and beginning to swell. Obviously, the wrist was broken.

I changed into the civilian clothes and looked at myself in the mirror. It was really true then, I was no longer in prison. It was an extraordinary feeling. I could hardly believe it. But the most dangerous and difficult part lay still ahead. The alarm must have been sounded by now and the hunt was on. It was 7.30.

When Sean returned, it was nearly nine o'clock. He had driven round for a while and finally left the car parked in a street in Kilburn. On his way home, he had called Michael and Pat and told them the good news. They were elated. He had bought a bottle of brandy. He poured out a drink for us and switched on the television. We sat down to watch the news. My bearded photograph appeared on the screen as the announcer read out 'High drama in West London' and went on to report the discovery of the escape. All ports and airfields were being watched. Iron-curtain embassies had been put under special surveillance. Ships from those countries in the Port of London were being searched. Police teams with dogs were combing the area of the prison. The hunt was on in a big way. I was wondering whether my family was watching television and how this news would burst upon them.

Sean went off to the kitchen to fry two enormous pork chops and heat an apple pie. While we had supper, he told me what had happened that afternoon on his side of the wall.

Shortly after he had given me the go-ahead to get out of the hall, a man on a bike with a large German Shepherd dog on a leash had cycled past and at the end of Artillery Row had checked the doors of a sports pavilion on the Common. He was, evidently, some sort of security guard. On his way back, he had got off his bike and stood watching Sean, who was sitting in his car with a pot of chrysanthemums on his knee. He just stood there and did not go away. Sean thought that the only way to get rid of him was to drive off and come back again later. He had done this and on the way had nearly got mixed up in a heavy traffic jam in Hammersmith. Fortunately, a helpful policeman had waved him on just in time and he was back near the prison about a quarter of an hour later. The man with the dog had gone and Sean decided the coast was now clear.

He had just answered my call and was about to get out of the car to throw the ladder when another car had driven up and pulled up along-side the wall, facing Sean's car. Inside was a couple who had apparently no intention of getting out and were soon engaged in a petting session. Sean, knowing I was now desperately waiting outside D Hall for the ladder to come over, could do nothing. At his wits' end, he decided to try and stare the couple away. He turned his headlights full on and sat stolidly looking at them. It took some time, but, in the end, they got embarrassed and drove off.

He was just getting ready to get the ladder out of the boot and climb on the roof to throw it when headlight after headlight began to swing into the road. Visiting hour at Hammersmith Hospital was just starting. He realised that we did not have another moment to lose and resolved to go ahead, come what may. Making use of a momentary lull, he climbed on the roof of the car and threw the ladder.

That evening we sat talking until late into the night. Though exhausted, we both felt an extraordinary elation and could not decide to bring this remarkable day to an end. At last we went to bed but had a restless night. Sean kept on muttering, 'Christ, we have done it,' and turning on his mattress. My head and my wrist were hurting and I was too excited to sleep.

When I woke up next morning, my wrist was swollen and hurting badly. I had little doubt that it was broken and something had to be done about it. Sean said he would get in touch with Michael and Pat. Perhaps they could get hold of a doctor who could set it. Otherwise, he suggested, we should have to go to the casualty ward of a hospital. I didn't like this idea at all and hoped that another solution might be found. After breakfast, Sean went out to buy the Sunday newspapers. He came back half an hour later and said he was going to Michael's house and ask him to see if he could find a doctor. He brought a copy of every newspaper with him, all reporting the escape in big headlines and carrying large photographs of me.

Sean returned in the early afternoon with the news that our friends were trying hard to find a doctor who would be willing to help. This was a development which had not been foreseen and it was not particularly easy to find somebody as it was a Sunday and many people were away. He repeated his suggestion that we should go to a hospital to have the wrist set. This I was determined not to do, especially after seeing the newspapers with my photograph splashed all over their front pages. I preferred to carry on without it being set, if there was no other way out.

At seven o'clock in the evening, there was, at last, a telephone call from Michael saying that we could expect a visit within the next hour. When the doctor arrived, carrying a black bag and accompanied by Michael, there were no effusive greetings or any introductions. The doctor got down to business at once, looked at the wrist and confirmed that it was broken. He then made a short statement: 'The normal procedure is that you should go to hospital to have it set. However, I understand that for some reason or other you are allergic to hospitals. Therefore I consider it my duty to help you. This, I take it is understood?' he said, looking at me. 'Of course, I fully understand this and appreciate it very much,' I replied.

'I shall need some hot water for the plaster and newspapers to cover the table,' the doctor continued. The only newspapers we had were that morning's with my photograph on the front pages. The doctor pretended not to notice this and proceeded to set the wrist after having given me first an injection. Sean helped him by holding my arm in a firm grip. It was painful, but not as painful as I had expected. It took about five minutes to get it right and then he put on the plaster. Though the pain was not entirely gone, the arm felt much better now. The doctor gave us some sleeping tablets and then left, accompanied to the front door, by Michael. There was no mention of a fee.

While the doctor was still there Pat arrived, followed shortly afterwards by Michael's wife, Anne. She was an attractive young woman, tall and dark, who reminded me very much of my wife and whom I liked a lot right from the start. They had brought something to drink with them and now that we were amongst ourselves it turned into a bit of a celebration party, with Sean and me filling them in on the details of the escape.

One thing we decided that evening was that I should move as soon as possible to more secure accommodation. The flat we were now in was never to be more than a temporary hiding place, somewhere to go to straight from the prison, to be out of sight as soon as possible. Two days later, I moved to other accommodation. This proved equally temporary. What with the hue and cry following the escape, my new host and hostess were, not unnaturally, very nervous and we thought it was better, both for their peace of mind and ours, that I moved. Pat then suggested that the simplest solution would be if I stayed with him in his small bachelor flat in Hampstead. In the absence of any other viable alternative, this seemed, indeed, the best solution and the same evening Michael took me there in his car.

Before the week was out I was joined there by Sean. The police were looking for him and it had become too dangerous to remain living in the neighbourhood of the Scrubs, where he might easily run into somebody who knew him.

The abandoned car had been found and, from tyre marks near the wall and chrysanthemum leaves inside, it had been identified as the car used in the escape. Sean had bought it from a man who had been at the hostel with him, but who had not known what it was to be used for. So, simply by tracing the previous owner, the police discovered Sean was involved. It was as easy as that. His description appeared in the newspapers and Scotland Yard was now as eager to get him as it was to get me. This meant that our friends, instead of having one fugitive on their hands, now had to cope with two. What we didn't know, and learned much later, when Sean's book *The Springing of George Blake,* came out, was that Sean himself had telephoned the police to tell them where they could find the abandoned getaway car. Had we known this we would, of course, have been horrified and had he consulted us beforehand we would have turned down this suggestion as madness. Sean maintained that by doing so he had put the police firmly on his own trail and away from any peace activists with whom he had no known connections. This is a moot point. What was important in my opinion was not whether the police knew or did not know that Sean was involved, but that from the very beginning they got it into their head that the escape had been organised by the KGB and that, therefore, they were up against professionals with considerable resources at their disposal. This paralysed their efforts as they were, already beforehand, convinced that they didn't have a chance in hell of catching me. If you say to yourself that you have no hope of finding what you are looking for, you usually don't find it. I have a feeling that it never even occurred to the police that some of the 'Wethersfield six' might be involved. If it had, they would almost certainly have found me. Be this as it may, Sean would have saved himself and all of us much aggravation if he had not taken this rash step.

Once in Pat's flat, I felt much safer and the three of us got on well together. Pat was at work all day and when he came home in the evening he often brought something tasty back for supper and there were always new developments to discuss. From time to time, Michael and Anne would join us. They always brought a few bottles of wine and the evening turned into a little party though none of us, with the exception of Sean, drank very much. Sometimes the conversation turned into a political discussion. All my friends, though appreciating the ultimate aims of Communism, condemned its practice, the lack of individual freedom in Communist countries and the ruthlessness with which any dissent was crushed. They particularly asked me, were I to arrive safely in Moscow, to use my influence to obtain the release of two well-known dissident writers, Mr Daniel and Mr Siniavski, about whose fate they were deeply concerned. I promised to do this, but was not at all certain whether my influence, if any, would reach that far. In turn, I disagreed with my friends on the complete banning of the bomb. It was my conviction and still is, that if we have enjoyed forty-five years of peace in Europe this is entirely due to the nuclear parity between the two superpowers. If the bomb were abolished, assuming this were possible, it would only be a matter of time before a major world war broke out, a war which would then certainly turn into a nuclear war because each side would immediately start manufacturing the bomb and the side which got there first would use it before the other side was ready. The lengthy and bloody wars between Iran and Iraq and in Afghanistan, since, where the threat of nuclear bombs did not exist, have shown convincingly, in my opinion, that humanity is not yet ready to live in peace and that only the threat of a nuclear holocaust deters it from a major conflict. These discussions among us, though lively, never turned acrimonious.

The only worry we had during this period, apart, of course, from the constant strain of the danger of being discovered, was caused by Sean. It proved almost impossible to keep him indoors. Occasionally he would disappear during the day and return in a state which clearly indicated that the temptation of entering a pub had been too strong for him. This predilection for strong drink had been a side of his personality which I had, naturally, not been able to observe in prison conditions. Sean was, by nature, a hail-fellow-well-met type and we shuddered to think what remarks he might drop in conversation with a casual pub acquaintance, all the more so as he had no sense of caution and, deep inside him, was burning for everyone to know that it was he who had sprung George Blake from prison. Pat and I frequently remonstrated with him and for a while he would stay indoors, but never for very long. We would have been even more horrified had we known that, on one occasion, he actually walked into a police station to make sure that his photograph was on the board of wanted persons.

Shortly after our move to Hampstead, we began serious discussions on the next and most difficult part of the operation; how to get Sean and me out of Britain and where to go to. My friends had worked out a plan to turn me into an Indian or an Arab and leave the country on a forged passport. To make the disguise almost foolproof, I would temporarily have to change my skin pigmentation. This involved taking a drug called meladinin over a period of about six weeks, in conjunction with treatment under an ultra-violet lamp. They had purchased the lamp already and would get the drug through friends in medical circles. Sean was confident that he could procure a false passport through contacts in the underworld. Right from the beginning, this plan didn't inspire any confidence in me, though I didn't say so outright. I didn't fancy the idea very much of having my pigmentation changed. One could never be sure, after all, that one would revert to one's original colour again. As to the plan of getting a false passport through contacts in the under-world, that appealed to me even less. Fortunately, because of my inju-ries, it was not advisable to start the drug treatment at once. Meanwhile there was no harm in sitting, from time to time, under the ultra-violet lamp. Soon, to my great relief, the plan had to be abandoned altogether when it became clear that, once Sean was wanted by the police himself, it would be too dangerous for him to contact people in the underworld to obtain the passports.

It was at this point that the suggestion was made, I don't remember by whom, that I should try and get into the Soviet Embassy in Kensing-ton Gardens. It shouldn't be too difficult to get in through the back gardens and once there I could ask for asylum. This seemed to me a counsel of despair and I turned the suggestion down out of hand. I would only be a burden and an embarrassment to them. I didn't want to do a Cardinal Mindszenty. If it came to that I preferred to be a prisoner in Wormwood Scrubs where, at least, I would be doing my time rather than a prisoner in the Soviet Embassy and remain on the escape list.

My friends then hit upon the idea of concealing me in a false compart-ment in a car or van and driving me themselves to a safe country. This plan seemed to me to offer a much better chance of success and I welcomed it from the start. Pat and Michael lost no time and began at once to explore the practical problems involved and shortly afterwards purchased a Dormobile. Friends of Michael and Pat, who possessed the necessary skills, expressed their willingness to do the conversion work which consisted of building a compartment at the back of a small kitchen cupboard in the Dormobile.

The way the money problem was settled to pay for the van and other operational expenses is quite extraordinary in itself. At the time when Michael was already planning the escape, a young woman, whom he calls Bridget and who was a good family friend, approached him one day and asked him for advice. She had inherited some money from an aunt and wanted to donate it to a deserving cause. As a socialist, she did not believe in inherited wealth. Could he suggest a suitable project or organisation. He did not give an answer at once but, when the need arose, told her how the money might be used. She agreed at once and wrote out a cheque for the necessary amount.

The next question was where to go. At one time, I had thought of Egypt, but this was, obviously, too far and too complicated. Yugoslavia was nearer, but involved crossing many frontiers. Switzerland was out, in view of the close co-operation between SIS and the Sûreté. To me the solution seemed obvious; East Germany. It was the nearest safe country and I knew the situation in and around Berlin extremely well. It had one other great advantage. I knew that my friends wanted to avoid any contact with the authorities of a Communist country. This was a matter to which they attached great importance. They did not want that it could ever be said that they had acted from other than purely humanitarian motives and had been in the pay, worked on behalf of, or even been in contact with a Soviet Bloc government or organisation. The Berlin route would make any such contact completely unnecessary. I explained to them that they could drop me off on the autobahn, at some distance from the East German frontier post on the outskirts of Berlin. They could then drive on without me to West Berlin and arrive there before I contacted the East German frontier guards. As they were British and had a British registered vehicle and thus were citizens of one of the four occupying powers, the East German frontier guards had no right to search or question them and would let them through unhindered. This plan appealed to them and was at once adopted.

As Michael was the only person who had a valid driving licence, he would have to drive the van. His wife, Anne, at once volunteered to come too and they decided to take their two little boys, aged two and three, with them. That way, they argued, there would be less risk of arousing suspicion. When I heard this, I was put in a difficult position. Obviously, if the occupants of the vehicle were a family with small children this would greatly reduce the likelihood of searches and discovery. But could I burden my conscience with responsibility for the fate of this remarkable couple and their small children if they were caught smuggling me out of the country? I had already ruined the life of my own family. Could I now put another at risk? Was that not asking too much? For a long time, while preparations were already in hand, I worried about this and hesitated. In the end, my friends persuaded me that this was the safest way not only for me but for them as well.

Now the only problem that remained to be settled was Sean. He obviously could not remain in hiding indefinitely. If he tried to live normally in England under an assumed name the chances were great that sooner or later, and most likely sooner, because of his tendency to be rash, he would fall into the hands of the police. Shortly after it was discovered that he was involved in the escape, two Special Branch officers had been allowed to visit his mother in Ireland and question her. This pointed to full co-operation on the part of the Irish authorities with the British police. It seemed to us very doubtful whether he would find sanctuary in Ireland.

In these circumstances, though up to now this had never been en-visaged at all, I suggested that the best solution for everybody would be if he came to the Soviet Union with me.

I felt confident that my friends there would look after him and help him in every way they could. Sean, at first, resisted this suggestion and argued that he should return to Ireland. He felt sure that the Irish authorities would never extradite him to the British. Even if they did, we need not worry, he would never give away his friends. This we did not doubt, but, as I pointed out, if his interrogators injected him with a truth drug, he would not be able to hold anything back with the best will in the world. For Pat, Michael and Anne there was another compli-cation. As a matter of conscience, if Sean stood trial, could they simply stand by and see him take the rap and be sentenced to a long term of imprisonment on his own?

Eventually, Sean agreed to follow me to the Soviet Union and stay there for a while to allow time for the excitement to die down and the clues to go cold. He was never happy about this decision and accepted it only for the sake of our friends' safety. How to get him out? The idea of making a second journey with the van was rejected. Sean was much bigger and heavier built than I and we thought it unlikely that he could remain shut in a cramped, dark space for about eight to nine hours, the time the journey from London to Ostend would take. Since obtaining a false passport was also out, Pat suggested that his passport should be used with his photograph replaced by that of Sean. About a week after my safe arrival in East Berlin, Sean would leave by train for Paris and from there fly to Berlin. There he could cross unhindered through check-point Charlie into East Berlin with his British passport, make his way to the Soviet Headquarters in Karlshorst and report to the sentry at the gate. As soon as I arrived in East Berlin, I would make arrangements with the Soviet authorities so that they would be ready to receive him.

After some experiments on an out-of-date passport, Pat, who is a printer by profession, succeeded, with great skill, in changing the photograph on his passport and reproducing the embossment in such a way that it was impossible to detect with the naked eye.

When the conversion work on the van was completed, all was ready for the journey. The date of departure was fixed for Saturday the 17th of December. It was the Christmas season and there would be a lot of tourist traffic to the continent so it was hoped that controls might be more superficial. A week before, Michael had taken me for a trial run in the van. I crawled into the compartment, the floor of which was covered with a piece of foam rubber. I was quite comfortable there, if a little cramped and the moment I got into that space, I felt sure the operation was going to succeed.

We were booked for the midnight ferry from Dover to Ostend and at 6.30 on the appointed day, Michael and his family drove up to collect me. Before leaving, we all had a final supper together. I proposed a toast to our success, but found it difficult to find words to express my deep gratitude to these brave and exceptional men and women who put their liberty and happiness at risk to help me escape from prison, hide me and smuggle me out of the country. I said that when I arrived in Moscow I would have some difficulty in explaining to the Soviet authorities who they were and why they had chosen to help me. It seemed to me that only in England could people like this be found. If all that had happened in my life had been necessary in order to have known such people, even if for only a short time, I considered it all to have been well worth it.

We left immediately after supper. I climbed into the van after having said a fond farewell to Pat and *au revoir* to Sean. Just before I disappeared into the hiding space, Michael handed me a rubber hot-water bottle. On purpose, I had drunk hardly any liquid that day, but I would be in that space for nearly nine hours and I might need it. I wriggled to find the most comfortable position and then the compartment was closed, the drawer put in place and the bed folded down. Shortly after that, Anne came down with the children and put them at once to bed. Then we left.

At first I felt quite comfortable, but gradually my breathing became difficult and I got a choking feeling. I was sure it was the rubber hot-water bottle, the smell of which was becoming more and more overwhelming. It was, anyway, useless as in the cramped space I could not possibly have manoeuvred it in the right position. I had no idea how long we had been driving, but I felt I could not hold out much longer. I needed fresh air otherwise I would faint. Reluctantly I decided to knock, as we had arranged I should do in an emergency. At first, they didn't hear the knocking above the noise of the engine, but, at last, Michael pulled up. The children had first to be moved by Anne to the front seat and wrapped up in a blanket before Michael could open the compartment. I crawled out of the space feeling sick and retching. 'I need some air badly,' I said, handing the hot-water bottle to him. 'It is this that is the trouble.' I stumbled out of the van and at once began to feel better. We had stopped on a high, lonely stretch of road, some ten miles outside Dover and the cold breeze felt wonderful. After a short while, I felt sufficiently recovered to return to the compartment, this time without the hot-water bottle.

Soon we reached Dover and the tension mounted as we passed through the customs, before boarding the ferry. With bated breath I tried to follow what was going on from the noises outside and the movement of the van. We slowed down and then stopped. I heard a voice asking for passports. A moment later, I heard Michael say 'Thank you,' and then we slowly moved on again. Shortly afterwards, I felt a few bumps and realised we were driving on to the ferry. It was done. I had been successfully smuggled out of England and was now on Belgian territory. The most dangerous part of the operation was over.

On the ferry, Michael and Anne and the children had to leave the van and sit in the lounge during the sea journey. Then I heard orders being shouted and suddenly I realised we were underway. After the removal of the hot-water bottle, I hadn't felt any more discomfort, but now the need to relieve myself was beginning to become urgent. There was nothing for it but to hold out. The sea was calm and I did not suffer from seasickness. Then the engines stopped, we were no longer moving and I heard the passengers returning to their cars. We had arrived in Ostend. Michael and his family got in and cars were starting up. There was a long delay and then I felt the bumps, indicating we were driving off the ferry. Another short stop as Michael showed their passports to the Belgian customs man and we were on our way.

About half an hour later, when we were well out of Ostend, Michael stopped by the roadside. The children were moved to the front again and I was, at last, able to crawl out. I had been in my hiding place for eight and a half hours, apart from the short break on the Dover road.

Michael and Anne were both very relieved to see that I was all right. It had been so quiet that they feared I had died on them. It was early morning, but still dark. I got out of the van and had what must have been the longest pee in my life.

The rest of the journey was uneventful. While we were driving through Belgium, there was no particular need to hide and I sat in the seat behind Michael and Anne, chatting to them and the children who took it all in their stride and had shown no surprise when I had suddenly appeared from nowhere.

When we approached the Belgian-German border, I got into my hiding place once more. There was a perfunctory passport check and about a quarter of an hour later I was able to crawl out again. All that Sunday we drove through West Germany. It was a dull, rainy day. We had some trouble with the windscreen wipers, which a garage, where we stopped on the way, could not put right. So Anne and I had to take it in turn to operate them by hand whenever it was raining.

By about 8.30 that evening we approached the border between West and East Germany, near Helmstedt. Michael stopped and I got into my hiding space again. This was the last border to cross. It might well prove the most difficult one. A short stop at the West German check-point and then we entered East Germany. Here the delay was much longer. I could hear the back doors of the van being opened and German voices. They must be looking inside. I held my breath; but a moment later the doors were slammed to again and I heard Michael climbing into the driving seat. Then we were on our way again. The last stretch of the journey had started. To be on the safe side, we had arranged that I would stay in hiding till we had crossed the Elbe near Magdeburg. At last Michael stopped and let me out. We had made it. But where was the elation? We all felt tired after the strain of the long journey and the lack of sleep, especially Michael who had been driving almost non-stop for more than twenty-four hours. As we got nearer to the point where we had to part, Michael and Anne got more and more worried about my fate. The barbed wire, watchtowers and searchlights on the East German border had done nothing to raise their spirits. Had they rescued me from one prison to deliver me into another? I tried to put their minds at rest. I felt completely confident that all would be well, at any rate after I had succeeded in convincing the East German and local Soviet authorities who I was. This cheered them up a bit, but I could feel doubt lingering.

Then, suddenly, I recognised, in the distance, the lights of the East German check-point near Berlin. Our journey had come to an end. I told Michael to pull up and switch off his lights. It was nearly midnight. The children were fast asleep. I once more explained to them the formalities they would have to go through at the two check-points ahead and told them where to turn off at the end of the autobahn in West Berlin to get to the Kurfürstendamm, where I had recommended a hotel. Then the time had come to say goodbye. With a heavy heart, I took my leave from Michael and Anne and, with them, from England and a whole part of my life. 'Thank you for everything you have done. We should be celebrating in champagne. I am sure that day will come.' They wished me luck and we shook hands once more. Then the door closed. One more wave and they drove off. I watched the rear lights disappear while I waited on the side of the empty road to give them ample time to get through the East German check-point, before setting out myself. For an instant in time I was free and alone in the dark night, poised between two worlds, belonging to neither. As I stood there among the sighing pine trees, I reflected on all that had happened, on the people and events which had worked together to bring about this instant and on those other people and events, which, just as ineluctably, had worked together to bring about my arrest and trial. And I remembered the words of Ecclesiastes: 'To everything there is a season and a time to every purpose under heaven. A time to weep, and a time to laugh; a time to mourn, and a time to dance. A time to get, and a time to lose; a time to keep, and a time to cast away.'

Then I started towards the check-point. I stepped out of the darkness into the harsh light of the arclamps and walked up to the East German border guard, standing near the closed barrier.

Chapter Twelve

Without any documents to identify myself, it took some time and effort before I could persuade the East German border guards to contact the local Soviet authorities. So much so, that I had to spend the night at the check-point in a room made available to me. The next morning at about eight o'clock, I was woken by an officer who brought me a tray with sandwiches and coffee. While I was still in bed having breakfast, the door of the room suddenly burst open. Three men stood in the doorway looking at me. One of them I immediately recognised as Vassili, the young man – now no longer so young – with whom I had had many a pleasant stroll through the suburbs of London. The moment he saw me, he shouted excitedly, 'It's him! It's him!' and rushed forward to embrace me. I was very surprised. I couldn't possibly understand how he could have come all the way from Moscow in the short time I had been at the check-point. In the car, on the way to East Berlin, he told me that it was pure coincidence that he was in Berlin. He had been attending a conference and been due to leave that day. In the middle of the night, he had been rung up by the Chief of the KGB in Berlin, who knew that he had been working with me in London. A man who claimed to be George Blake had arrived at the East German check-point on the autobahn near Berlin. Could he go out there and identify him?

In Berlin I was treated somewhat as a hero and the comrades

seemed especially pleased that I had chosen their city to surface. Though I never for a moment thought that I would be turned away or not looked after well, I had not expected such a warm welcome.

While I was in Berlin, I was fitted out with a complete set of new clothes. Every day one of the officials, detailed to look after me in the villa where I had been put up, would go to West Berlin and purchase various items of clothing for me there. If they didn't fit, he would return and change them for a smaller or bigger size, as the case might be. I was extremely puzzled by this procedure which seemed to me both complicated and unnecessary. I had been told that in a few days I would be flown to Moscow in a special aircraft. Why couldn't we wait to fit me out till I was there? I could then go to the shops, try everything on and buy what I needed myself. Today, having lived more than twenty-four years in Moscow, I am no longer puzzled. The comrades wanted to fit me out with good quality clothing while it was still possible to do so. In Moscow, as I was soon to find out, this would have been very difficult.

I was put up in a large, comfortable flat with an elderly housekeeper to look after me. Two weeks later I was joined by Sean Bourke. He had managed to reach East Berlin safely, exactly according to the plan we had worked out.

The rest of Sean's story is, unfortunately, not a happy one. Over the period that we lived together in Moscow, our relationship soured. The main reason for this was a fundamental difference of opinion about his future. The ideal solution would have been if he could have settled in the Soviet Union. He would have been provided for and well looked after, while Pat, Michael and Anne could feel completely safe. But this, I soon realised, was quite out of the question. Sean was too much of an individualist, not to say anarchist, by nature, too impatient of any form of authority to have settled down happily in a state as authoritarian as the Soviet Union was in those years. Besides, everything was foreign and strange to him here. Television, radio, the cinema, theatres and newspapers were closed to him for he did not know the language. The only thing he might have found congenial was a wide-spread predisposition to the consumption of strong drink and a great tolerance of anybody who had had too much of it. At the same time, more than anything else he missed, I think, the warmth and conviviality of the English pub, an institution which here does not exist in any form whatsoever. Perhaps, in spite of all these obstacles, he might have settled down if he had been willing to make the effort and learn the language so that he would have got to know the people and their traditions, which in many ways were not all that different from his own. But he lacked any incentive to do so. He had neither the ideological commitment to Soviet society nor the imperative need to adapt to it which I had. I knew that I would have to spend a great part, and possibly, all of my life in this country and was intent, therefore, from the outset, on looking at the positive side of things and making the best of it. As I made my bed so I should lie in it. Sean's approach was not unnaturally quite the opposite. He had been reluctant to come here in the first place and wanted to leave again as soon as possible. He was determined from the start not to like it here and latched on to everything negative which could confirm him in his intention. For this I could not and did not blame him. Accepting that he was set on leaving, a plan was worked out whereby he could live anywhere he liked under a different identity. My friends in the KGB expressed their willingness to provide him with genuine documents and a sum of money enabling him to start a new life. This he didn't want either. Not only did he want to write a book about the escape and his prominent role in it – he could have done that here and have had it published in the West – but he wanted to be able to boast about it to his friends and drinking companions in Ireland and even, if necessary, to his fellow inmates in a British prison. This determination was so strong that he even went so far as to go to the British Embassy in Moscow to give himself up to the British authorities, but they turned him away. To have tried to smuggle him out of the country would have involved too much trouble to be worth it.

This thirst for publicity clashed directly with the security of our friends in England. They did not want their participation in the escape to become known to the authorities with all the consequences that might flow from this. After all, that was why we had persuaded Sean to come to the Soviet Union in the first place. So I was faced with an agonising choice: either to support Sean in achieving his personal wishes which, if carried out, could expose Pat, Michael and Anne to danger, or to ensure their security by opposing Sean's intentions.

It was Sean who had almost single-handed engineered my escape from Wormwood Scrubs. It was Pat, Michael and Anne who had found the money necessary to finance the whole operation, hidden me and finally managed to smuggle me out of England. I owed as much to them as to Sean, if not more. Faced with this dilemma I opted for the security of Pat, Michael and Anne and did everything in my power to persuade Sean either to stay here or to settle elsewhere, under a different name. This he strongly resented and he never forgave me for not taking his side.

As nobody intended to keep him here against his wishes, arrangements were made for him to return to Ireland. There he fought successfully extradition to Britain, though it was a close shave. He wrote his book in which, quite unnecessarily and for no understandable reason, he incriminated Pat, Michael and Anne in such a way that the British authorities had no difficulty in establishing their identity. For reasons best known to themselves, they decided, at the time, not to prosecute.

Sean, for a while, lived it up from the proceeds of the book and, no doubt, enjoyed the local celebrity he craved for. He died in his early forties from over indulgence in strong drink, living alone and destitute in a caravan in an Irish seaside resort. It was a sad end for a gifted, charming, brave, but unpredictable man, to whose memory I shall always remain grateful.

My determination to look at everything in the Soviet Union through rose-coloured spectacles, a tendency common to many Western Communists, sometimes led to rather hasty and naïve conclusions. In the Sixties and Seventies champagne was easily available and quite cheap. At special counters in many food stores one could buy a glass of very good Soviet champagne for about forty kopeks. I found this very impressive and interpreted it at once as a sure sign that Soviet society was about to enter the Communist era. Here drinking champagne was no longer the privilege of the very rich, but open to the man in the street. During the recent anti-alcohol campaign when one had to queue for up to two hours to buy any kind of strong drink at all, I told this story to my Soviet friends and it caused much bitter mirth and amazement at how I could have been quite so naïve.

Soviet society differed considerably from what I had imagined it to be. When I had been fitted out in Berlin, I had not only been struck by the complexity of the procedure, but also by the lavishness of the purchases. I had thought that I would be given one or two, at most three, suits and such other personal possessions as were strictly necessary. I had furthermore imagined that in Moscow I would probably be given a flat of one or, possibly, two sparsely furnished rooms. To my surprise, I was housed in a spacious flat of four high-ceilinged rooms with oriental carpets, heavy mahogany furniture and crystal chandeliers. Taxi drivers and waiters, to my astonishment, accepted tips without batting an eyelid and were as put out as their counterparts in the West, if these weren't quite as large as they felt was their due. When, on one occasion, during my first months in Moscow, I did some translation work for one of the large publishing houses and I refused the fee on the grounds that I was already amply provided for Stan, my KGB colleague who was looking after me at the time, gave me a severe ticking off and pointed out that this was a socialist society where everybody was paid according to his work and not his needs, that I had quite the wrong approach which, moreover, nobody would understand or even appreciate and would lead to all sorts of difficulties. For instance, what was the publishing house going to do with the fee which I had refused? I would throw the whole administrative machinery out of gear.

Another instance of this same bureaucratic approach, I encountered about a year later when I started my first regular job as a translator in another publishing house. I had been working there for about a fortnight when I was told to collect the premium which I had earned. I thought there must be a mistake and pointed out that I could not possibly have earned a premium as I had been there only two weeks. It was explained to me that as a member of the staff, I shared automatically in the premium and had to accept it. What seemed to worry people most was that, if one did not take the money, nobody would know what to do with it, since the system made no allowance for such a contingency. Having been in prison for six years, I knew all about the system and the pointlessness of fighting it. So I took the premium without any further protest.

I have often wondered whether having come straight out of prison made it easier or more difficult for me to adapt to life in the Soviet Union. On the one hand, it is always difficult, after a long period in prison, to adapt to freedom and a normal existence. To have to do so in a society which has a completely different structure and conditions would seem even more difficult. On the other hand, had I come to the Soviet Union in 1961, straight from Beirut, as I easily might have done, I think the contrast would have been much sharper and it might have been much more difficult to adapt myself. In a way, Wormwood Scrubs acted as a kind of airlock which made the transition easier and the rough edges less painful. After prison, it was such a wonderful experience to be able to get up in the morning and dispose of one's day as one thought fit, to go wherever one wished, that it made the lower standard of living and other disadvantages inherent in life in the Soviet Union much less difficult to accept.

Talking about rough edges, one of the other things which surprised me, for I had somehow expected the contrary in a socialist society, was the rudeness of people to each other in public places. In the long queues, rows and altercations are a frequent occurrence – somebody has gone to the head of the queue, not waited for his turn, pushed somebody out of the way or made a disparaging remark. The salesgirls in the shops, with rare exceptions, are rude and sullen, both because they are overworked and have to attend to an endless stream of jostling and pushing customers who inundate them with questions and because, in an economy of shortages, neither they nor the people in charge of them are interested whether one honours their shop with one's custom or not. They can get rid of their stocks anyway. This universal rudeness and the sullen and tired look of the crowds in the streets are the result of the strain of daily life, the constant irritation and exhaustion caused by the queues and the frustration engendered by the endless obstacles, which the bureaucratic machinery, without which nothing can be done, puts in the way of solving the most ordinary, everyday problems.

I found this universal rudeness and indifference all the more difficult to bear as I, myself, have always attached much importance to courtesy which I look upon as the oil that lubricates human relations. A smile or thank you cost nothing and can do wonders and I find much wisdom in the biblical saying that 'a soft answer turneth away wrath'. But I learned my lesson early on. I remember, one day, entering a shop and standing aside to hold the door open for a young woman behind me. Not only did she pass without a thank you or even a glance, but before I had time to go in myself, she was followed by a long stream of customers, who gave me queer looks as they passed and saw me standing there holding the door open. I felt rather an idiot and never repeated that gesture again.

In sharp contrast to the grim-faced, sullen-looking crowd in the street, the individual Russian is warmhearted, kind, generous and extremely hospitable. Meeting him is like the sun suddenly breaking through on a cloudy day. The Russians have one other admirable quality which distinguishes them favourably from many other nations. They are extremely kind and helpful to foreigners, looking upon them as guests who, as such, should be given preferential treatment. It has happened to me in shops that my purchase is wrapped up for me in paper whereas to other customers it is just handed as it is, solely because my accent immediately gives me away as a foreigner.

It has been explained to me that this considerate attitude is due, in part, to a feeling of pity which most Russians experience for foreigners who, they think, must feel quite lost in another country and should, therefore, be helped. Given their own deep attachment to their homeland and the known difficulty they have in settling down in a foreign country, this may well be true. This admirable characteristic has, however, a reverse side of which I approve less. This is an excessive admiration for everything foreign. Although there is an excellent national drink called 'kwass' which, in my opinion, is much nicer and more refreshing, many consider it a matter of prestige to have bottles of Coca-Cola on the table on festive occasions. Any garments, especially jeans, even though locally manufactured, sell for double the price if they have a Levi-Strauss or Adidas label.

Another characteristic of the Russians which struck me quite early on is their attitude to law and authority. I was brought up in the great respect for the law shown in general by people in England and, even more so, in Holland, and the relatively scant regard for anybody in authority. In Russia exactly the opposite is true. There is but scant regard for the law and great respect, often amounting to servility, for anybody in authority. People don't even bother to circumvent laws, they simply ignore them. The nineteenth-century writer Saltykov-Shedrin wrote about his times: 'The multiplicity and complexity of the laws of the Russian Empire are redeemed by the fact that they need not necessarily be observed.' This, I am afraid, remains true to this day. Only very recently are serious attempts being made to raise the prestige of the law and the judiciary, which has to control its correct application, and place authority under the law, where it should be. But it is an uphill task and it will take much time and effort to overcome centuries-old traditions and habits of thought. What makes this task more difficult is that the Russians have undoubtedly an anarchistic streak in them. They positively enjoy going out of their way to break rules and regulations, which many people in authority think do not apply to them anyway. One can observe this every day in the streets. People are always crossing the road when the traffic lights are red or entering the Metro through the clearly marked exit and leaving through the clearly marked entrance. Rubbish is by preference dumped in those places where there is a large notice saying that it is strictly forbidden to dump rubbish. These are, of course, minor infringements, but they are characteristic of an attitude which extends to more serious matters such as the widespread custom in the villages of distilling 'hootch'. It is an attitude which makes the Russian nation difficult to govern and is, perhaps, the reason why, historically there has always been the need of an iron fist.

Russians are given to extremes and are inclined to see everything in black or white. They find it difficult to stick to the golden mean. They one day shower their leaders with excessive praise, adulation and flattery which at times acquire sickening proportions and, the next day, when they are dead or have fallen from power, subject them to merciless criticism and mockery. Either the country is flooded with alcohol which, for years, was the only commodity of which there was never a shortage or one has to queue for two hours for a bottle of vodka. During the anti-alcohol campaign the local authorities in the Southern regions, in a desire to demonstrate their zeal to Moscow, destroyed acres and acres of valuable vineyards which had taken years to cultivate and now will take as many years to restore, or destroyed modern brewing installations, imported at great expense from abroad. This lack of moderation is coupled with a certain unpredictability in behaviour. This is well illustrated by the following simile told me by a British expert on Soviet affairs: 'Europeans always write from left to right. Arabs write from right to left. The Chinese and Japanese write from top to bottom. The Russians write diagonally either from the left down to the right or from the right down to the left. Only nobody can say beforehand, including they themselves, which way it is going to be.'

Russians often do not have the patience or perhaps do not see the need for attending to small details. In this respect they are the exact opposite of the Japanese. Most houses and buildings in Russian towns, including Moscow, are painted in pastel pink, yellow and green colours which gives them a bright, cheerful appearance. Nevertheless, they look almost invariably shabby. The reason is that when the outsides of houses are painted – it applies to the interiors as well – nobody can be bothered to scrape off the old paint. I cannot remember having ever seen a blow-lamp used here for this purpose. The new coat of paint is simply applied to the dirty surface of the old one. The result is that it soon starts to crack, blister and crumble. Then a new coat is applied. In this way, an enormous amount of paint and effort is wasted while the result remains mediocre. This aversion to detail and lack of patience also shows itself in the attitude to tools and instruments. These are often used for purposes for which they have not been designed with the result that the tools are damaged and the end is not achieved.

The Russians themselves are well aware of these shortcomings and can laugh at them as is illustrated by the following anecdote: 'American scientists and engineers managed to manufacture a miniature atom bomb which fitted neatly into an attaché case. Shortly afterwards, Russian scientists and engineers succeeded in making an atom bomb of the same size and calibre. The only thing they just couldn't get right was the attaché case.' Another favourite approach is: why do things the easy way, if they can be done in a complicated way? The Russians themselves call this 'pulling out a tooth through the arse'.

All this makes Russia a country of paradoxes and contradictions. It is, to my knowledge, the only country in the world where the soup, in restaurants, is served cold and the Coca-Cola warm, where one has to queue two hours to enter a 'fast' food shop and where the term 'right-wing conservatives' stands for 'hard-line communists' and 'left-wing radicals' for supporters of private property and free enterprise. For a person brought up in the West who settles in this country, it is sometimes difficult to make out how far the negative aspects of life are due to the socialist system or to the Russian character. The answer, probably, is a combination of the two.

Though these strictures may give an impression to the contrary, I admire the Russians enormously. I have found them to be a gifted, resourceful, tough, and warmhearted people. In everyday life, they are easy to get on with and I feel completely at home among them. I can say, without exaggeration, that the twenty-four years I have lived in this country have been the most stable and happy period in my life.

The first six months of my life here were probably the most difficult. Most of the time Sean and I were cooped up in the flat, leading, in many ways, the same existence as in Hampstead when we were in hiding. We had both been given a generous allowance and a lot of time on our hands – in many ways a criminal's dream – but very little opportunity to spend it. Moscow is not the most famous place in the world for having a good time and for us it was even less so. As it was considered undesirable that our presence should become known, Sean and I had to avoid the large hotels, restaurants, theatres and other places of entertainment especially in the centre, which were frequented by foreigners. As a result, we spent most of our time walking, getting to know Moscow and extending our walks further and further as we did so. From the start, I liked everything that was old in Moscow, from the quaint little backstreets, the courtyards with their one or two storeyed merchants' houses, the fine old palaces of the aristocracy, the many churches with their golden or blue, star-sparkled domes to the fortress-like monasteries, and disliked everything that was modern which struck me as cold, ugly and impersonal. One notable exception was the Metro, with its stations looking like palace halls, adorned with statues and murals, lit by heavy chandeliers and kept spotlessly clean. I found the service also very impressive with trains arriving about every minute during the rush hours.

A question which preoccupied me very much at that period and made it an even more unhappy one were the relations with my wife. About six months before my escape, when it was already in the planning stage, my wife, on one of her regular visits, had asked me for a divorce. She had met somebody who very much wanted to marry her and she was anxious to take this opportunity to start a new life. She was to all intents and purposes in the position of a widow and had three children to bring up. Although, otherwise, I would never have dreamt of divorcing her, in the position both she and I were in, I could not possibly refuse or put any obstacles in the way. I agreed, therefore, at once, though her request, somehow quite unexpected, came as a heavy blow. I immediately informed my solicitor and the proceedings were set in motion. But these things take time and the case was to be heard only a month or so after the date set for the the escape. I, naturally, dare not whisper a word to her about this. I had secret hopes, however, that, if the escape was successful, she might eventually be willing and able to join me with the children in whatever country I might find sanctuary. While I was still in hiding in Hampstead, I heard that, in my absence, the hearing had been adjourned, so my hope remained alive. About two months after my arrival in Moscow, Stan, the man who was looking after me, one day brought me newspaper cuttings which reported that the divorce case had been heard in my absence and a decree nisi granted. This news dashed all my hopes of a reunion with my wife and children and caused me a great deal of grief. Later, when I knew more about life and conditions in the Soviet Union and, especially, after I became acquainted with my fellow-exiles, Kim Philby and Donald Maclean and their families, I realised that this blow had been a blessing in disguise and how wise my wife had been in not wanting to join me. It would have turned into a disaster and a traumatic experience for all of us. My wife, I am certain, would never have been able to adapt herself to life in this country and settle down happily. There would have been too many difficulties and, not having the ideological commitment I had, she would not have seen the need to put up with them. She was a very English person and would, for instance only wear clothes of English make. I remember, when we were living in West Berlin, she would not even buy clothes of German manufacture for the small children and would wait till we were back in England on leave to do all her shopping. During the first two years I lived in Moscow, the man who had been my friend at MECAS and with whom we had spent the last evening in Beirut, was Minister at the British Embassy here. Our wives had also been good friends and I can imagine how difficult it would have been for my wife not to be able to see her friend who was living in the same city.

So all I can say is that all is well that ends well and we have much to be grateful for. My wife's new marriage turned out a very happy one. She had one more son by her new husband who proved an excellent father to my sons. I too remarried two years later, also had another son and my marriage too turned out a happy one.

As soon as I was safely in Moscow, I was, of course, very anxious to inform my family of the fact for I could well imagine how worried they must be about my fate after the news of the escape burst on them. In February, two months after my arrival, I was able to send my first letter to my mother, informing her that I was safe and well. It was posted in Egypt to create, at first, the impression that I had gone there. A month later, I wrote another letter with an address in East Germany to which my mother could write. In it I invited her to come and stay with me for a few weeks in East Germany. She at once replied that she would be coming and on what day and by which train. One day in June of that year, she arrived at the Ost Bahnhof in East Berlin where she expected me to be waiting for her. She was met instead by Stan who told her that I was in Moscow, where he would be taking her the next day. When we met, it was a happy, though emotional reunion, the third in our life. We had a wonderful holiday together. By that time, Sean had been given his own flat and I had dispensed with the services of the housekeeper, so we had the flat to ourselves. Accompanied by Stan, we made a trip to the Carpathian mountains where we stayed in the house of a forester in a beautiful nature reserve.

My mother did not like the idea of me being on my own in Moscow, so she suggested that she should come and live with me, at least for part of the year. I accepted her offer gratefully. My mother and I have always got on very well together. We have a great deal in common, share the same attitude to life, and have much the same tastes. We both enjoy home life and the little recurring pleasures it offers. We both like cooking and creating a comfortable, cosy interior. I have also inherited her equable temper so that we hardly ever disagree on anything or quarrel.

She arrived the following November, this time by train because she had a lot of luggage with her. She came well prepared for the Russian winter and brought such things as electric blankets, hot-water bottles, fur-lined slippers and padded dressing gowns. All these things proved completely unnecessary, however, as the houses in Russia are extremely well heated. There are no cold corridors or bedrooms and one sleeps in winter under the same number of blankets as in summer. However paradoxical this may sound, I have suffered less from the cold in Russia than in England. Indoors it is warm and outdoors one is warmly dressed in fur hats, padded or fur-lined coats, gloves and boots.

Amongst the luggage my mother brought was a large trunk with all my clothes. Shortly after the start of my prison sentence, my wife had consulted her about what to do with my belongings. Give them away, perhaps, or sell them? Without a moment's hesitation, my mother at once decided that they should be kept. The time would certainly come when I would need them again. She sent everything to the cleaners and stored it away in mothballs in a large trunk. So, for many years in Moscow, I was able to wear my English clothes and one or two items have survived to this day.

Another thing she brought with her was a beautiful album of paintings in the National Gallery. This had been signed and presented to her by the officers of the Special Branch who had been detailed to watch her house after I escaped. They sat in cars watching the house and followed my mother wherever she went. The same watch had been set on my wife. My mother, knowing me very well, was absolutely certain that, whatever happened, I would not come to her house, and did not mind this surveillance. It was the end of October and the weather was inclement. She felt sorry for the police officers who had to sit all day outside in the car. So she invited them in for a cup of tea and soon suggested that, instead of waiting outside, they should sit in one of the rooms and be more warm and comfortable. They accepted with pleasure and gradually a friendly relationship grew up between them and my mother. Since they had to follow her anyway, they, in turn, suggested that they should take her in their car wherever she had to go. When, at the end of four months, it became known that I had left the country, the watch was lifted. As a token of their affection the officers involved in the surveillance operation presented my mother with the album signed by each of them.

After her first visit to me in Moscow, my mother decided to leave England and go back to Holland. She was given back her Dutch nationality which she had lost on marrying my father. So for a while she was in the possession of two valid passports, her old British passport and a new Dutch one. Whenever she came to England to visit her grandchildren, she used her Dutch passport as she was afraid that if she travelled on her British passport, she might not be allowed to leave the country again. On one occasion, arriving in Harwich on the nightboat, she passed the immigration through the channel for foreigners. The immigration officer, who belonged to the Special Branch, recognised her. Looking at her Dutch passport, he smiled and said, 'Mrs Blake, if you had used your British passport, you would have got through quicker.' This incident illustrates the attitude of the British authorities to my family. They never put any obstacles in the way of any of them visiting me in Moscow and didn't even question them on their return.

All that winter, our life in Moscow remained very restricted. We spent a lot of our time making the flat, which had the impersonal atmosphere of all safe houses, look more homely. In those days, it was still possible to buy carpets and bits of old or even antique furniture at a reasonable price so we spent a lot of time bargain hunting and so managed to give the flat a lived-in look and a character of its own. Because of the long winters and the relative dearth of places of public entertainment, I realised early on how important it is here to have a comfortable home with a cosy, warm atmosphere.

Occasionally, my friends in the KGB organised excursions for us to some old country house or famous beauty spot outside Moscow, but mostly we went for long walks which, fortunately, we both enjoy very much. Not far from us lived an elderly woman with her idiot son. Like us, they went for regular walks and so we quite often ran into each other. I couldn't help but be struck by the similarity and when I saw them, I used to say to my mother, 'Look, there we go. We are just like those two.'

Much of our time was inevitably taken up by everyday shopping. This is not so easy in Moscow and, if you are a foreigner, it takes some time to learn the ropes. To begin with there are always queues in the shops. If there aren't any, it means there is nothing to be had. This is partly because there is a shortage of consumer goods and food products and partly because the sales side is badly organised. There are not enough salesgirls to serve at the counters and often only one cashdesk is manned, even though there may be several, so that very quickly queues build up. This leads to irritability and frayed nerves, both on the part of the customers and the staff. What holds up proceedings further is that, although in most shops there are electric cash registers, the cashiers, for some reason, don't quite trust them and invariably check the amount on an abacus. This means that the operation of paying takes nearly twice as long as it should do. A foreigner in a Soviet shop feels quite lost in the clamouring crowd of customers at the various counters and doesn't know where to start. There is however a logic to this apparent chaos and, after a while, one gets the hang of it. One important thing to know is that the shop only sells the goods which are on display that day. If you don't see what you need it is no good asking because it isn't there, at least not for the ordinary customer who is not a friend of a member of the staff. If, say, you want to buy cheese, you queue up at the appropriate counter. When your turn comes, you say how much you want (people seldom buy less than half a kilo or a kilo) and the girl will weigh it for you, wrap it up and tell how much it costs. You then go to the queue at the cash desk and wait your turn. When you have paid, you can now go to the head of the queue with your cheque and hand it to the girl who will give you your purchase, in between serving the customers still in the queue. If you need something else which is sold at another counter, you have to go through the whole procedure again.

My mother, though she doesn't speak a word of Russian, mastered this system very quickly and soon did much of the shopping on her own. Since there are special shops for foreigners, it is very rare for any of them to buy articles of food in a Soviet shop so that my mother stood out and soon became a well-known figure in the neighbourhood. In spite of the general lack of courtesy, the shop attendants were very helpful and nice to her. She would point to what she wanted and say how much of it (the word kilo is the same in Russian). The attendant would then write the price on a piece of paper which my mother would give to the cashier. She became so well known that for several years after she left some salesgirls in the neighbourhood remembered her and would ask me how she was.

Though there is a shortage of food this does not mean, of course, that people do not get enough to eat, only that the choice is limited – certainly as compared to Western countries – and that many things are difficult to get. The paradox is though that, whereas the shop shelves give an empty impression, the tables on festive occasions in Russian homes are groaning with food. But it takes much effort and time to get what you want and from time to time certain food products simply disappear. You can never be sure what there is on sale. You may decide that you want chicken, but on that particular day there is only beef or pork to be had. Things like cheese, mayonnaise, sausage or what-have-you suddenly disappear from the shops. If it isn't available in one shop, you can be sure that you won't be able to get it anywhere else either. The other day, I went out to buy a few bottles of buttermilk and came back with bottles of beer. There was no buttermilk, but beer, which had not been on sale for a long time, suddenly appeared again. We never go out without taking a shopping bag with us for we never know what we may unexpectedly encounter on our way. This shopping bag is, therefore, quite appropriately called a 'just in case' in Russian. When you see something you need, you buy always in far greater quantities than you actually require, knowing that it may disappear again for a long time. This habit in itself is one of the causes of shortages. If you are carrying a bag of oranges or tins of fruit or peas, it is quite common for people to accost you in the street and ask you where you got it. This struck me as very strange at first. These difficulties are due not only to the fact that the existing agricultural system is unable to feed the population adequately but also to the inefficient way supply and distribution are organised. The trouble really is that nobody is personally interested in the actual results of his work, but only in being covered and able to claim that he has formally complied with instructions from above.

You can, of course, buy almost everything in season in the markets, of which there are several in Moscow, but there the prices are four or five times higher than in the state shops so that very few people can afford to buy there. An additional factor that makes life difficult is that many items can only be bought in specialised shops of which there are few. For instance, there is only one shop in the whole of Moscow where you can buy spare parts for cars (in so far as they are available) or two shops where you can buy batteries for electronic watches. The service in laundries, cleaners, hairdressers and various repair shops is bad and the work done often shoddy. So, whether you like it or not, you have to become a do-it-yourself man and learn to do most repairs yourself. A do-it-yourself man, by the way, without do-it-yourself shops. I have even learned to cut my own hair. At the hairdressers, I had to wait too long and the man who helped me used to smell of vodka and herring. This was not only unpleasant, but slightly frightening.

As to the obstacles in the way of getting any permit or decision from a government or municipal agency, these are absolutely staggering and it needs a really strong resolve to see it through. There is, for instance, only one place in Moscow where you can apply for a driving licence and this is located, as if on purpose, in one of the last houses of the city near its very boundary. So much time and energy is taken up with the simple process of living that people often have not enough left to do their actual work properly. Thus you get a vicious circle where the difficulties of daily life lead to inefficient work and inefficient work to further difficulties.

From all this it is clear that the first years of my life here were taken up with learning to adjust myself to the new conditions. I had been living here nearly two years before I was allowed to go for the first time to the Bolshoi Theatre, half the audience of which is always made up of foreigners. For this purpose, I was driven up to the artistes' entrance and taken through several back passages to the artistes' box, overlooking the stage, where I had to take a back seat so that I could not be seen. That evening, they danced 'Giselle' which made a deep impression on me and I shall always remember that first visit. Since then I have often been to the Bolshoi as an ordinary member of the audience, but have never been recognised or approached by foreigners.

Apart from the opera and the ballet, I go quite often to a concert or a play. I am very fond of the classical Russian theatre and like plays by Gogol, Ostrovski and Saltykov-Shedrin, but have been, on the whole, disappointed by modern Soviet playwrights. I am, I must admit, rather conservative in my tastes and prefer when a scene takes place in a drawing-room that the stage actually looks like a drawing-room and not, as is usual in the modern theatre, that every act is played in the same, rather abstract setting.

The initial isolation in which I and my mother lived was broken when I met my wife in the spring of 1968. Her name was Ida and we got acquainted during a boat cruise on the river Volga. After our return to Moscow, we continued to see each other and got married the following year. This encounter brought about a great change in my life. My wife is a very active person – a real outdoor girl – who loves swimming, skiing and going for long walks in the country. As I am fairly active myself – though not quite as much as she – I allowed myself gladly to be drawn into these activities, which I think have contributed to keeping me fit. She is in that way very much like my first wife who was also essentially an outdoor girl and loved riding, skiing, walking and, when a schoolgirl, playing hockey. What they also have in common is that they are both very honest and given to speaking their mind, irrespective of persons. It is perhaps a paradox that I, having a less straightforward nature, should twice have married women of this turn of character. The fact that I had something to do with intelligence did not surprise her. She had suspected it from the beginning. The point is that, though I was obviously a foreigner, I did not live like a foreigner. They have special houses and shops reserved for them and, especially in the mid-Sixties, could not mix freely with ordinary Russians and the latter even less with them. So the only conclusion she could draw was that I must be in a special position and, therefore, have something to do with intelligence. She herself is not especially impressed with the intelligence world, finds frankly speaking anything to do with it downright boring and prefers to speak about something else. But there is an old Russian saying 'Love is blind and makes you marry a goat' so we got married and lived happily ever afterwards. My son Misha shares this attitude although, from his early boyhood, he has been aware that his father had something to do with intelligence. He used to accompany us on our trips abroad to the socialist countries and was frequently present at lunches given in my honour when toasts were pronounced referring to the work I had done in this field. It evidently did not impress him very much for at the age of fourteen he firmly made up his mind that he was going to be a physicist and on his own initiative, though with our consent of course, he transferred from the special French school he had been attending to a school specialising in mathematics and physics, subjects for which he obviously has a talent.

Our marriage met with a certain amount of opposition on the part of my future mother-in-law, who is a widow and my wife's step-mother. This was not because she had anything against me personally, but because I was a foreigner. She had lived through the years of the Stalin repressions when any connection with a foreigner could be fatal. She had two sons, my wife's half-brothers, who are engineers working in the defence industry and she was afraid that they might lose their jobs if it became known that their sister had married a foreigner. When it was explained to her that I was an honoured guest here and *persona grata* with the KGB, her reaction was, 'That's all very well. Today he may be *persona grata*, but who can guarantee that tomorrow he will not be *persona non grata*.' Our relations with my mother-in-law are now normal and we visit her from time to time in the village where she lives, not far from Moscow, but she herself refuses steadfastly to this day to set foot in our flat and does not encourage her sons to do so.

This incident led to an amusing misunderstanding. Factories working for the defence industry keep their addresses secret and are designated by a Post Box number. It has become the habit therefore to refer to people who work there as working in a Post Box. When Ida told me about her mother's apprehensions, she said it was because her brothers worked in a Post Box. I received my letters at that time and still do through a Post Box at the Central Post Office so I naturally took her to mean that her brothers were Post Office employees. This puzzled me greatly. I appreciated of course that to be a Post Office employee is to hold a position of trust, but not to such a degree that it precluded all contact with a foreigner, especially one who was, after all, still *persona grata* with the KGB.

Ida had a wide circle of friends, acquaintances and relatives by whom I was very quickly accepted as one of them. I was now able to observe at first hand how Russian people live and become part of that life myself.

My mother continued to live with us during the winter, but spent most of the summer in Holland. We live in a house which has no lift and as our flat is on the top floor, it became increasingly difficult for her, as she grew older, to climb the stairs. Fortunately, by that time, we were able to spend our summer holidays in one of the socialist countries and, instead of her coming to Moscow, we now began to meet every year, sometimes in Hungary or Czechoslovakia, but mostly in the DDR. Ironically, since the democratic revolutions in Eastern Europe, this is something I can no longer do freely.

A few months after my arrival here, Gordon Lonsdale came to see me. We were both very pleased to meet again in freedom and I reminded him of his extraordinary prediction. After that we met from time to time for lunch and enjoyed reminiscing about life in England and our days in the Scrubs. He was happily reunited to his family and had resumed his work in the KGB, where he had been welcomed back as a hero. He found it difficult, however, to settle down to life in the Soviet Union after such a long absence. The truth is that, apart from being a first class intelligence officer, he was also a highly successful businessman. In his cover capacity of head of a Canadian firm dealing in juke boxes, he had made millions which he had, of course, not kept for himself, but faithfully paid into the account of the Soviet state. He found it far from easy now to get used to the restricted life of a KGB official and was impatient of many aspects of Soviet reality. He was particularly critical of the inefficient and often incompetent way Soviet industrial enterprises were run and international trade was conducted. Being an outspoken man who had the good of his country at heart, he made his views known. Criticism of any kind was not appreciated in those days and he soon fell from favour and found himself relegated to a position of relatively minor importance. He was spared further disappointment by sudden death from a heart attack while he was picking mushrooms with his family in the woods near Moscow. In him I lost a friend whom I admired greatly and who had helped me much with good advice in the early years of my life in the Soviet Union. This country lost a devoted servant, who, had he lived to the days of *perestroika*, could have done work of great use.

Lonsdale had been a so-called 'illegal resident'. I have always had the greatest respect and admiration for this class of intelligence officer. To my mind there is no higher. They have to live their cover so completely that, indeed, they have to become another person. They have to give up their own life and become somebody else. Every time they attempt to recruit a new agent and put the fatal question to him, every time they go to a secret rendezvous, they risk their liberty and sometimes their life. They have to be continually on guard and live in a state of constant tension. Only during the very rare and short periods when they can return home and be with their families can they relax. Sometimes they are accompanied by their wives who in that case, have also to become another person and are henceforth not just their life companions, but their companions-in-arms. Lonsdale was a perfect example of what an 'illegal resident' should be. Only a man who believes very strongly in an ideal and serves a great cause will agree to embark on such a career, though the word 'calling' is perhaps more appropriate here. Only an intelligence service which works for a great cause can ask such a sacrifice from its officers. That is why, as far as I know, at any rate in peace time, only the Soviet intelligence service has 'illegal residents'.

In the spring of 1970, not long after Lonsdale's death, I met Kim Philby. Although we had both worked in Head Office in Broadway Buildings, during the last year of the war and, later, had been at the same time in Beirut, our paths had never crossed and we only knew of each other's existence from what we had read in the newspapers. The occasion we met was a lunch party, given in our honour by the Chief of the Soviet Intelligence Service, in one of the KGB's more sumptuous flats. From then on we saw each other regularly. Kim was rather lonely at that time and he appreciated the homely atmosphere of our flat, created by my wife and mother, with both of whom he got on very well. He was going through a difficult patch as his relationship with Melinda Maclean, which had lasted not more than two years, had come to an end and he was drinking heavily.

In the course of that summer, his youngest son, Tommy, who was a jockey by profession, came to spend his holidays with him. He was a nice, easy-going boy whom we all liked very much. In order to help entertain him, we managed one day to get two tickets for a show on ice and thought it would be nice if we could find a girl to accompany him. This was not so easy as all my wife's girlfriends were in their thirties and nearly all married. Rufa, however, a very attractive woman, who worked with Ida in the same institute, was not married and would, we thought, make pleasant company for the young man. She was quite willing to help out and took Tommy to the ice show. As he, naturally, did not know his way about Moscow, she had to take him back to his father's flat and that is how Kim met his future wife. He was immediately taken by her in a big way and did not keep this to himself. My wife and I thought a friendship with an attractive woman would relieve his loneliness and make him drink less and decided to encourage further meetings. I had just acquired a car, a 1971 Volga – a car strong as a tank – and was anxious to try it out. We planned to make a trip to Yaroslavl, an old town on the Volga with many churches, monasteries and old merchant houses. We asked Kim and Rufa to come with us and they both accepted. My mother was also there, so we set out, all five, on this trip, which was rather an adventure as far as I was concerned, for it was the first time that I drove a car for any distance on Russian roads. It turned out a great success from every point of view. We had no mishaps with the car, Kim and Rufa got on famously together and my wife told me, while we were in Yaroslavl, the happy news that she was pregnant. Immediately on our return, Kim proposed to Rufa who was, I think, rather overwhelmed by the suddenness of this offer of marriage and hesitant at first to accept. But Kim was a very persistent suitor and soon she overcame her initial doubts – he was nearly twenty years older than she – and accepted. It proved a very happy marriage and Kim's salvation. From the very beginning, Rufa insisted, on the threat of leaving him, that he stop drinking or, at any rate, greatly reduce his intake. For her sake, he managed to do this, although it cannot have been easy. If the last fifteen years of his life were happy and peaceful, he owed this entirely to her. Her health was not very strong and they both enjoyed a rather retired life in their comfortable flat. Both liked travelling and they regularly visited one of the socialist countries. Kim didn't work in any Soviet organisation and spent most of the day at home in his well-stocked library, listening to the BBC World Service and solving *The Times*' crossword puzzle. In the beginning, he had tried to write articles on the Middle East for a Soviet publication, but his approach to journalism was so different from what was considered acceptable here that he soon gave it up. He never tried to get another job, did not make any great effort to learn Russian well and was clearly not interested in integrating himself in Soviet society. He did, however, do a lot of work for the KGB, in his capacity as a consultant, but as he was a rather secretive man I never discovered what he really did. In the last years of his life, we saw little of each other. We fell out because of a difference over the publication in the British press, without my permission, of a number of family photographs taken by one of his sons during a visit to my dacha. I did, however, go to his funeral service to pay him my last respects.

The life led by Donald Maclean was quite different. I got to know him through his wife Melinda, who was still seeing Kim occasionally, though their relationship had ended and she had returned to her husband. Donald and I at once felt a strong sympathy for each other and we soon became close friends. Unlike Kim Philby and Guy Burgess, he had made a deliberate effort to integrate into Soviet society and help build Communism. With his characteristic energy, he mastered the Russian language which, by the time I got to know him, he spoke and wrote faultlessly. He became a member of the Soviet Communist Party and took an active part in the work of the party organisation of the Institute of World Economy and International Relations where he worked. He established himself as one of the leading experts on British foreign affairs and wrote a doctoral thesis entitled 'British Foreign Policy after Suez' which was later published in England in book form. One of his great achievements was to persuade the Soviet Government, which had been extremely reluctant to adopt this point of view, that the European Community was here to stay and constituted a third force and economic power which had to be reckoned with. He was also a long-standing member of the 'Learned Council' of the Institute, the body before which dissertations are defended and which awards degrees.

Donald had a wide circle of friends and acquaintances and was much loved and respected by the people who worked with him. What made him so attractive to many, in this age of cynicism, was not only his sincerely held belief in Communism, but, above all, the fact that he lived a life which was in full accord with his principles. He eschewed all privileges and comfort and dressed and ate simply. All the fourteen years that I knew him, I never saw him touch a drop of alcohol, though there had been periods in his life, including after his flight to the Soviet Union, when he drank heavily. 'Instead of an alcoholic', he used to say of himself, 'I have become a workaholic.'

Indeed, he was always writing analyses, reports, articles and books or taking part in conferences or round-table discussions. Under his guidance a whole generation of experts on British foreign and domestic policy was formed. He was, I think, the only man in the Institute whose work was always ready on time. There was a strong Calvinistic streak in him, inherited from his Scottish ancestors and this gave us something in common.

In spite of his great height – he stood six foot six in his socks – he had a very gentle nature and was always ready with a kind word or smile for the people with whom he came in contact. He was very considerate of other people and anybody who needed help knew that they would not turn to him in vain. His great interest in life was politics and he followed closely the developments in this country and in the Communist movement as a whole. He did not like what he saw and thought little of the coterie of aged gentlemen who ruled the Soviet Union in those years. He continued to believe, however, in the ability of the Communist movement to reform and renew itself. He was confident that when, by the very nature of things, the generation of senile leaders would have passed away, a new generation of technocrats would take over who would see the urgent need for reform. In this way he was a prophet of *perestroika*, which unfortunately he did not live to see.

This is what he wrote in 1981 in a private memorandum which he gave to me for safekeeping:

Indeed the ruling élite has at times to such an extent acted directly against the interests of Soviet society that one can say without too much exaggeration that the socialist formation has for long periods survived despite the nature and deeds of the leadership. The record of the leadership and its penumbra shows, it seems to me, a persistent and regressive tendency to substitute the aim of preserving its own power for the aim of finding ways of realising the energy of society which they rule. They do not see and cannot see that this is not what the road to the prosperity and security of Soviet society requires, that their interests and the interests of the Soviet Union do not coincide. What has fallen into discredit is not the socialist mode of production upon which the entire Soviet structure rests (it is nowadays almost universally taken for granted) but the political apex of that structure, the small group of men who make all the key decisions on how Soviet society is run. Many have become aware that the highly complex problems of running the Soviet

Union are now beyond the range of the present arbiters at the top, that a new quality of leadership is required. During the last two decades there has been a steady increase in the absolute and relative value of the material and other privileges of the wielders of authority and their families which of course has the effect of increasing among them resistance to change and risk-taking. This system of privileges which is as far as possible concealed from the public gaze also both reflects and contributes to a certain erosion within the ruling stratum of Soviet society of the moral, ethical and intellectual norms lying at the heart of the classical Communist view of human society. There is evidently a connection between this form of organised semi-legal corruption at and near the top and the spread of spontaneous illegal corruption in Soviet society at large. All the same, thirty years of living and working here tells me that the idea of each for all and all for each which gives socialism its moral leverage is still deeply embedded in the consciousness of most of those who wield various forms of authority in the Soviet Union and is likely to remain so.

In this country the immediate initiative for creative change is still likely to come from inside the Party-State hierarchy rather than from below. It seems more probable than not that the next five years, owing to favourable changes at the top, will see an improvement in the political, cultural and moral climate in the Soviet Union and the introduction of a complex of reforms affecting most major aspects of the life of the Soviet Union.

Donald was particularly scathing of the foreign policy conducted by the Brezhnev régime. This is what he wrote in the same paper:

To me it seems that the feature of contemporary Soviet foreign policy which, contrary to the intentions and expectations of its authors, does most damage to the interests of the Soviet Union is an undialectical one-sided conception of the role in world politics of the country's armed forces, the inability to establish in this field the right proportions and priorities in order to obtain the right result namely the security and well-being of Soviet society. What appears to have happened during the last five years is that at certain crucial turning points in policy-making the views of the military authorities with their natural professional interest in maximising the armed strength of the country, have with the support of the top leadership prevailed over the views of those who are called upon to assess the overall influence of military policy upon the international interest of the country.

The Soviet Union, as if it were hypnotised by the size and variety of American nuclear forces is continually adding to its own overkill capacity not only with no advantage to itself, but with seriously harmful consequences.

The latest instance of this is the introduction, now well advanced, of a new generation of nuclear rockets targeted upon Western Europe and its adjacent areas. The Soviet leadership evidently believed that the introduction of the SS-20 rockets would not compel the FRG, Britain and some other Western European states to accept upon their territories a new generation of American weapons of roughly comparable capacity, but in fact it has. The next result, or shortly, will be, unless the Soviet Union changes its policy, a rise in the level of nuclear confrontation in Europe with no compensating advantage to itself, indeed quite the reverse. As it is, the behaviour of the leadership suggests the absence of both a valid conception of what forces are sufficient for this purpose and also the ability correctly to foresee the reaction of the Western Europeans.

When he was asked to write a paper justifying this decision, i.e. to deploy SS-20 rockets, he declined with his favourite saying on these occasions, 'I refuse to take part in anti-Soviet propaganda,' as he considered this step contrary to the interest of the Soviet Union.

He felt solidarity, therefore, with the dissident voices who called for renewal and democracy and a reduction of the power of the party apparatus and the bureaucracy. To show this solidarity, he contributed regularly part of his income – which was not small by Soviet standards – to the fund established for helping the families of dissidents who had been sent to prison. He also wrote repeatedly to individual members of the Soviet leadership to intercede on behalf of dissidents and to protest against the practice of forcibly detaining some of them in mental hospitals.

The beginning and the end of his life were marked by sacrifice. The first sacrifice he made was when he had been a student in Cambridge. It was his ambition then to become a university don. When he joined the Communist party in the Thirties and was, subsequently, recruited by the Comintern to work in the interest of the Soviet Union, he was given the assignment of joining the Foreign Office. Although the life of a diplomat, with its obligatory social round, did not appeal to him at all, for the sake of serving the cause in which he believed, he set aside his personal ambitions and feelings and became a member of the Foreign Service.

By an irony of fate, he was able to fulfil his original ambition when he came to the Soviet Union and had to choose a new profession. He became an academic after all, and achieved notable distinction in this field.

Towards the end of his life, he was called upon to make another great personal sacrifice. His wife Melinda and their three children had followed him to the Soviet Union two years after his flight. They had found it difficult to settle down and had never been quite happy here. All his life Donald suffered from a sense of guilt towards his wife and children whose lives, he thought, he had deflected from their normal course. When, towards the end of the Seventies, his children and their Soviet partners expressed a strong desire to emigrate to England or the United States, he felt it his duty to do all he could to help them to do this. It was the Brezhnev period and the Soviet authorities were reluctant to let people go. Donald had accumulated a great deal of goodwill with the KGB however and he realised that he was in a position to bring moral pressure to bear on the authorities to let his family return to the West. Although he knew he had cancer and did not have all that long to live, he felt he had to arrange their departure while he was still alive. He was afraid that once he was no longer there, the authorities might not let them go. As it turned out, this fear proved totally unfounded. They would have let his family go in any case though we did not know this at that time. I say we, because Donald and I consulted each other on all important matters and I, too, had strongly advised him to use his influence while he was still able to do so.

So they all left with their families, one after the other. He particularly missed his little granddaughter to whom he was strongly attached. For the last two years he lived alone, looked after by his faithful housekeeper, Nadezhda Petrovna, and surrounded by his many friends and colleagues. He bore his illness cheerfully and with great courage, working to almost the last day on a collective work of which he was the editor.

During the last months of his life which he was able to spend at home, he was visited by his younger brother Alan, of whom he was very fond, and by his eldest son, Fergus. Fortunately, he was never in great pain and the only sedative he allowed himself was valerian. Suddenly one day his condition deteriorated and we had to take him to hospital. When we got there, I helped him to undress and saw him comfortably installed in his bed in a single room, which the KGB had arranged for him, in one of the best hospitals in Moscow. I left him, promising that I would visit him the next day. That was the last time I saw him alive. The next afternoon when I called he had already died and I was not allowed to see him.

On the day of the funeral I went to the morgue with Nadezhda Petrovna and another old friend to collect the body. He looked much younger, very peaceful and almost majestic in death. In accordance with his wishes, I asked that the coffin be closed before we left. This is contrary to the Russian tradition which requires that the coffin be left open until just before it is lowered into the grave.

His funeral service, which was held in the assembly hall of the Institute, of which he was such a distinguished member, turned into a touching farewell to a man who was much loved, admired and respected by all who knew him, not because he was a famous spy, but because he was a good and just man, a true English gentleman, in the best sense of that term. Many people spoke among whom were several academicians who paid tribute to him as an outstanding scholar. I know that is how he would like to be remembered. In my farewell words I recalled the biblical legend about the forty just men. Though God wanted to destroy the world because of man's sins, he promised not to do so as long as forty just men could be found for whose sake he would withhold his judgment. I said that it seemed to me that we, who had been Donald's colleagues and friends, had had the rare privilege of knowing personally one of those just men for whose sake mankind would be preserved.

Due to the usual administrative mix-up Donald's son Fergus arrived too late to take part in the funeral. The next morning I went with him to the crematorium to collect the ashes of his father which he took with him that same day to England to be buried in accordance with his last wishes in the family grave in the village of Penn. Usually one has to wait two weeks before the ashes can be called for, but this arrangement was expedited with the help of the KGB.

His portrait hangs today in the library of the Institute, alongside those of many other famous Soviet scholars. Even now, five years after his death, there are always fresh flowers in the vase under his portrait, renewed every time by his many friends and admirers in the Institute. To me his death was a great personal loss. He had been a trusted friend, a wise counsellor and most interesting company with whom conversation never lagged.

In my conversations with both Donald and Kim, we hardly ever spoke about our respective intelligence activities, though with Kim we sometimes recalled SIS personalities we had both known. I suppose that was the unconscious effect of years of training not to speak about one's work. Donald's attitude to intelligence and intelligence officers in general was that which is commonly held by members of the Foreign Service, slightly disparaging. Contrary to Kim, who I have a feeling, apart from his strong commitment to Communism, spied because he rather enjoyed it, Donald agreed to spy only out of a stern sense of duty. With him it went rather against the grain and he had constantly to overcome his inner reluctance. Nevertheless, I am sure his contribution was considerable. In Washington he had access to atomic secrets and if we have enjoyed peace for the last forty-five years and are likely to do so for a long time to come, I attribute this in a large part, to the activities of the so-called 'atomic spies' to whom he belonged. They made sure that the Soviet Union was able to build the atom bomb in record time and achieve nuclear parity. It is this 'mutual deterrence', though I hope on a much reduced level from the present, which will guarantee, I am convinced, 'peace in our time'.

Donald and Kim, as far as I could see, had only one thing in common. They both smoked a lot and had a preference for heavy tobacco, Gauloises if they could get them, but usually 'Dukat', the cheapest Soviet brand of cigarettes which have a particularly pungent smell. Neither Kim nor Donald ever mentioned or even hinted at the existence of a 'fifth' man. About the existence of Anthony Blunt, I learned for the first time when I read about him in the English newspapers. Only after that did Donald occasionally refer to him and his role in his and Guy Burgess's escape. As to the latter, I never met him as he died before I came to Moscow. Donald often spoke about him and their difficult relations when they shared a flat in Kuibyshev during their first years in the Soviet Union. I heard even more about him from Nadezhda Petrovna, Donald's housekeeper, with whom I am still in touch and who worked for Guy before he died. All these stories confirm the well-established image of him. He must have been a very clever and daring man, with great charm, but who, according to all accounts, positively enjoyed making mischief among his friends and, in order to do so, was not above opening their letters.

About two years after my arrival in Moscow, I started on my first job. I was found work as a Dutch translator with the 'Progress' Publishing House, but did not find this occupation very inspiring. Apart from the fact that the material I had to translate was not very interesting, the main trouble was that it was the kind of work which prolonged my isolation. I did all my translating at home and only once a fortnight or so would I go to the publishing house to hand in my work and collect new material. This way, I had little opportunity to get to know my colleagues and become part of a collective. This is important in any country if one wants to integrate, but particularly so in the Soviet Union, where social activities outside work are relatively limited.

Donald saw this at once and suggested early on in our friendship that I should come and work in his institute, where the atmosphere was quite different. With his help and that of the KGB, this was arranged and it turned out to be another important step towards making my life more interesting and giving me the feeling that I was an accepted member of this society.

From the beginning, I found the work interesting and the staff friendly. The people in my department were all experts in their own field of foreign relations and many of them had lived or been abroad. They were, therefore, much better informed and their outlook was broader than that of most Soviet citizens. I found among them people with a great fund of knowledge with whom it was interesting to converse and in whose company it was a pleasure to be. I can not imagine now what my life here would have been like if I had not had the good fortune of being able to join the institute. Certainly, it would have been much more dull.

The particular field of study assigned to me was the Middle East and its conflicts, particularly the Arab–Israeli conflict. This was an area with which I had some acquaintance. From time to time, I have to write articles or memoranda analysing new developments in the situation. In these I have, for a long time, urged that the Soviet government re-establish diplomatic relations with the state of Israel. If one aspires to be a mediator, one must have good relations with both sides. It seems to me that the Soviet government would be in a better position to help the Palestinian cause if it could talk directly to the Israeli government than if it deprives itself of this possibility. The unconditional and often uncritical support of the US Administration for Israel has not barred it from maintaining good relations with almost all Arab countries. As a result of the 'new political thinking', relations between the Soviet Union and Israel have started to improve in recent years. Consular officials have been exchanged and cultural exchanges between the two countries are becoming more frequent, but so far full diplomatic relations have not been restored.

About three years ago, as a result of *glasnost*, our institute started to put out a yearbook *Disarmament and Security* in which the whole range of problems connected with curbing the arms race, lowering the levels of military confrontation in different regions and lessening the danger of war are analysed. The book is published both in Russian and English and I was asked to become its English editor, in addition to my other work.

The pressure of work however was not very great and, in this respect, the institute was no exception, and could not be, to most other Soviet organisations. These all tend to be grossly overstaffed and, in general, the rhythm of life in this country is much slower than in the West. This has, to my mind, two advantages. There is greater social security and no unemployment and one does not have the feeling that one is caught up in the rat race. On the other hand, as a result, the standard of living is noticeably lower. But one must choose. One cannot have everything in life. One can either aspire to a high standard of living, but then one must be prepared to work hard for it, or one can prefer a more leisurely pace, but then one must be content with much less. One cannot have it both ways, as I have often explained to my Russian friends. This law is as true for nations as it is for individuals. Most of the researchers come to work only three days a week. These days are called 'the days of attendance'. The remaining two days of the working week are known as 'library days', when most people stay at home. It is left to one's conscience whether one does any work on those days or not. It is true, of course, that much of the work involved in political analysis can best be done at home, in one's study. The important thing, after all, is to get the work done in time, though here again deadlines are pretty flexible. The atmosphere in most Soviet institutions, as I can confirm from my own experience and from what I have heard from others, is decidedly relaxed. Much time is spent in general gossip, discussing domestic problems, and, in our institute, debating international affairs. Donald and I had adjoining rooms so we saw a lot of each other and always had our morning coffee and afternoon tea, which we made ourselves, together. The time set aside for drinking coffee in the morning and tea in the afternoon is as sacred in Soviet government offices as it is in British ones.

Discipline, in general, is slack. People turn up late and leave early and, as so many of the problems of existence have to be solved during working hours, because that is the only time the agencies concerned are open, it is not considered a very serious offence if one disappears occasionally during the day.

In order to help their staff avoid queues and provide them

occasionally with products which are in short supply, many factories and offices have private arrangements with food stores or supply bases where they regularly place orders on behalf of their staff. This, too, is a time-consuming process. A member of the trade union committee has to put the list of products available that week on the announcement board. The orders and the money have to be collected and sent to the shop. When delivery day comes, once a week or a fortnight, as the case may be, the institute is in a turmoil. The items have to be packed in individual bags and everyone who has placed an order has to go to a special room or place to collect it. After that, a lot of barter goes on with people exchanging between themselves items in which they are especially interested. For several years, I was the member of the trade union committee responsible for supervising the distribution of orders. I found this a headache which took up most of a working day. Later, I changed and became responsible for organising office parties on the occasion of big national holidays, such as the Day of the Revolution and Victory Day, or when one of our colleagues celebrated a jubilee. Before the anti-alcohol laws, I was famous in this capacity for the mulled wine which I made on these occasions.

Soviet institutes also frequently organise excursions for their staff, sometimes quite far afield, and it is not unusual for one day, either the Friday or Monday, to be added to the weekend to make this possible. I myself have never availed myself of this facility as my wife and I prefer to spend most weekends at the dacha.

When I bought my car, which would not have been possible without the help of the KGB as the waiting lists are very long, we had intended to use it mainly for long journeys to explore the Soviet Union. I don't think, in retrospect, this was a very realistic project. Travelling by car in this country presents many snags. Petrol stations are few and far between and often not easy to find. There are even fewer service stations and spare parts are difficult to come by. Unless one is a good mechanic oneself – which I am not – and has contacts in the car world, it is a problem to have one's car repaired. Setting out on a long journey is therefore a hazardous enterprise. In the event, my skills and endurance in this field were never put to the test. As I have already mentioned, on the first trip we undertook, my wife told me we were going to have a child. That put paid to any plans of exploring the Soviet Union by car. Now I use the car exclusively in the summer for driving to and from our dacha. I do not like driving in the winter. The roads are slippery, one has difficulty in starting the car in the morning or has first to clear the snow away before one can get in. So, at the end of October, I put it away in the garage, attached to my dacha, and don't take it out again till the middle of April, when I am sure there will be no more snow.

As soon as my friends in the KGB heard that there was going to be a family increase, they offered me a dacha. It is considered very important here that children should spend the summer in the countryside. Having a dacha is not in itself a particular privilege. Many people in Moscow have a dacha and all the villages within a radius of about a hundred miles around the city are what is known as 'dacha places'. Of course, there are dachas and dachas. The word covers a wide variety of dwellings from a one-room garden shack to the large, comfortable, brick villas standing in extensive grounds, allotted to senior government officials. Most dachas, however, are wooden houses in the Russian style standing in the woods on plots of land of varying size. Many people have their own dacha, inherited from parents or relatives or share one with friends. Others, less fortunate, rent a couple of rooms with a veranda in the summer. One way or another everyone, especially people with small children, try to spend the three summer months when the schools are closed in the countryside. The dachas are often interspersed with pioneer camps and summer kindergartens for children whose parents have no dacha. An important role in dacha life, as in life in general in the Soviet Union, is played by grandmothers, who look after the children while the parents are away at work.

At first, I wasn't particularly keen on having a dacha. I was not used to the idea of leaving the city for three or four months at a stretch, all the more so, as this involved commuting three days a week to work. But my wife was very keen and pointed to the benefit to the health of my little son, who was born in the spring of 1971. This was an argument I could not oppose and so I accepted the KGB's kind offer. Now I am so used to the dacha that I cannot imagine life without it. Ours is a typical Russian wooden house, standing in a fairly large garden which looks like part of a wood as we have allowed it to grow wild. We use it very intensively as we not only spend the summer months there, but nearly every weekend throughout the winter. We are able to do this because the dacha has gas-heating so that it is always warm there. We usually leave early on Saturday mornings and return on Sunday evenings. It takes us two hours from door to door to get there. As we have a dog – a beautiful cocker-spaniel, called Danny – we cannot use the Metro and have to walk to the station which takes about twenty minutes. From there, it is one hour by train and then another half an hour's walk from the station. In summer we go for long walks and swim in the many small lakes in the vicinity. In autumn we go mushrooming in the woods – a national Russian pastime – and in winter we ski for hours on end. What with one thing and another, our dog gets plenty of exercise and we are able to witness and enjoy every subtle change in nature, as season succeeds season.

Donald Maclean also had a dacha of his own. For him its great attraction was the garden. As a true Englishman, he loved gardening and spent all his leisure hours growing flowers, fruit and vegetables. His dacha, however, could not be properly heated and had to be closed down in winter. As he was also a keen skier, he used to come and stay every winter for a few weeks at my dacha. He usually brought a friend with him, a colleague from the institute, and his faithful Nadezhda Petrovna to cook for them. I have many pleasant memories of these winter vacations, with the long ski trips in the snowy forest and the many interesting conversations in the cosy warmth of our sitting-room afterwards.

When my wife was expecting the baby, I had, somehow, made up my mind that it was going to be a girl. I was at first somewhat disappointed, therefore, when it turned out to be a boy. I had already three boys and I thought it would be nice to have a daughter who could look after me in my old age. This disappointment didn't last long, however, as very quickly I got attached to my little boy. In a way, he replaced the three boys in England from who I had been separated and in him I was able to go through all the phases of development, which I had missed with the other boys. He did well at school and is now a tall, good-looking boy of nineteen who is studying physics at Moscow University and is a constant source of satisfaction and pleasure to my wife and myself. In him I have been given not only another son, but a very good friend.

My wife, who studied mathematics and physics at one institute and French at another, worked for many years as a French interpreter at the Central Mathematical Economic Institute, located in a building immediately next to my own institute. Then a few years ago, as a result of *perestroika* and the subsequent reorganisation of her institute, she was made redundant and she decided to devote herself entirely to her household duties. I have always liked cooking, which I learned from my mother, and when Ida was still working I did a lot of the cooking myself, particularly sweets and puddings of which I am very fond. Russian cooking, putting the emphasis on 'zakuskis' or hors d'oeuvres, is rather weak on sweets. In restaurants, here, the only sweets they serve are either rather good icecream or what is called 'compote' which consists of a few pieces of stewed fruit in rather a lot of liquid. Now that Ida has more time and learned a number of my recipes, she does most of the cooking herself though I continue to help with the shopping as that is a rather burdensome chore. Nothing at all, except some pieces of heavy furniture, is ever delivered to the door and one has to carry everything oneself. So in time, Ida has become an excellent cook. Since *perestroika* and *glasnost* she has, however, also become passionately interested in politics and reads most of the numerous publications which now exist on that subject. Often she reads the more interesting articles to us aloud, accompanying her reading by sharp commentary. We now call her 'the cook who is capable of ruling the state', after Lenin's famous dictum that every cook should be able to run the state.

Only one pudding I always insist on making myself and that is the Christmas pudding. I used to make two. One for ourselves and one for Donald who, like us, always celebrated Christmas with his large family of children and grandchildren. We have a tree, a turkey with all the trimmings, or nearly all, and of course, a pudding. What helps to create the right festive atmosphere here is that, at that time, Moscow and the countryside is covered by a thick layer of snow and when you look out of the window the picture is like a Christmas card, especially at dusk when here and there a window is lighted up. We always invite friends to our Christmas party which they enjoy as for them celebrating Christmas in this way is a novelty. One of the reasons is that the calendar of the Eastern Church differs from that of the Western Church by thirteen days. The 25th of December falls on the 7th of January therefore. That incidentally is why the October Revolution which broke out on the 25th of October (old style) is celebrated on the 7th of November (new style). Another, more important, reason is that for the Orthodox Church Easter has always been the most important Christian feast. In this country, in spite of many years of official discouragement – to put it mildly – of any religious manifestation in the past, this feast still lives on in the popular tradition and, especially of late, is widely celebrated. Special Easter dishes are prepared, such as beautifully painted and coloured eggs and Easter bread. It is also the custom to visit the graves of relatives on that day. Moscow transport lays on extra buses and trains and the traffic police are out in force to direct the traffic and the crowds to the various cemeteries. People put coloured eggs or scatter grain on the graves and sometimes drink a glass of vodka there as if in the company of the dead. They then place their hand on the grave and repeat three times 'Christ is risen! He is risen indeed.' I have always thought this a rather touching ceremony. It is as if people are reassuring their dead that they will not be in the grave for ever.

So today I can say that my life has fallen on pleasant lines, perhaps more so than many would say I deserve. For though I was cut off for many years from my children in England, I was granted the day when, after I had almost given up hope of ever seeing them again, we were united once more. All those years, my mother had remained in contact with my wife and continued to see the children regularly. Through her I was getting news and the occasional photograph so that I could follow their development. When they were in their early teens, my wife had told them the whole story about their father, since this could not be kept from them indefinitely. For a long time, they did not show any signs of wanting to see me. But then, first, the boy in the middle, who at that time must have been about twenty-four, expressed a strong desire to meet me. So it was arranged that he should accompany my mother on a summer holiday to the DDR, where we would all meet to spend three weeks at a seaside resort on the Baltic. It was a complete gamble how we would take to each other for he did not remember me, of course, as he had been only two when I disappeared from his life. The visit turned out a great success. I had to tell him my whole story, which I did much in the way I have set out in this book. Although, like all the members of my family, he probably did not approve of what I had done, he did understand the motives and it constituted in no way a barrier between us. From the very beginning, we got on extremely well together and it was as if we had always known each other. He also got on well with my wife and with his Russian half-brother, who speaks English well, but, like his father, with a slight accent.

The following year the other two boys, the eldest and the youngest, no doubt encouraged by what their brother had told them, decided to come too. The eldest, who was four when I left, still vaguely remembered me, but the youngest had never seen me at all. It was the end of March and the snow was still lying when they arrived in Moscow from Berlin at the White Russia railway station. I was waiting with my youngest son, Misha, on the platform to meet them. As they stepped out of the train we at once recognised each other and from then on, for a whole week, we never stopped talking. It was a slow getting-to-know-you, talk and more talk. They found my English quaint and old-fashioned but something that helped break the ice was that my youngest English son had some of my mannerisms even though he was seeing me for the first time. The oldest boy noticed this and saw the likeness in us. But again the whole thing was a gamble. Would we click? Would they understand? Again I told my story in great detail and again they understood. Three things I think contributed to this. Firstly, my wife had never spoken to them about me in any disparaging terms. For this I am deeply grateful to her. Secondly my mother had always discussed me in a normal way, certainly when they were older and conveyed to them the interest I showed in them. Finally, my boys happen to be committed Christians and, however paradoxical this may sound, this gives us something in common. So it worked. It was a measure of the success of the visit that when I met them on arrival at the railway station we shook hands. When they left, I kissed them.

Since that first visit, they have come every year to Moscow for a few weeks and they regularly write to me. On these occasions I have been able to take them with me on journeys and show them some of the more interesting parts of the Soviet Union.

I must record one more remarkable and, in a way, unexpected reunion in my life. In February of this year Michael and Anne Randle and Pat Pottle and his wife Sue, whom he had married since the escape, came to see me in Moscow. We had all of us often wanted to meet again, but had felt the risk involved was too high and so had not taken any active steps to bring it about. This problem had now been solved for us. On the basis of the information contained in Sean Bourke's book on the escape, H. Montgomery Hyde, in his book *George Blake Superspy* for the first time positively identified Pat and Michael without actually giving their real names. The story was taken up by the *Sunday Times* which, in an article, concluded that there was no doubt that Michael Randle and Pat Pottle had helped to organise the escape. The British police had known this, of course, ever since the publication of Sean's book, but had decided that there was not enough evidence to prosecute and had let the matter rest.

As a result of the *Sunday Times* article a spate of rumours started, involving people who had had nothing to do with the escape, and alleging that Pat and Michael had variously acted on behalf of the KGB or MI6 or the two services jointly. This was, of course, utter rubbish as they had been moved solely by humanitarian motives and had not been acting on behalf of any intelligence service whatsoever. In order to put paid to these rumours once and for all, Pat and Michael decided to write a book in which they admitted their participation in the escape, told the whole story as it happened and set out their reasons for helping me. Once the book was published, it became more difficult for the British authorities to do nothing. Even so, it was not until a campaign was started in the Commons, in which more than 110 Conservative MPs took part, and a private prosecution was threatened that the Director of Public Prosecutions took action and charged them.

When Michael and Pat and their wives came to Moscow they brought their legal advisers with them. They were anxious to get a proper statement from me confirming that they had had no connection with the KGB or received any financial assistance or reward from that organisation. Since I knew this to be true and they expressly asked me to make such a statement, I agreed to do so, though I realised that it confirmed their participation in the escape and could be used against them. I fully understood, however, the reason why they wanted this statement and felt that the least I could do was to help them in this matter.

We had a wonderful week together. I was able to show them the sights of Moscow and we had several pleasant family parties during which we at last were able to raise our glasses to the success of the escape. It was amazing how, at once, we took up the threads again which had been broken off twenty-four years earlier. Discussing the problems involved in their trial and the statement they wanted from me it seemed as if we were simply continuing our discussion in Hampstead about the best way to leave the country. For me their visit was an exhilarating experience. I felt I was in the swim again, though my joy at seeing them was overshadowed by worry about the outcome of a forthcoming trial. I was again deeply aware of the inadequacy of words to express what I felt towards them, now that I was in safety and they might be about to stand trial for my sake.

If I owe my freedom to them, the fact that I have been able to integrate so successfully into Soviet society is in a large measure due to the help which I received from my friends in the KGB. From the very beginning, they have done everything they could to make life as easy for me here as possible, as, of course, they have done for Kim and Donald and others like us. At first I thought, perhaps rather sceptically, that their concern for my welfare was bound to come to an end and that in time I would have to fend for myself. To my great surprise, I have been surrounded all these years by the same care and attention as in the beginning. Gratitude for what I have done? Yes, no doubt, but gratitude is a rare commodity in this world and, therefore, all the more appreciated when one experiences it. The help of my friends has been particularly welcome in overcoming the many administrative difficulties with which life is beset in this country. I often wonder how I would have coped without that help. Again, through them, it was possible since 1975, for me and my family to spend our holidays every year in one of the socialist countries. This became especially important when my mother was no longer able to make the long journey to Moscow as she would join us, usually accompanied by one of my sisters. We were always received with great hospitality by the local comrades and in this way had some unforgettable holidays together. We particularly remember my mother's ninetieth birthday, when the whole family gathered at a seaside resort on the Baltic in the DDR and the German comrades organised a birthday party for her which, I am sure, made up for much that she had been through because of me. But all things in this life come to an end, the good as well as the bad, and for the last three years we have not been able to meet. Although her general health is still good, considering her advanced age, and she still has all her faculties, she is no longer able to travel. So now we talk regularly on the telephone and remember the good times we had together. We both feel that we have much to be thankful for.

Two KGB officials, one senior the other more junior, are permanently charged to look after me. When they were still alive Kim Philby, Donald Maclean and I shared the same officials. If we have a problem we can turn to them for assistance. To enjoy such protection in a country where everything belongs to or is run by the state is of course invaluable. On the whole, if at all possible, I try to solve my problems myself, however, and I know Kim and Donald did the same. Only in exceptional circumstances do I ask for help. Before *perestroika*, for instance, in the good old Brezhnev days, it would have taken a lot of time and required numerous visits to various government offices and endless patience to arrange for one of my relatives to come and visit me if I had tried to do so on my own. With the help of the KGB, all the formalities were taken care of in the shortest possible time. When my car, after sixteen years of faithful service, was in need of fundamental repairs, the KGB decided that it would be easier to provide me with a new one. On my own, not having contacts in the underworld, it would have been nearly impossible to have the repairs carried out and as to buying a new car, I would have found myself on a waiting list for at least ten years or more.

My relations with these and other KGB officers is always very cordial. Due to the exigencies of the service, they change about every three or four years and so in the forty or so years that I have been connected with the Soviet intelligence service, I have met a great number of officials from the top chiefs to the drivers, starting with Boris Korovin and his assistant Vassili. The latter, now himself a general, I met the other day at an official function. We were very pleased to see each other again and thought that in both our cases the years had dealt kindly with us. Of course, the relationship with the officers with whom I was in contact in the field and with those whom I have known in Moscow differs. Those I knew in the field I called by their first names, true or not, and they called me George. The fact that we shared a common danger and were very dependent on each other for our safety as well as the feeling that we were working for the same cause, created an unspoken bond between us. On the other hand, the limitations imposed by clandestine meetings made a close personal acquaintanceship impossible. Relations with officials in Moscow are more formal in so far as we call each other by our name and patronimic which is the Russian equivalent of calling someone Mr So-and-So. At the same time, as we meet mostly in my flat while enjoying a cup of tea or on some festive occasion a glass of wine, the atmosphere is much more relaxed and it is possible to get to know each other much better. In some cases, truly friendly relations have been formed which have been kept up even after the officer in question has been moved to another job.

As a veteran intelligence officer, I am often asked to attend official functions and meetings on the occasion of a national holiday and usually invited to sit in the presidium. From time to time, I am asked to give talks to young KGB officers about my life and activities as a Soviet spy. Although this makes me feel rather like an old gramophone record which has been played over and over again, in the circumstances, I find it difficult to refuse. I am glad to be able, even in a small way, to do something in return for what they are doing for me. Incidentally, the Soviets don't like the word 'spy' used for their own agents. They call them 'scouts'. 'Spies' are the agents of the other side. They are very sensitive on this point. This is much the same approach, after all, as that of other governments who call the guerrilla bands of which they approve 'freedom fighters', 'partisans' or 'patriots' and those of which they do not approve 'terrorists', 'extremists' or 'bandits'.

Approaching the end of my story, looking back on my life, it is legitimate to pose the question: What has happened to my dream of helping to build a Communist society, a kingdom of justice, equality and peace, the universal brotherhood of man? One must be blind or wilfully close one's eyes, in this fifth year of *perestroika*, not to see that the noble experiment of building such a society has failed. Nobody today, in the Soviet Union or elsewhere, can seriously claim that we are advancing towards Communism. On the contrary, we are moving away from it towards market relations, private property and private enterprise. No euphemisms such as talk about a 'socialist' market or 'individual' instead of 'private' property can hide this fact.

It is difficult to forecast, today, what will emerge from the processes which have been set in motion. One thing is certain, it will not be a Communist society. If all goes well and there are no violent upheavals on a national scale what we may end up with is a mixed economy and the kind of society to which no social democrat could find objection.

Why has the experiment failed? Why has it not proved possible to build a Communist society? As I see it, the answer is this: Communist society is indeed the highest form of society imaginable in this world, but to build the highest form of society, the people who build it must possess the highest moral qualities. They must be able to put unreservedly the interests of the community, the interests of others, higher than their own. They must really love their neighbours as themselves. Therein lies the crux. Neither in this country, nor anywhere else, have people at the end of the twentieth century grown to the moral stature required to build a Communist society. The founding fathers of the Communist movement believed that it would be enough to fundamentally change the economic system, to change the relations of production, to do away with private property and people's mentality would automatically change and they would become ripe for Communism. The experience of the last seventy years in the Soviet Union and in the last forty years in the countries of Eastern Europe has shown that this is not so. The central idea of socialism 'each for all and all for each' has not proved a sufficient stimulus to raise productivity to the level required to create a prosperous society, all the members of which enjoy both social security and a high standard of living. The fact that in recent years it has become necessary in the Soviet Union to appeal to private charity to assist the state in providing adequate care for orphans and abandoned children, the aged and the disabled is both a sign and an admission that socialism has, in a large measure, failed. Under socialism there should be no need for private charity.

With my dislike for competition, it came as a particular disappointment to me when I found that in the Soviet Union it had been deemed necessary to introduce an artificial form of competition. It was a device, in the absence of the stimulus engendered by a market economy and unemployment, to make people work harder and better. It was used both within factories and institutes and between them. It was called 'socialist competition' but was neither competition nor socialist and apart from causing a great deal of bad feeling and jealousy between people, was quite ineffective in stimulating production.

Perhàps my greatest disappointment in coming to this country was to find that this society had not given birth to a new type of man. Underneath the varnish – and the varnish here was often less bright than in the West because of the difficulties of living – people here were essentially the same as people everywhere. Socialist man did not differ fundamentally from capitalist man. I found the same instincts, the same desires, the same ambitions, the same virtues and the same faults. What difference there was was only superficial. No 'new' man had been born and until this happens no attempts to build the kingdom of righteousness can succeed. Of course, there are some exceptional people who are ripe for the new society but they have existed at all times and in all countries. There have always been people like Alyosha in the *Brothers Karamazov* or Prince Myshkin in the *Idiot*, like Donald Maclean, or Michael and Anne Randle and Pat Pottle, like Mother Teresa, but they have been the first fruit, the harbingers of times to come. They are the sure proof that man carries in him the potential of building the perfect society. When that will be, nobody now can say. After all, 'a thousand ages are but an evening gone'. But of one thing I am certain: mankind will return to this experiment, it will try again. Now here, then there, it will make new attempts to build Communism, for, deep inside us – all of us – there is an instinctive yearning for it. Ask anybody who believes in a life hereafter, how he visualises this. He may be an arch reactionary or Mrs Thatcher herself, but he will describe to you what is, in fact, a Communist society where all are equal, where there are no rich and no poor, where there is no more war and strife, envy or hatred. This means that this ideal lives deep inside all of us and that it will move mankind again and again to strive for it. Then the October Revolution will be studied anew, lessons will be drawn from it and mistakes avoided. One of these mistakes, a cardinal one to my mind, was to think that people can be forced into a socialist strait-jacket. If the experience of the last seventy years in this country has taught us one thing, it is that Communism cannot be implanted by force, by strict discipline and terror. People have to develop naturally the high moral standards it requires. Only when this transformation in people has taken place as the result of a natural process of spiritual growth can Communism be established and will it endure.

What then about the sacrifices, the untold human suffering this experiment has required? Was this all in vain? I shall answer it by a question. Has there ever been a human endeavour of any magnitude which has not involved suffering and sacrifice? What about the creation of mighty colonial empires? What about the French Revolution or the industrial revolution? What about the spread of great world religions – to name but a few examples. Were all these events not accompanied by great sacrifices and untold suffering?

As to my views on religion, they have not changed. From time to time I attend a service at the Russian Orthodox Church. I do this because I find the liturgy beautiful and enjoy the singing, not because I have again become a believer. On the other hand, I am not an atheist either. I find that the atheist and the believer have this in common that they both assert what we cannot know. Whether there is a God and a hereafter or not we shall only know in the hour of our death or we shall know nothing at all. Having said this, I must admit that, while holding to this position, I am more inclined to believe that there is a Supreme Being, a Maker of Heaven and Earth, than that there is not. That this amazing Universe, of which we are an integral part, should have come about accidentally, I find difficult to believe. But my God, if he exists, is not the God of the Christians, though I can fully abide by the description of Him in the beautiful rhymed version of Psalm 90: 'Before the hills in order stood, Or earth received its frame, From everlasting thou art God, To endless years the same.' God, as I see Him is not a God to whom we can pray and make supplication to grant favours or avert calamities. He is immutable and His eternal purposes can no more be changed by the working of our free will than that He will change them because we ask Him to do so. To my mind only one prayer is acceptable to Him and that is 'Thy will be done', said not in supplication, but as a statement of fact, in total acceptance and humble submission.

As I have already said, the years in this country, living among the Russian people as one of them, have been the happiest and most stable period in my life. I hope my Russian friends will forgive me the comparison, if I liken my relationship with that people to a love affair with an immensely attractive woman with a somewhat difficult character to whom I have linked my fate and with whom I will stay, come what may, for better or for worse, till death do us part.

I have made arrangements that, after my death, I shall be cremated and the ashes scattered in the woods near our dacha, where I have walked and skied so often with my wife and son, so that it may be said: 'Neither shall his place know him anymore.'